Sing Me to Sleep

Terence Lavelle

Published by New Generation Publishing in 2014

Copyright © Terence Lavelle 2014

First Edition

www.newgeneration-publishing.com

New Generation Publishing

Cover photograph – Kings Own (Lancaster) Territorial's at summer camp, Rhyl around 1911. Front right is my wife's great uncle, George Haslam at summer camp with the East Lancashire Regiment. He has taken the cap from one of the King's Own lads and is wearing it himself. Just a few years later they were in the trenches.

Contents

Page

Foreword
Introduction

1. How the poems and ditties were collected   19
2. Background to War.   38
3. European Rivalries.   58
4. Germany's Ambitions.   67
5. Opening Moves.   74
6. The Precautionary Period.   87
7. The Curragh Incident.   91
8. War is declared.   97
9. The Rush to arms and the problems it caused.   102
10. Mobilisation.   109
11. The B.E.F. goes to France.   121
12. The Retreat from Mons.   143
13. The Ind. 4th Division at Le Cateau.   153
14. The Battles of the Marne and Aisne.   172
15. The 1st Battle of Ypres.   187
16. The Effects of Ammunition Shortages   217
17. A Ministry for Munitions.   225
18. Munitions Production.   240
19. Battalions, Brigades and Divisions.   248
20. The 1st Somme. July – November 1916.   257
21. 4th & 8th Battalions East Lancashire
    Regiment.   281
22. The Battle of Arras – 9th April 1917.   285
23. Battle Of Messines.   309
24. 3rd Ypres – Passchendaele – Cambrai.   321
25. Germany Prepares for Victory Offensive.   332
26. 2nd & 3rd Somme. 21 March 1918.   339
27. Chemin des Dames & the 2nd Marne   371
28. Final roundup Armistice   387
29. Conclusion.   406

Poems and Ditties

		Page
Sing me to sleep		13
1.	The Message.	29
2.	Billy Clough's poem.	44
3.	Afghanistan.	55
4.	A game of Nap.	65
5.	The Fly.	73
6.	Church Parade.	88
7.	A Soldier's Lament.	103
8.	Kings Own.	114
9.	Letters.	118
10.	Dugout Proverb.	147
11.	The Open Door.	165
12.	Super Sniper.	170
13.	"K" (1).	193
14.	An awful Predicament.	199
15.	La Bassee Road.	200
16.	A Soldier's Letter.	207
17.	Starshell.	210
18.	On Active Service	222
19.	Daily Routine in the Army.	238
20.	Our Humble Request.	255
21.	Matey.	260
22.	A.D. 1916.	267
23.	The Rifle.	281
24.	Friday night in the Billet	283
25.	Soldier's Prayer	288
26.	Marching.	293
27.	I oft go out at night.	307
28.	The return.	373
29.	The spoils of War	391

Photographs

		Page
1.	Poets Corner trip to Chester Zoo	26
2.	Four Generations	26
3.	Celebrating Homecoming	33
4.	The Book of Poems	34
5.	George Haslam at St Lukes War Hospital	50
6.	42nd Division Burial Party.	263
7.	A Tank at Cambrai 1917	263
8.	4th Batt. East Lancashire Regt.	264
9.	British Heavy Field Gun	264
10.	A Firestep in the British Trenches	265
11.	East Lanc's saphead at Givenchy	290
12.	British 18 Pounder Field Gun.	290
13.	Chateau Wood 1917	325
14.	Wounded awaiting transport	325

Young Squaddies in their homes of clay;
The parapet of the trench all blown away.
Around them craters and fields of mud,
The trees no more than splintered wood.
They dream of home so far away,
If they ever again will see the day.

When early morning breeze has blown,
And skies are bright and blue.
To meadows fair we haste, to mow
The grass all fresh with dew.
We're mowing the flowers and hay
The birds are singing,
The church bells ringing,
Whilst mowing the flowers and hay.

Foreword

Sometime in the 1980's I received a large envelope postmarked, Queensland, Australia. It was from my elder Brother who had emmigrated to Australia in the mid 1960's and was, what the Aussies call, a 'ten pound Pom'. When I opened the package I found a dog-eared notebook with no back or front to it, somewhat larger than A5 in size, the sort used as a ruled hard backed record book in the past, black with a red spine, included was a note saying 'thought you would like this'. I knew instinctively what it was; the boards were missing and the hand written lines in pen and ink were barely legible on the front and back pages where they had torn, feathered and faded, but of course I knew what it all said. This was a handwritten book of WWI poems collected by my father when he was a regular soldier between the wars and had a great significance for me.

My brother had visited the UK with his family in 1978 and stayed with my wife and I at our home in Marple, a dozen or more years had gone by since he had left, and as we reminisced about life at home when we were younger at some stage we touched on the subject of dad's book of poems. I had given little thought to it since leaving home and assumed my father still had in his possession at that time. There was no further discussion but he obviously decided at some stage that he would send it to me when he got back home, my first reaction was that I was appalled at the state of the book, but as I read the poems again I just felt that I was fortunate to have it.

The incentives for writing this book were twofold, one is the poems; the other of course was the sacrifice made by my ancestors. After having briefly spent time accumulating information in a piecemeal fashion about the involvement of my family members in the Great War, and also following the movements of the regiments in which they served, the idea evolved that I should try to get this information into some sort of order. In the late 1980's, early 1990's I had been in touch with the King's Own Regimental Museum and was helped by the then keeper Stuart Eastwood, he was very knowlegible about all things to do with the regiment and at that time he was in the process of writing a book 'The Lions of England'. When I acquired a copy it increased my enthusiam in looking for information and what I had eventually was a random collection that gave me some in depth information about the wider aspects of WWI. On my retirement in 1998 I dreaded the prospect of leaving a structured daily routine and not going to work each day, so I hit on the idea of designing and building a summerhouse. I lofted out the detail, angles, dimensions etc on the garage floor with chalk, and spent the latter end of 1998 happily going out to work each day, in the garage! My wife referred to it enternally as 'the shed'. That finished, I thought about the rhymes and wondered if I could incorporate them with the exploits of my forebears in an essay, not for publication but simply to set thing out in written form. I took that as my next project and started to write, but spring was here and I was tieing myself down when I should be out walking or caravanning so I put it aside to finish later. More recently, being conscious of the approaching 100th anniversary of the outbreak of WW1 the idea struck me that I should finish off what I had started; to relearn what I had started some 14 years earlier.

Setting out to write non-fiction within set parameters, assuming these have been identified, can become terribly frustrating because of related factors that continually pop up tending to pull the writer away from the main subject, it was now beginning to look like a book and I suppose that deciding how many side avenues to pursue is really dictated by how much the person wants to write. I set out with the idea that a brief account of the war would set the poems etc. in the context of the time in which they were created, it would also offer the chance to refer to the Lancashire Regiments that my family had served in. Some how the 'brief account' did not quite work out as planned.

I have included some salient points about our place in Europe and how we arrived at where we are, it was never my intention to cover in any detail the history of the Great War, detailed information on that subject is available in scores of books written by others with far more extensive knowledge of our history. I would like to think however that this might be an interesting, easy reading introduction to WWI, its causes and the events that brought it about, of life at that time, and most of all, in Sir John French's words of the 'The good Yeomen of these islands'. I have referred to the actions that my forebears were involved in, The Battle of Arras where my paternal Grandfather, John Lavelle was killed on April 11th 1917 and the Third Ypres where my grandmothers brother (my great uncle) Benjamin Leaver, was killed at Zonnebeke, Passchendaele on the 9th of October 1917. My maternal Grandfather, Wilson Clough and his brother William Clough (my great uncle), were also in the front line in the 2nd and 3rd battles of the Somme, both were casualties and died as a result of wounds within a year of the war ending. I could not write this book without paying some respect to them for the contribution that they made in the Great War, the ultimate contribution. For me it is simply a vehicle that will allow the rhymes to be published in a suitably fitting, informative background.

Sing Me To Sleep

Sing me to sleep where the bullets fall,
Let me forget the War and all.
Damp is my dugout, cold are my feet'
Nothing but bully and biscuits to eat.

Over the sandbags helmets you'll find,
Corpses in front and corpses behind.
Far, far from Ypres I long to be,
Where German snipers can't get at me.

Think of me where the worms creep,
Waiting for the Sergeant to sing me to sleep.
Sing me to sleep in some old shed,
The rats all running around my head.

Stretched full out on my waterproof,
Dodging the raindrops through the roof
Dreaming of home and nights in the west,
Somebody's overseas boots on my chest.

Introduction

There are many people, particularly the younger generations, who know little about what actually happened in the two world wars, many living through, and born after WWI will be aware to some extent of various aspects of the Great War, but because of the sheer magnitude of that historical event few would have a reasonably clear understanding of its origins or about the war itself, and in view of the fact that for a long time now British history has been something to be swept under the carpet, now might just be the time to dust it off and bring it to the forefront. Many will know little if anything of the origins of conflict in Europe, the rivalries that existed, the events that led on to the build up of war, of the treaties and loyalties that caused the countries of Europe to declare one after another such eagerness to go to war in 1914. Perhaps it would be an important topic for today with the coming of China and the turbulence in the Middle East. WWI is a first class example of how the momentum towards a world war can grow exponentially out of the most obscure events that at the time seemed insignificant in the light of what followed, Syria and Iran and North Korea might be examples of that line of thinking today.

The Great War was the most complex, life-changing event in the history of Europe. How did it start what were the causes, how did Britain get drawn in are questions that I have touched on. But since there were so many factors involved, not only in 1914 but going back through the Napoleonic period, opinions vary greatly, so it is for the reader to come to their own conclusions about what part Germany played. What is clear is that in 1914 Germany was becoming a major world power both militarily and economically, and worryingly so for the other great nations, that growth in stature, without doubt, was set to continue by its increased expansion in world markets. It seemed therefore, that to actually provoke a war with European neighbours unnecessarily was a particularly short sighted policy. Germany was always in a position to influence the outcome of the Austria/Serbia confrontation, however, had a peaceful settlement been endorsed, the opportunity for Germany to go to war in Europe would have been lost, at least in the short term.

I believe that no amount of searching for mitigation on the part of Germany would ever produce anything to to show that the other involved nations were at fault as Germany was, and if confirmation of that were needed, they provided it in 1939 when they did it all again, perhaps for added reasons. Traditionally France was the belligerent in Europe but that was brought to an end one hundred years before WWI by Wellington at Waterloo and in 1870 the Germans made an attack on France that saw the annexation of Alsace and Lorraine. In 1914 it was said that Germany's concern was a possible attack by Russia and because of the Franco Russian treaty and the Entente Cordial, that fear increased, they now felt that they were opposed by a tripartite of three potential enemies. That line of reasoning seems rather weak considering that Russia had a peasant army, ill equipt and spread over a vast region from the Baltic to Vladivostok. *A clear indication of Russia's inability to successfully enter into war with Germany is the fact that Churchill, in spite of opposition from senior staff at the admiralty, mounted the disastrous Gallipoli campaign in order to get vital supplies to Russia* Germany would have all the time they needed to prepare for a Russian attack if there was to be one, but of course there was nothing to indicate that was even a possibility. France had a large but poorly trained and motivated army and had shown no signs of aggression toward Germany, of course they hoped for the day that their annexed territories would once again be under French rule, but in the 44 years since 1870 had made no efforts militarily to win them back. Britain was not a threat to Germany and at that time had no thoughts of going to war with any nation other than to defend her shores.

The reverse of the situation that France, Britain and Russia found themselves in was however true of Germany who had the largest, the best equipt and trained army in the world, they were also building their Kreigsmarine to match or better the Royal Navy. Considering that there was not another nation on earth planning to go to war with Germany one has to ask why would they need such vast military resources? Lloyd George had already said at his annual speech at the Mansion House in 1911, that he understood Germany's aspirations with regard to building an Empire, and that Britain was prepared to ease the way to that end in any way that she could. The problem was that Germany was envious of the fact that these other major countries had large Empires and Germany was being left behind. The easy way would be to make Europe the German Empire and they set out to do that twice militarily, now it is being achieved by other means. We in this country have paid twice over for that gratuitous bullying. I wonder what those who went to the Great War would think now about the sacrifice they made.

The part that the B.E.F. (British Expeditionary Force) played in two world wars is not touched on in French schools as it is in Belgium, only the part that France played in the Great War is of any significance to the French, America did not become active in the war until the Spring of 1918 and their first taste of real action was in June 1918, but one would be hard put to not to think that the part they played is of greater significance to the French than was the British contribution.

By the time of the 3rd Ypres (Passchendaele) the British forces in France had grown to more than 1.5 million men, equalling the French and Germans and by now carrying the brunt of the allied fighting, taking more prisoners and guns than the French. I was interested to read a recent report stating that Francois Hollande the newly elected President of France, had made a visit to a British War cemetery in Normandy on 06/06/2012, and in the light of Britain's contribution and sacrifice in liberating France in two World Wars, it came as a great shock to know that he was the first President ever to visit a WWII British War cemetery in Normandy. Neither did it go unnoticed when the 60th anniversary of the D Day landings were held in France, the Queen was not invited and the celebrations were held in the Cherbourg area where the Americans landed, the Canadians and the British were conveniently airbrushed out.

It is impossible to travel any distance in Picardy or the Pas de Calais without coming across a British burial ground, it is simply littered with them as any IGN French map will show. I may be wrong but to my mind there has been a deliberate non-recognition on the part of the French of the sacrifice made by two generations of young Britain's, who gave their lives on French soil fighting to prevent Germany from dominating the Channel ports as to free the French from the yoke of German aggression. De Gaulle after WWII had no time for the British who along with the Americans after fighting on the Normandy beaches, at Caen, through the Falaise gap and the on to Paris with huge casualties and loss of life, stood back and allowed the Free French Army to march triumphantly into Paris as liberators, just as the French had arranged for the Belgians (supported by General Plumers 2nd Army) to march into

.

Brussels at the end of the Great War and take the credit. It seems clear that the powers that be in Europe would be only too pleased for the British to forget their glorious history and just wrap themselves in the EU flag as another number in the Union. I sincerely hope that 2014 sees our patriotic flame rekindled, along with a newfound pride in our past, something that for too long has been pushed under the carpet. I do not believe that we are still a major power, but we do have useful world diplomatic skills. Far better that we relinquish all grandiose ideas of world policing once and for all, but perhaps the loss of Britain's seat on the Security Council at the UN would be a bar to that.

1

How the poems and ditties were collected

My father, James Lavelle, was a Warrant Officer with the Kings Own Royal Regiment (Lancaster), and it was he who, as a young soldier, handwrote the poems and ditties gleaned by rubbing shoulders with old sweats from WWI. His early life would have been very similar to so many young people whose families suffered first hand as a result of the Great War. At age thirteen he started work half time, there was little work to be found but he was taken on as a lather boy in the local barbers shop. He then went on to work at Ordnance cotton mill, Blackburn learning to be a tenter on mule spinning frames until he was seventeen when he signed on with the colours. The prospects for advancement in the army between the wars was literally nil, they referred to it as 'dead man's shoes' so he served seven years and took his discharge to a civilian life that ironically, offered even less prospects than the army, the depression was biting and life in the 1930's was very hard, he had no skills and was therefore permanently on the dole. In those days ex servicemen were looked on favourably and he was soon offered a council house, one of the first with a bath and a garden back and front, the problem was that he could not find work and the rent was much higher than a terraced mill house, this resulted in my parents having to relinquish their lovely, modern semi after only a couple of years. How different the expectations today, that someone will pay your rent, waive your council tax plus a weekly benefit payment and more for each child! But then, they lived in the real world where, if you could not afford it you had to do without it.

I was roughly the same age at the end of WWII that my father was at the end of WWI, his war was 4 years long but his father never came back, my father was away 6 years and came back a stranger, discounting the years in between our experiences must have been very similar. Virtually a single parent family in each case with pathetically low income from the husband away in the war. My own mother was a full time machinist in an engineering factory given over to munitions, living close by us were several families where the father had a reserved occupation, and I only knew of one other family in the streets around where I lived in which the father had been called up and was away at the war. The father in these families had lots of overtime, it was not unusual even after the war to be working overtime of 3 nights a week till 9pm plus Saturday and Sunday work so they could earn a good income. In many cases the wife also worked, they lived a normal family life and save for the rationing, went short of nothing. It has to be remembered that life before the war was a frugal existence for most working people anyway, rationing was hard of course, but were it to occur now the impact would be devastating.

For some reason my father never spoke to me about his father, my grandfather, neither did my grandmother or any of my father's siblings and of course the older generation just never spoke about those who served in the Great War. My father did talk a little about his experiences during the retreat from the Escaut at Tournai on the French/Belgian border to Dunkirk with the British Expeditionary Force, and although I have a good memory I recall only a few things that he said about that period, probably these were related to the sort of questions that a little boy would ask. He was a postman and when he came home, having learnt to drive in the army, he was Royal Mail van driver delivering mail, mainly covering the Ribble Valley, Whalley and Great Harwood and I used to go with him. He would pile a heap of folded mail sacks on the passenger seat so that I had a good view and probably thought it a good time to get to know each other, I was ten and he was a stranger to me after six years away, the relationship on my part was one based on respect and fear rather than love.

On one of these trips out I remember asking if he ever killed any Germans, and he told me that the one occasion that he ever fired at anyone in earnest was early one morning after the small detachment he was with had marched all night. The 5th Kings Own was with the 126th Brigade and had been guarding a bridge that the Royal Engineers had mined for demolition on a section of the Escaut near to St Amand, Tournai in Belgium. His detachment had got out after being left as Mary Ward (rearguard) covering the bridge as the endless stream of troops withdrew from across the Dendre. It was 28th May 1940 at Tournai when they received the order to get out, there was a lack of transport and somehow during the bombing this section was split from the battalion, it was then 'everyman for himself'.

The small group that he was with had marched most of the night and found an abandoned farm before daylight, there they settled down for some kip and to wait for darkness to continue the long march to Dunkirk. After only a short time they were stood too by the sentries on 'stag', it was early morning and German soldiers had been seen skirting the cornfield with the obvious intention of clearing the barn and farmhouse before moving on. It seems certain that the Germans knew that there were British soldiers in the barn and had opened fire. The group would, I am sure, have preferred to quietly withdraw without making contact but in the event, having been seen first, they had no choice but to withdraw under fire, and they managed that without casualties.

My Father said that he had fired at a German and he saw him go down out of sight at the far edge of the cornfield, he never knew if he had injured or killed the man because the group beat a hasty retreat. He was a platoon sergeant at that time with what I would assume to be a mixed group of stragglers, it was late afternoon on that same day when they were on the road and heard vehicles coming toward them, in a state off near panic they all threw themselves into the ditch by the roadside in the hope that they would not be seen. As the vehicles approached silhouetted against the light my father half thought that they might be British and with his heart thumping he stepped out onto the road. The lead vehicle stopped and someone spoke to him in a cockney accent and told them to jump aboard, they were a patrol sent out to look for stragglers along the corridor that the British were squeezed into. My Dad said that he was so overcome by relief and elation he nearly cried, something he felt he would never forget. They were taken on the back of a 3 tonner to the outskirts of Dunkirk and left to march the last few miles to the beach. There were several incidents that he spoke of at various times that I remember clearly, about being on the beach, how together with another soldier they dragged along an exhausted comrade through the water by the belt of his greatcoat, so weary he almost did not make it as they literally dragged him to the gangplank and onto the ship. He also mentioned that there was an officer standing on the roof of a vehicle with lists calling up groups and directing them to assembly points on the beach as if it were a football match, even while the Germans were bombing and strafing. Generally however he said little about the B.E.F. and Dunkirk, it irks me at times that I never sat down with him to talk about the past as

I did with my mother shortly after he died.

When he came home in Dec 1945 he had a wristwatch that he had acquired after Dunkirk, the only clock we had in the house in those days was an old red alarm clock with bells on top, so he knocked a nail in the wall by the fireplace and hung his watch on it and that is where it lived. He had arrived at Dover from Dunkirk and then on by rail to Reading, on the way he was with a soldier, he may have been of the Kings Own or not but he had a wristwatch that he had taken from a German soldier, presumably dead, and my father was very keen to have it as a souvenir, I do not know how he managed it, what perhaps he was able to give him, but somehow he persuaded the chap to let him have the watch. It is a very small 15 jewel Movado with a military dial and adjusted to four positions, obviously a very expensive watch when new in the early 20th century, the fact that it was adjusted to four positions indicated a need for chrono like accuracy and probably was made for military use. The exterior looks very cheap and small now and it is only on opening the watch that the quality of the movement can be seen; it probably was a prized possession to the original owner. Now it has my dad's name, rank and number crudely etched on the back along with his denomination, a mechanical dog tag as it were.

My dad was an old soldier In the Kings Own between the Wars having joined up at the age of seventeen and he was recalled in 1939. After landing at Dover from Dunkirk on June 1st 1940 he went to a dispersal camp at Reading, Berkshire and then to Winchcombe in Gloucestershire, he remembered the Plaisterers and the landlord there in his diary with some affection, a pub I was pleased to visit some years ago. He then spent a couple of years based at various camps in Yorkshire and Lincolnshire, Thirsk, Leyburn,

Woodhall Spa and places like that. His battalion the 5th battalion (Territorials) Kings Own had been redesignated the 107th Tank Regiment Kings Own, Royal Armoured Corps and was now an armoured regiment. As a Sergeant he undertook training in tank Warfare and became a tank commander on Cromwell and Churchill tanks. He moved up the ranks and in 1943 he was promoted to Warrant Officer and seconded to the 6th Gold Coast regiment, Royal West African Frontier Forces. After landing by troopship (bound for the Cape and India) at Accra his first unit was at Ashanti and then up country to Kintampo posted to a training battalion for recruits that were shipped out to India and destined to join Allied troops in the War against the Japanese in the Burmese jungle.

I was almost five when he went away, my brother was a little older than me and nine days after my father had gone my sister was born, he possibly managed to get a compassionate 48 to see his new born baby, and 3 days after that on the 15th of September he went off to France to what was dubbed 'the phoney war'. I suppose that it would be around 1942 when my mother started to read the poems to us on occasions in the evening, my brother and I both used to enjoy listening to her reciting them, having washed ready for bed we would sit by the fire with a mug of oxo, they were memorable times, just us by the fire oh! So cosy, I did not realise how poor we were at that time, and although times were very rough for my mother, working full time, moving house, my brother six months in isolation hospital with Diphtheria etc, as children we accepted things as the norm and felt we were a happy and contented little family. Alas! With the end of the war those happy days would come to an abrupt end.

In all probability my father did not know or remember much about his own father, after all he was only about 8 years old when his father went away to the Great War, two years later he was killed. I knew all about my father, where he lived and where he had served in the army but the only thing I knew of my grandfather was that he and my grandmother had a small confectioners shop on Nab lane in Blackburn, that he was a founder member of St Paul's club, a local men's social club in the town, and was also a member of 'Poets Corner' at the Bradshaw Arms on the corner of Nab Lane, he was a bit of a dandy by all accounts, seen in a photo with a cane and a straw hat on a 1912 charabanc trip to Chester zoo. He had a very lucrative window cleaning business having most of the big business's, shops, banks, offices in Blackburn town centre on his books, he was killed at the Battle of Arras in April 1917 leaving my gran and six children. There were Poets Corners throughout the country in those days and perhaps that could have been the basis of the poems that were written in the war by ordinary private soldiers. The fact that my father knew little about his father, this lack of information about those that went to fight, is probably typical of most families and what they knew about relatives in the Great War.

Poets Corner, Bradshaw Arms Blackburn, on a trip to Chester Zoo 1912
John Lavelle front right in a light jacket.

Four generations 1905. Right of photo, my grandparents, John Lavelle with
his wife Maria, and first-born child John. Left of photo, my great, great
grandfather James Lavelle and my great grandmother, Mary Ann Lavelle.
The latter knew constant peace during their lifetime, the former had their
whole lives blighted by two World Wars.

There was always great national patriotism with regard to Britain's role in the salient points of European history, Nelson at Trafalgar and the Nile, Wolfe at Quebec (The French and Montcalm) or Wellington at Waterloo, these were battles not wars and were more easily understood. By contrast The Great War was a long and complicated affair in which battles were fought virtually in static situations, a series of battles over a four years where there was no loss or gain to either side, only horrendous numbers of dead and injured, it is likely that people knew of the battle in which a relative was killed or wounded but not much more than that. Perhaps the little they knew was sufficient, or perhaps it had to be because so enormous was the loss that no one wanted to talk about these things.

There had been enough pain and life was hard enough, my paternal Grandmother was left with six children to provide for and no husband with whom to share the burden, my maternal grandmother was in the same situation with four children, they were amongst thousands who lost their loved ones and so they had to put it behind them. Life was infinitely harder and more frugal in those days and there was little room for sentiment, unlike the over emotional modern generations, they were well able to face the reality of the situation in which they found themselves. Neither was there any point in burdening others with your own problems when they themselves suffered the grief of those very same losses, and they too had to find the means to cope. For those unfortunate enough to have lost a husband, father, son, or loved one, there was little talk of that loss, nevertheless they had a deep understanding of each other's sorrow that inevitably drew them closer as a community.

On the other hand in some way, it seemed to be part of the make up of those old soldiers not to talk about their traumatic experiences, in the vault of the local pub they might tell each other yarns and pull each others leg about this and that in the war, those who had been there and experienced it all, not to go over the suffering but to simply recall army life and the level of comradeship. But they would often clam up in the presence of others. Perhaps those that did not go and never experienced what it was like to be in the army let alone at the 'front', felt that the old sweats were obsessed with it all, so those who had been and experienced army life kept it to themselves rather than have someone wet behind the ears swinging the lampshade and saying 'here we go again'.

I knew a couple of old neighbours in the street when I was young, one was 'owd Breakall, he would sit on a kitchen chair at the front door in the sunshine with his shiny boots on, fustian pants and union shirt, he wore a navy blue waistcoat with his braces showing below. His waistcoat front was all shiny from going in the pockets for his penknife to cut tobacco, or his watch on an Albert. He would cut his twist with his old penknife and puff at a clay pipe with only half a stem that butted out beneath his bushy nicotine stained moustache. He and old Mr Brierley were much of a muchness after a lifetime 'int' mill'. They lived round the corner from each other and both had been in the Boer War and the Great War, I knew that, but that was all anyone knew, they never spoke of it to anyone. I just wonder if it was to do with the fact that only those that had done military service ever travelled anywhere and that those who never had the opportunity envied them the fact that they could speak of these exotic places and experiences.

As a young recruit of 17 my father signed on in the King's Own, they sent him away from the recruiting office the first time he went to sign on and told him 'come back tomorrow when you are eighteen'. The next day he filled in the forms showing himself one year older and took the Kings shilling, his army record shows his birth a year earlier than his birth registration certificate, that of course was not unusual in those days, the recruiting sergeant was not interested in seeing a birth certificate. My Father had decided that the Royal Artillery was what he wanted to be in, but the recruiting sergeant was a regular with the Kings Own and doubt-less told my dad all about the regimental battle honours that filled him with pride at the thought of serving with the 4th of foot, the Kings Own, the senior regiment in the Kings division. I have no doubt he learned of Pte. Miller VC. Of Withnell (a village in the Blackburn Hundred) and how he earned his VC.

Pte. J. Miller V.C. Kings Own Royal Regiment (Lancaster).

THE MESSAGE

Now put away your books my lads, come sit you by my side,
And I'll tell you the glorious story of how 'Miller of Withnell' died.
I've told of the Spartan boy, how the Spartans no-bly bore,
To guard the narrow pass in the grand old days of yore.

You've read great Nelson's story of Trafalgar cross the foam,
And also of the noble three who kept the bridge of Rome.
I've told you of Gordon's death, the bravest of the

brave,

And of the noble Kitchener now in his ocean grave.

But none fell more nobly than this lad, of Lancashire the pride,

So let your children's children, tell how Jimmy Miller died.

We had shelled the Hun from his dugout; our guns had smashed him in style,

We had hurled the foe from his trenches, driven him back a mile.

But many a hero has fallen, and many a husband and son,

Who'd gone to their rest left us weakened,

Could we hold that which we had won?

So our captain cried out 'here Miller, a message to company 'D'

I know you and trust you brave Miller, so bring back the answer to me.

You never have shirked a duty, you never have reasoned why,

For God's sake do not fail me now, but bring me back the reply.

I hate to ask you to risk your life, but it's the only way,

If you but get the answer back you'll save some lives today.

A brief salute to his officer, he cleared the trench with a bound,

He darted out into the open, onto the shell swept ground.

With a hearty cheer from his comrades, the rest is hard to tell,

But scarce a score of paces had gone, when an an-

gry bullet fell,
And struck him through from back to side, he halt-
ed for a span,
(Ye shot not well O'marksman to stay so brave a
man).

Then with his hand pressed to the wound, he strug-
gled gamely on,
And got his message through at last, his short life
all but gone.
'Now stay you here good Miller, you have nobly
run your race,
And you are sorely wounded; let another take your
place.

Don't ask it Sir, why waste a life? You're open to
attack,
I've brought this message right through hell; I'll
take the answer back.
Brave men sobbed as he started back, across that
danger zone,
They could not, dare not queer his pitch, that's a
creed in the old 'Kings Own'

Now he reels along in his agony, now on his knees
he crawls,
With his life blood ebbing drop by drop, a dozen
stumbles and falls.
And the goal is reached as he murmurs, 'relief Sir,
all is well'
Then he dropped at the Captain's feet and died, so
Miller of Withnell fell.

His name is off the roll call now, so brave where
all were brave,
He's laid by gallant soldiers in his lonely, hon-

oured grave.

He saw his duty plain and straight; he went for it there and then,

I think 'Our Saviour' wont be hard on a man who died for men.

Cheer up you ye hearts of England, cheer up ye Britons all,

Bear up ye wives and mothers, so sick at duties call.

The soul of our race lies in men like those who fight to their last breath,

And like the sentinel of old stand faithful unto death.

But this deed stands aloof from all, heroic, grand, alone,

The pride of the entire British race, the pride of the old 'Kings Own'.

So when you folk talk of heroes, tell the story far and wide,

The story of The Message, and how Miller of Withnell died.

Pte. Miller was with the 7th Service battalion and was killed in the 'Battle of Bazentin Ridge' at Bazentin-Le-Petit on July 30th 1916. He was one of The groups of battles (Bazentin Ridge, Delville Wood, Pozieres) that were 'the First Somme'. He was awarded a posthumous V.C. The village of Withnell is situated about 6 miles west of Blackburn on the road to Chorley.

By the mid 1920's my father found himself for a period at Dover Castle waiting for a contingency to sail by troopship to India where he spent the next four years with the 2nd battalion at Rawalpindi, the twin city of Islamabad. The summer months were spent in the Murree Hills, the foothills of the Himalayas, away from the hot plains at two hill stations, Gharial and Kuldana. My

Dad mentioned the Himalayan mountain, Nanga Parbat and the fact that on occasion's expeditionary parties from the Garrison went climbing there, but somehow I doubt if my father ever did. At some stage he was seconded to the Gurkhas and he had lots of interesting photographs, things like trooping the colour at Gharial in 1929, he brought home with him two Gurkha khukri knives in black scabbards that were always in the house when I was a boy. He also had sepia photos of the Ghurkha's using a khukri to behead a goat, and even a bullock, the latter with a huge two handed Khukri about 36 inches long. On the battalion's completion of their tour in India they embarked ship for Suez, there they disembarked and travelled up the Nile to Khartoum. Sudan was a hardship posting and whereas India or Burma would be a 3/5 year minimum posting, a tour in the Sudan lasted only one year. It was during these years that he listened to the old regulars and painstakingly wrote down the poems they recited.

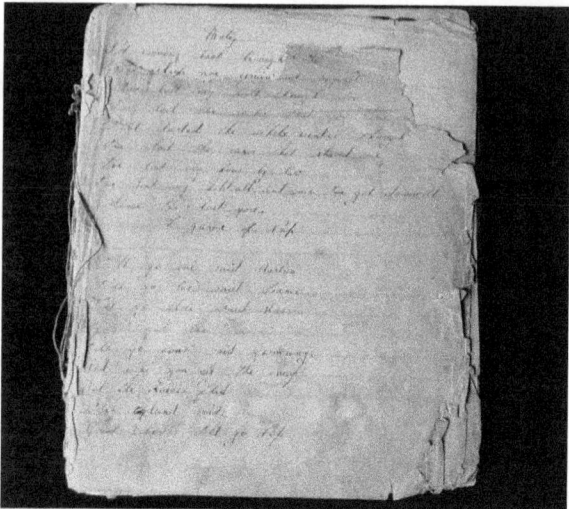
The book of rhymes and ditties, it was sent to me in a very bad state.

There is no doubt that Germany was the prime mover in starting WWI even though the incident that started it off was not primarily a matter of immediate concern to to that country. Having said, that Germany did not necessarily cause the Great War, what they did was to turn an opportunity to their advantage by manipulating events, by keeping the pot boiling. There is perhaps a more modern style of thinking in the present day with regard to this, but my belief is that war served the Kaisers interests and war was what they had planned for over a long period of time.[1] The origins of why Germany had a need to be so involved does in fact go much further back in history. It just so happened that at that time Germany was particularly agitated and afraid real or imagined, that Russia was posing an increasingly greater military and economical threat to her security.

Early in the 20th century Russia had signed a treaty of alliance with Germany's traditional enemy, France

and the assassination of the Austrian Archduke Ferdi-
nand and his wife at Sarejevo was simply the spark that
eventually lit the tinder of underlying problems be-
tween the leading nations of Europe. It was Germany
that felt at odds with the other great European nations
and had an urgent need to improve its world status, it
was this that brought about the manipulation events at
Sarajevo, a situation that could have been resolved am-
icably had Austria listened to the advice of other na-
tions than Germany. Besides the Franco Russian treaty
there was now the Entente Cordiale that for Germany
posed a long-term serious threat to expansion and
world power at the level that the tripartite enjoyed. Ac-
cess to the North Sea was limiting, it was access to the
English Channel that Germany wanted and eventually
to challenge the might of the British Navy, there was
only Austria with which Germany was on friendly
terms.

The Great War saw the annihilation of a generation
of young and middle aged men, and others in their
thousands were casualties, some died and some lived,
some lived and then died soon after the war ended from
wounds or gassing as both my Grandfathers and great
uncles did; some lived on and never really recovered
from their injuries. My forbears suffered all of these on
both sides of the family and they are remembered with
the thousands of British soldiers killed and wounded in
the Great War. These young men were at the front in
the trenches, in a situation where they witnessed vio-
lence and brutality on an unbelievable scale. It has been
said that war is the ultimate violence and of course they
had no choice in what they did and why they were
there; they were completely powerless to do other than
what was bid of them and so perhaps poetry was a sat-
isfying means of relieving their feelings.

To have a better understanding of the suffering and

anguish brought to all those who have lived through war, and to recognize the significance of that in relation to the comfortable life we all now enjoy thanks to their selfless sacrifice, it is necessary to read about it. We have had more almost 70 years of peace and unlike most other countries in Europe we still have never been occupied by a foreign power, but it has come at a great price and all these years later it is so easy to forget that. It has made us what we are; an island off the coast of Europe that never was fully integrated with the mainland, but this great nation of ours still punches above its weight and is an influence for good and right in the modern world, and would be equally so without the role of world policeman that the senior politicians of this country are so keen to perpetuate. Economically however we seem to be in terminal decline, we now seem to be at low ebb as we were when we entered the Common Market in 1973, then we were the sick man of Europe, nevertheless we are owned to a large extent by other countries, I believe that with a common market level of membership and free of the shackles of Europe and the Human Rights circus etc. we can again be a nation to be proud of. It seems that too many years have been spent by British Institutions trying to make money in less honest ways than the hard working people of days gone by. Nowadays everyone you speak to has a major worry of some sort about the way the country is changing, the abused welfare state is bloated and untouchable, immigration and its effect on the nation over the last 5 years particularly is a huge concern for the indigenous population. The lack of following in the Christian Church made worse by the politically correct attitude of the establishment, same sex marriages, the curtailment of civil liberties, the burgeoning of Police power and the widening gap between parliament and the people, all are matters for serious concern today.

There is no doubt that what they fought for is not what we now have, in many ways it is exactly the opposite, i.e. a country run by diktat from Brussels, This is not what I set out to write about, but it is directly related to the idea that they had then, of a 'better tomorrow'.

Above From left. Bert Gregson, the Landlord of the Queens Hotel across the street, a fellow drinker wearing my dad's slouch hat, my dad and an RAF chap. In front of Tony's New Empress Ballroom Town Hall St. Blackburn after VE day.

2

Background to War

For anyone growing up as I did during WWII military aspects of life was the norm, it was all around us as the whole nation knuckled down to the War effort. I suppose that for the most part of my early life the subject of military service was always ever present as it was for my parents and grandparents; now I am taking the time to look more closely at the effects of war on family life, in those days it was a matter of getting on with life, we were living it rather than studying it. I do recall that in my last year at school in the late nineteen forties aspects of the Great War being introduced to our history lessons, never before had WWI been a subject at the school that I attended and it was not a popular subject, it was not seen to have the romantic appeal, the dash and the colour of other aspects of British military history such as, The Crimea, Trafalgar, India, or the Peninsular Wars.

A large part of the poetry that we learned at school was about past glorious history before that seemingly black, decadent period of WWI. The élan of soldiers and cavalry at Waterloo and the Crimea was depicted in paintings, dashing heroes, flamboyant Hussars on horseback in blue and gold braid, sword raised, or foot soldiers in red tunics, forming the thin red line. Compared to that WWI was eternally static and depressive, worn out soldiers in drab khaki battledress wearing hose tops and puttees, surrounded by treeless landscapes and mud. It is not surprising that nothing romantic was ever recorded in oils as they did for previous battles.

As youngsters we really had no detailed knowledge of the Great War which of course seemed at the time infinitely more complex than other aspects of our history, certainly there was no easy means of absorbing all the wealth of information that is now readily available via television and the mountain of books that have been written covering every aspect of the two world Wars.

Anyone born in the 100 years between 1850 and 1950 had their lives changed and to a large extent dominated by war, virtually everyone had one or more relatives involved in some aspect of war. It is easy to understand that the people of those generations who suffered the deprivations of war were only too glad when it was over and could put it behind them, to forget about it and get on with living a normal life. Of course it was not to be, another world war and the Wall St. crash saw to that. But all this becomes only of real interest when it is history, when it can be looked at from a more comfortable, affluent viewpoint, and although we English revel in stories of the war, books, newspapers and on TV, I wonder if many really understand what they gave up for us later generations, or is it just some sort of pride in being on the winning side. There were no winners.

They said the Great War was a 'War to end all Wars', 'a war to make the world safe for democracy', Government of the people, for the people, by the people. It has to be said that we now know that democracy is something we enjoy to the point where it clashes with individual human rights and at that point it goes out of the window, democracy is for the people, human rights is for the individual whose rights are upheld by laws concocted by judges whose qualifications and level of experience leave a lot to be desired. Those laws are then applied to the letter in this country by judges who are increasingly isolated from the values of the general public, and for what seem to be to the man in the street, unfathomable and absurd reasons. Democracy and individual human rights as they are now, do not sit well together.

After the Armistice Germany found itself in a situation where to them, the victorious nations were seeking unreasonable compensation and by doing so heaped humiliation on the German people through the constraints of the Treaty of Versailles. In 1919 the signatories to the Versailles Treaty were making punitive demands that Germany had been forced to accept, these terms were carefully drawn up to make sure that Germany would never again be in a position to make war. The financial demands were so severe that they were never met, America, flexing it's new found muscles, was the chief architect of the Versailles Treaty but it was France that made the severest demands, in the end and having no other choice, it was America, having made loans for the reparation of war damage that allowed Germany to pay only half of what was demanded. The very fact that the conditions laid down in the Treaty of Versailles were brought to bear, made it inevitable that Germany would again go to war, if only to lift the burden that the nation toiled hopelessly to repay.

The Great War was fought by huge citizens armies, families were proud of what their men folk did, the courage and loyalty to their country, but they were also saddened and appalled at the waste of human life and the devastation from which no nation gained, there was only losses for all the countries involved, and they were enormous. To the bitter end of the war Germany held out in the hope that they could somehow bargain with the Allies, and as they retreated behind the Rhine the Germans laid waste to everything they could. It is difficult to criticise those who set the terms of the Versailles Treaty, they were acting on behalf of a public that demanded that Germany, the principle belligerent in this epic struggle that was felt across the world, be punished and prevented forever from waging war on it's neighbours, no demands made on Germany could be too severe after what they had done. Whilst the common people wanted retribution, they also wanted simply to forget, the politicians however made sure that it was not forgotten and placed Germany over a barrel, they were blind to the fact that what they did ensured that war again was inevitable. Even whilst the Allied occupation Forces were on the Rhine from 1919 until 1929, the clock was ticking, the countdown to WWII was under way, but the West could not, or did not want to see it. At the end of WWII, and having learned the lessons of the Versailles Treaty, the allies bent over backwards to help Germany and Japan recover, so much so that Germany now, once again dominates Europe, has one of the world's largest economies and finds itself in a totally different situation than it was in 1919 and 1945 without having even mobilised it's armies.

It is easy to point out that it would have been better to have helped Germany in 1919 as the west did after WWII, but in 1919 that lesson had yet to be learned in order to be understood, it was the reason for treating Germany differently the second time around by the support of American lease lend. I recall when I was serving my apprenticeship in engineering, there was still food rationing, Britain was virtually bankrupt and also needed American lease lend, (America was the only country to have made a fortune out of both world wars) but it seemed that there were conditions attached to the loans we had from America, we had to spend the money supporting Germany, and although we had heavy machine tool industries in Britain, in the early 1950's the new machinery brought into the heavy and light machine shops of the engineering company where

I worked, came not from British machine tool factories but from German factories. At that time Britain had an Empire that was falling apart, the colonies needed policing and there were costly campaigns in Malaya, Cyprus, Kenya, Aden not to mention the countries commitment to the Korean War. America was anti colonial, and not disposed to helping relieve the British financial situation other than to lend money with strings attached, money it could well afford since we provided a massive export market for the US long before it entered the war in June 1942.

The fact is that given the same circumstances as those in 1918, the same public feelings would exact the same sort of revenge on an aggressor that had caused so much death and misery and heartache, as much to its own people as the other nations involved. So from that point of view, who is to say that the architects of the Versailles Treaty were wrong? In 1945 the West again wanted retribution but this time had to embrace the vanquished rather than punish them, and that was as difficult for the people of bankrupt Britain and France as it was for Germany.

I remember as a child that the feelings of remembrance were always very strong within the community where I lived. When I was growing up in the street of terraced mill houses where my Grandmother lived[2] there was a framed, polished wood roll of honour screwed to the gable of the end house opposite, paid for by the residents of those four streets. It had two bronze vases one each side on a little pedestal and there was always flowers or sprigs of holly in them, someone would always take the time to polish these wooden plinths and keep it all neat and shiny. The children in the street knew that the names of their relatives were on that Roll of Honour, and that included my grandfather. Beyond that there was no talk of the Great War, nobody wanted to talk about it perhaps because it was too painful.

Both of my grandmothers had large framed pictures of their husbands hung on the front room wall, my maternal granddad with his medals in the large photo frame. In the early 1970's I started to become curious about my two grandfathers, what regiments they had served with and where exactly they had been in the Great War. I have a photograph of my grandmother with her mother and sisters and brothers when she was about eighteen years of age, in it the photo my grandmother's older brother wore a red army tunic, it was taken as he was about to go off to the Boer War. I later became curious as to the regiment he was with and his regular army service at the time of the Boer war before being called up and killed in action in 1917. My mother knew by heart the poem that someone had written and was sold round the streets to raise money for my maternal grandfathers younger brother William 'Billy' Clough, he had suffered severe facial injuries by shrapnel and was taken prisoner at Gommecourt on the 23rd of March 1918, he had his eyes taken out in by German medics and was a prisoner of war for six months. An obituary in the Bury Times reported 'he was hit in one eye by shrapnel and taken prisoner where the Germans removed both his eyes', a bit of harmless sensationalism perhaps. He was included on a prisoner exchange in September 1918 arranged by the Red Cross and was admitted to St Dunstan's (now renamed Blind Veterans). This sort of thing was not uncommon where families lived on meagre incomes because the breadwinner was no longer there. This is the poem written to collect money for Billy Clough's wife who lived at the village of Stubbins near Ramsbottom in Lancashire.

Billy Clough's Poem

On August 4th four years ago when the Britons
declared war,
The lads from Ramsbottom, every one, were
loyal to the core.
They joined up in hundreds to fight for Britons
cause,
And how they fought and bled, has need for
some applause.
Some were the 'old comtemptables', in the re-
treat from Mons,
Mothers of such lads as these, aren't you proud
to have such sons?
While out there in the Dardanelle's, with the lid
of hell took off,
Ramsbottom again recalls how we possessed
the stuff.
On every front throughout the War, some lads
from Rams' have been,
In Egypt, Salonika, France and Russia, fighting
seen.
And when the War is over, what are we going
to do?
To help these gallant lads of ours who have
helped to pull us through.
Some will be cripples many ways one we know
is blind.
We must try to help poor Billy Clough, and also
bear in mind.
The Govt. may provide an arm or a leg, and
make it work all right,
But it's beyond the power of human aid to give
a blind man sight.
Then there are those who will not return, those
who fought and fell,

Some died from pneumonia, dysentery or gas,
some in their prison cell.
We think of these brave lads, and we know why
they are gone,
They've paid the supreme sacrifice, for the victory that was won.
To the wife who lost her husband, to the mother
that's lost her lad,
To the girl that's lost her sweetheart, and the
child that's lost it's dad.
We offer our deep sympathy; it isn't much we
know,
But it might just help a little to heal the cruel
blow.
They were heroes every one, full of English
pluck and grit,
And as England expected went and bravely did
their bit.
For they fought as the old song used to say, like
a soldier and a man.

***

From a very early age I had been aware that my paternal Grandfather was killed at the Arras, but nothing more than that. I started to wonder why my father never mentioned him; more odd still was the fact that 21 years after the Great War ended my father went to France on September 15th 1939 with the advance units of the B.E.F. (British Expeditionary Force). It was during what was dubbed 'The Phoney War', he returned to England in December 1939 to attend an NCO's course and then went back again to France in April 1940 taking with him his small Post Office diary, it was given to all workers at the GPO each Christmas, my father kept brief notes in it during his second period in France and

Belgium from April right up to the retreat from Dunkirk and getting back to Blighty.

When the German army massed on the Belgian border in May 1940, the British Expeditionary Force (B.E.F.) had been training and building up its ranks for more than six months waiting for Germany to move into Belgium. The notes in my father's diary record that on the way from Le Mans the 5th Kings Own travelled via Reims and Arras to the allocated area around Frelingheim on the Belgian border. On the 26th of April 1940 somewhere between Arras and Douai the train passed a huge memorial, "I think it must be Vimy Ridge" he wrote. Vimy Ridge of course, was an objective taken by the Canadians in fierce fighting at the 'Battle of Arras' and on the same front within 3 or 4 miles of where his own father was killed alongside the Arras – Cambrai road, close to Moncy le Preux. The same day that his father (my grandfather) was killed, 11th of April 1917, just a few miles to the north The Canadians moved up as part of the same push but on the other side of Monchy, they took Vimy Ridge. 23 years to the month later and for the same purpose, the B.E.F was taking up positions to fight the Germans. It is significant and yet sad that Vimy Ridge struck a chord with my father, and yet, having passed virtually the spot were his father was killed in action, he made no mention whatever of it in his diary. He had made almost a repeat of the movements that his Father had made in the Great War and there ought to have been some recognition of that on my father's part but there was none.

This perhaps indicates the huge need of people who had suffered such tragic loss in the Great War to be allowed to forget. Like many other families where the father or son had been killed the issue was put behind them and they moved on. Life was a struggle anyway and everyone was in the same dire situation, there had to be ways of suppressing the grief and anguish of a generation of young men being wiped out and they had to help each other in order to find any meaning in the lives they lived, that was only possible by burying the past and moving on.

For me it is sad to think that I probably knew more about my grandfather's time in France than my father did, he of course had no means of knowing what happened other than what was in the telegram sent by the War Office on his demise, there would normally be an obituary in the local newspaper 'The Blackburn Times' but there appears to have been none for either of my grandfathers. Now we take for granted the sea of information at our fingertips. Sometime in the late 1970's an elderly relative of my wife[3] died and my wife and I went to clear some of the things from his house, amongst the collection of odds and ends were some photographs of him in uniform. They spanned a period from being a young man in the Territorial Army to his being in St Luke's war hospital at Halifax, brought back from the Front with severe shrapnel wounds in 1917, his second serious injury by shrapnel. He had been transferred from the East Lancashire Regiment to the Kings Shropshire Light Infantry to make up numbers lost and was twice injured at the Western Front; the first time was an upper arm wound from shrapnel, he was patched up in a field hospital and after a period of convalescence was sent back to the front, the second time his shoulder blade was shattered by shrapnel and it was all over for him, he had his 'Blighty ticket'. After an extended period of hospitalisation he was discharged in November 1917 from St Lukes War hospital at Halifax as medically unfit. During the time that George was at St Lukes Hospital he met a young women who lived at nearby Sowerby Bridge, she may have worked at the hospital, anyhow they fell in love, George had never been married but she had, and she had two boys, their father had been killed at the front, she and George had found something that provided for them a strong bond and they lived together to a good old age, he outlived her and was devastated when she died, so much so that he lasted only a short while after her death.

Of the family members whose military background I have followed he was the only one to live, he was, relatively speaking, one of the lucky ones. I say he was lucky and in that respect he was but he lost his only natural son Maurice when he was killed at the 1st Alamein, the Battle of Alam Halfa, when Auchinleck routed Rommel and turned the tide against the Africa Corps in the Western Desert. Things had been going badly for too long and Rommel was within 60 miles of Cairo, Auchinleck an Indian Army officer and Commander in Chief of the Middle East Land Forces, decided that he would personally take over command of the 8th Army from the G.O.C. Lt. Gen. Neil Ritchie. At the 1st Alamein (30th June 1942) Auchinleck repulsed Rommel and turned the tide in a decisive battle that eventually saw the Africa Corps driven out of North Africa. Auchinleck rarely gets praise for that, sadly all the praise goes to Montgomery because Churchill was too intolerant, during the battle he had continually bombarded Auchinleck with requests for tactical information and now would not allow Auchinleck the time to regroup his exhausted troops and supplies before the main battle of El Alamein itself. In the end Churchill waited a month longer until October for Montgomery to strike. Maurice Haslam was a trooper in 4th CLY (County of London Yoemanry) with the 22nd armoured brigade. Like his father he had been transferred from his own unit just as his father had in WWI, from the 5th Inniskilling Dragoon Guards, to fill the gaps in the ranks left by casualties in earlier battles in the Western Desert. In learning of his son's death I am sure there were moments when George wished he himself had died of his wounds at the Front, and his poor wife who had lost her husband in the Great War now suffered the loss of her son in WWII. When later he knew that I had actually been to the war cemetery at Alamein in 1962 whilst working in Egypt, and been so close to his sons grave he was very upset, at the time I knew nothing of his sons death, he on the other hand had never been in a position to visit his sons grave and the irony of the fact that I had been so close really did upset him. There must be countless ironical episodes of a similar nature that families throughout Britain could tell of, resulting from both wars.

George Haslam (the young man on the cover of this book six years later) with comrades at St Lukes Hospital Halifax. They are wearing the war service badge, it was a solid silver badge inscribed on the edge with the recipients name, rank and number. It was intended to show that the wearer had done their duty and in particular to stop young women accosting them with white feathers.

Between the Crimean Wars and the Boer War there was perfect peace in England, all the battles relatively small and they took place in far off parts of Empire, we had a very small standing army compared to France and

Germany, but we were of course a great maritime power and that was all we needed to ensure security of our islands, it was taken care of by the most powerful navy in the world up to the end of WW1. Again since 1945, for us there has been relative peace, my grandparents, parents and my generation, lived through the period up to 1945, or should I say the ones who survived did and so their lives were greatly affected.

Looking back at the experiences of these older generations I realised two very significant things, one was the incredible hardships that they and their comrades had suffered, some making the supreme sacrifice and yet those who survived the war made no bones about it. Neither did those left behind at home to cope with life and their great losses. The job had to be done, it would be understandable if there were great bitterness and anger, but that somehow it was not in them. It was left to people like Wilfred Owen, Rupert Brooke and Seigfried Sassoon to write that sort of thing in poetry about the battlefield, many who wrote poetry would not call themselves poets but they made a serious attempt to express themselves in the poetry they wrote. The other point was the realisation that a person born before or during the Second World War was about to leave a way of life that had existed with only minor changes since the onset of the industrial revolution and they had now to adapt to a new order.

Life was about to change and a whole new modern era would give those born from the fifties a different expectation from life. An easier life with no wars, lots of labour saving devices, better communications, more money for less hours worked, better housing conditions, free medical care, a welfare state, a wider variety of food to in the new self serving supermarkets, a greater portion of their income spent on home ownership with inside toilet and bath, washing machine, vacuum cleaner, television, motor cars and holidays bringing greater mobility and personal travel; none of which existed before 1950 for the ordinary person, but most of all there was a lasting peace. There would also be a greater emphasis on individuality, and consequently an air of selfishness, '---- you Jack' which is so much a part of present day life, Jumped up 'uns as some of the older ones like Owd Breakall would say, self-opinionated might be the word that best describes these newer generations. The possibility of someday having to go and fight for your country and lay down your life would be anathema to so many today, it is no longer part of the deal in being a member of the present day society, where taking, not giving is the name of the game. Nevertheless those born since the fifties and sixties have also had to adapt to change, the age of technology has moved things on at a breathtaking pace in every sphere of life, no one has a minute to spare in the high speed, increasingly scrutinised world we now live, the stability that once existed in the family, in the workplace is not there any more. The people looking for that better life these days are immigrants, and if they will work and not scrounge then why should they not.

In the main, those who had been at the Front did not have the means to take pictures, neither could they write home of what they saw since everything was heavily censored. It could well be one reason why so many turned to poetry as a means of expression. What they wrote gives some idea of what they felt a the time and curiously so much of it is humorous; so whatever the poems are they are not intended to shock in the way that a picture might, nevertheless they do have a very strong impact, and more than anything they are honest, the word 'spin' was for later generations. The men who wrote the poems were not 'poets' per se, they were just ordinary working men conscripted and shipped out to fight in the front line, increasingly bewildered, wearied, saddened, many frightened by the violence of war and a military regime that had a complete disregard for human life.

They lived with a deathly routine, living and sleeping in the trenches with persistent enemy shelling and mortar bombing, over the top, advancing to the wire, in 'reserve', in 'support' and then back into 'the line', they were conditioned to 'stand too' 'go over the top' and die, living in the most horrific conditions, sinking in mud, the blood, the bones and the smell of the death of their comrades, dead horses, smashed carts, remnants of uniforms and bodies, the ground littered with uprooted trees and water filled shell holes. They had a need to write of what they saw, what they had to endure and to record it in the only way available to them. From that point of view we owe them a great debt and should therefore hold their memory sacred. How can we live in what to them would be such extravagant comfort and forget about them when not only did they have nothing, they gave their lives to boot? These and the many other WWI poems give us a good insight into what they really saw and felt. Understanding how the war came about and the huge impact it had, and following some of the exploits of the troops involved, might give some small inkling into just how 'they gave their today for our tomorrow'. I never cease to be impressed at the way that some of the poems from the WWI trenches are written in such a light hearted, matter of fact way, almost mocking their own existence as they suffered a living hell, and yet others speak of the extreme sadness of it all.

There is a new way of thinking now, that self-flagellation is good for us and will make us better in the eyes of others, there is a tendency to apologise for what our forefathers did, indeed there is an expectation that we will do that. But I feel that is simply to mock them, a display of arrogance on the one hand and political correctness on the other, we did not live in those times but more to the point the generations from the 1950's have never suffered the conditions that they had to cope with. We should all be ashamed of the efforts of so many that seek to apply the standards of today to what was in effect another world. War demands a different set of rules, for instance making decisions now about what happened then to my mind just cannot be done. They did what they did because it had to be done and who are we to judge? Can it be that we have learned from the mistakes they made and now take a high-handed approach in assessing what they were about? Well we are now so clever that having twice been at war with Afghanistan in the past and had no lasting influence we find ourselves there again, and have been for 10 years, that does not speak of learning in my book especially when one considers the dreadful loss of fine young soldiers, (465) and the heart rending sight of so many fine young men back in civvy street with terrible injuries. The Taliban are at the door and when the Nato forces pull out they will be back as if those 10 years never happened. The politicians of this century cannot resist the opportunity to bask in the glow of world statesmanship and invariably the impression they leave is that of the old adage, put your hands in a bucket of water, the impression you leave when you take them out -------.

This is one of the little verses from my fathers hand-written book of poems and ditties.

AFGHANISTAN

When lying wounded on Afghanistan's plains,
And the women come out, to cut up your remains,
Just roll to your rifle and blow out your brains,
And go to your God like a soldier.

Britain was totally unprepared

In the early stages of the Great War the supply of ammunition was a serious problem for Britain and also France, the difference was that France had lost her industrial north and the coalfields that fed her industry. France knew that ammunition was a key issue and strove to create alternative means of production in order to ensure that adequate supplies reached the front. That was far from the case in Britain, the military leaders of the British High Command had been trained to wage fast mobile war in which heavy field artillery played little part and for that reason, in the early stages of the war no priority was given to ammunition supplies for heavy field guns. Lloyd George wrote in his memoirs that Kitchener was more concerned with the high level of artillery shells being expended than he was in the number of casualties being inflicted on our troops by the enemy; the reality was that the British forces did not have half the ammunition that they required. Commenting during a meeting of the cabinet on the 'Battle of Neuve Chapelle' Kitchener made the comment "this is terrible" and when asked if the casualties were high he said, "I am not thinking of casualties", he was appalled at the extent of the use of ammunition, by this time of course the British regular army had been virtually wiped out.

In a reply to a memo from Sir John French, G.O.C. of the B.E.F. berating the authorities for the appalling lack off ammunition supplies and stating the case for his being unable to carry out attacks, Kitchener made no bones about the fact that Sir John French was expected to do whatever was required whether or not ammunition was available, if the ammunition wasn't there he would just have to get on with it, the numbers of casualties were to be regretted but could be no excuse for not doing what was necessary, ammunition shortages or not.

I think that it was Napoleon who once said something like 'when you aim to hit the target you have to close one eye', and so throughout the war the British and French General Staffs literally did just that, the consequences were horrendous in terms of dead and wounded. Not all died in action; more than three thousand British soldiers were sentenced to death by Courts Marshal, fortunately only some three hundred sentences were carried out. One breach of army regulations that was subject to capital punishment was falling asleep on 'stag', sentry duty. I recall one night when I was on stag in Germany; in those days BAOR employed Polish refugees on security. At the Osnabruck Garrison where I was stationed a dark green uniformed, armed Polish militiaman accompanied each soldier on stag; in other circumstances it would have been two soldiers. The stags operated at shifts of 2 hours on and 4 hours off over 24 hours, in this instance I was awakened to go back on at 2am, it was January with a very thick hoar frost covering everything and huge globules of ice hanging from the cap comforter around my face where I breathed. The Pole was used to extreme cold and anyway he was built like a battleship, but towards the end of the 2 hours I was literally shivering from head to toe even with my army greatcoat over my BD and army issue woollen Long John's. At one stage we passed the ablutions block and the Pole said to me, 'go in for a few minutes and get warm, I'll keep watch. The blanco room was in darkness, there were two four inch steam pipes running around the lower walls and above were heavy slatted shelves, it was a place to dry out webbing and very, very warm. I put my rifle on the shelf and sat down and within a few minutes the heat overwhelmed me, I was dosing off, fortunately the Pole popped his head in and said the Orderly Officer was doing the rounds, which he wasn't, but it did the trick. I know how easy that was but I don't think that anyone was ever Court Marshalled for it, and certainly not in peacetime, more like jankers, a few extra fire piquet's if you were caught.

3

European Rivalries

One may wonder what Britain was doing fighting in a European War; Britain of course had her Empire and was not at any stage threatened by events in Europe, she could afford to sit on the sidelines and not get involved; or could she? The security of the Channel Ports had been of supreme importance to England for centuries and her preoccupation with Belgian neutrality and free access to the channel ports had gone back to before the days of the Spanish armadas. England had fought with the Spanish, the French and the Dutch for that very reason and now it was no less important an issue. From the French revolution emerged Napoleon who was bent on dominating the whole of Europe, the five major European powers of that time, France, Germany, Austro/Hungary, Russia and Great Britain were very much distrustful of one and other, trying to hold on to, and where possible, expand their Empires in order to survive.

There were endless rounds of conferences in the capitals of Europe continually sorting out problems and making concessions to each other. Britain alone, although contributing to these discussions, stood aloof and had little need as the others did to enter into defensive treaties since she had no common borders with any other country. Until 1904 and the Entente Cordiale, Britain took no part in the pandering by European states to each other, making every effort to get others on side and seeking to set up set up alliances in order to protect themselves. The Entente Cordiale was readily entered into by France and was an agreement that the French gained most from. Britain was a powerful nation with a huge Empire and France was only too happy to have Britain on her side, but although Britain would no longer have conflict with France in North Africa, it brought her prospects of war with Germany a great deal closer, it was inevitable that Germany would go to war at some time, and the time had come when Britain could no longer sit in isolation on the fringes of Europe.

The Entente Cordiale brought to an end the long-standing conflict between the Britain and France, and the newfound cordiality between the two countries had its origins in the upper Nile valley. When General Gordon was assassinated at Khartoum in 1885 the British were forced to pull out of the Sudan along with the Egyptian forces leaving the area to be controlled by the Mhadi. Some thirteen years later in 1898 Britain, along with Egyptian forces decided to re-conquer the Sudan and after the battle of Omdurman Kitchener again took Khartoum. The British had created a great deal of animosity by ousting the French from Egypt where the Suez Canal was the lifeline to the British Empire in the Far East. France had traditionally colonized North Africa but Britain had no interest in that sphere other than the control of the Canal; that was a major problem for France. The retaking of The Sudan and control of the upper Nile however was part of a British plan to link the colonies and protectorates under British rule from Cairo to the South African Cape and to control passage through the canal. Contrary to this the French, who virtually controlled the whole of north West Africa had dreams of linking the territories from Morocco down to the Congo in the West with its colonies on the Red Sea and the Gulf of Aden in the east, the key to both British and French aspirations was of course the upper Nile. The British were concerned that the French, still smarting from the loss of Egypt, might send a force from

Dakar in the French West African Colony of Senegal to take the strategic town of Fashoda situated on the Nile between Uganda and the southern Sudan

In the House of Commons Lord Grey had said that 'Any move by France to take control of the upper Nile would be considered by the British Government as an act of aggression'. Nevertheless as Kitcheners was striving against the Dervishes to retake the Sudan, France had already dispatched an expeditionary force under Captain Baptiste Marchand to capture the fortress. It took Marchand all of twelve months to carry a dismantled gunboat through the jungles of the Congo to Fashoda where on arrival he persuaded the local tribal chief to place the area under French rule, with that he was able to raise the French flag over the Fort. Very soon after his arrival he received word that Kitchener was close to Fashoda with a force of 2000 men and five gunboats, far greater than the small force of French Colonial troops. On his arrival Kitchener told Marchand that he would raise the British flag alongside the French but Marchand refused to allow it. Kitchener spelled out the consequences, that Britain and France would be at war if it became necessary for Kitchener to take Fashoda by force, Marchand did not respond to Kitchener's statement but later they did talk. They eventually arrived at a diplomatic compromise allowing Kitchener to raise the Union Jack over a corner of the fort. It was owing to the good sense of the French and British commanders that war between the countries was averted, peace had broken out at Fashoda and the matter was passed on to the British and French Governments to sort out.

The struggles between the European countries in the 18th and early 19th centuries were aimed at defending their positions at home whilst not losing out on expansion in Africa, Asia and the Middle East and this state of affairs generally continued for the next hundred years. The British and French eventually ended their longstanding backbiting following the Fashoda incident when they came to an agreement over the Sudan, out of which eventually came the 'Entente Cordiale' in 1904. England finally ended her isolation from Europe and ensured that the Channel coast of Belgium and France would be secure, this was always what Britain had sought when she had sent her armies into Belgium over the centuries, never to occupy that country but only seeking to prevent occupation by any other power. Britain now found herself again in that same role, tipping the balance in favour of a neutral Belgium and a free France.

Britain traditionally had been interested only playing a preventative part in any one European State dominating others and gaining too much power, not only for the benefit of the oppressed but ultimately to protect Britain's own interests. Safety from attack or invasion of the English channel ports along with safe access to the North Sea and the Western approaches has always been a fundamental cornerstone of the English security. The home defences were dependent on a powerful navy and coastal defences particularly after the French revolution and the rise of Napoleon. When it became clear in 1805 that France had every intention of threatening the free movement of British shipping in the Channel and in the Mediterranean, Nelson was ordered to seek out the joint French Spanish fleet under the Admirals Villeneuve and Gravina, he found them at Trafalgar and roundly defeated them, albeit at the cost of losing his own life in the process. This tremendous victory set the scene for Napoleon's eventual demise.

Sir John Moore commanded the first British Force to oppose the French in support of the Spanish, who were under French occupation, as was Portugal. The

campaign itself was a failure in which the Commanding
Officer of that small force, Sir John Moore, was killed
at Corunna. We learned at school of all these exploits,
the poem 'The Burial of Sir John Moore' written by Sir
Charles Wolfe is one that we learned by heart, the sort
of poem that stirred something within.

Not a sound was heard, not a funeral note
As his corpse to the ramparts we hurried.
Not a soldier discharged his farewell shot
Oer' the grave where our hero we buried.
We buried him darkly at dead of night
The sods with our bayonets turning
By the struggling moonbeam's misty light
And the lantern dimly burning.

Wellington continued the battles of the Peninsular War,
Badajoz, Talavera, Salamanca, Vittoria and San Sebas-
tian are all battle honours on the colours of many Brit-
ish regiments. (The Kings Own provided the 'forlorn
hope' led by Lt. Francis McGuire at San Sebastian). At
the battle of Waterloo, (Blucher named it La Belle Alli-
ance) Wellington commanded a coalition army of Brit-
ish, Belgian, Nederland and Prussian forces and finally
put an end to Napoleon's Grand Plan that he had man-
aged to resurrect during the hundred days freedom he
enjoyed following his escape from allied incarceration
on the Island of Elba. Although it is said that he dis-
missed the English as a 'Nation of Shopkeepers', a
phrase that he had apparently borrowed from the
French Ambassador to Italy, Napoleon whilst held at
Longwood on St. Helena and reflecting on his cam-
paigns said,

"The English Character is superior to ours. They are
in everything more practical than we are: they emigrate,

they marry; they kill themselves with less indecision than we display in going to the opera. They are also braver than we are. I think that one can say that in courage they are to us what we are to the Russians, what the Russians are to the Germans, what the Germans are to the Italians." And he also goes on to say "Had I an English Army I should have conquered the universe, for I could have gone all over the world without demoralising my troops. Had I been the choice of the English as I was of the French, I might have lost the battle of Waterloo without losing a vote in the Legislature or a soldier from my ranks, I should have won the game."[4]

At the outbreak of WWI France already had a pact with Russia that if either were attacked, the one would declare war in support of the other. This was a safeguard against a German attack that Russia feared and France already had suffered in 1870 with the loss of Alsace and Lorraine. Britain herself had no such commitment to France, but control of the French and Belgian coasts were as much Britains concern as theirs. Since 1904 Britain had been developing ever more friendly relations with France, a fact that led Germany to consider herself surrounded by potential enemies since the signing of the Entente Cordiale. Germany considered Russia to be the ever present threat, France the old enemy, and now Britain had, to all intents and purposes joined them in a tripartite. It meant that inevitably Britain would be drawn into conflict with Germany, it did not take too long for that to happen, and the cause was something no one could have predicted. The assassination of the Grand Duke of Austria and his wife during a visit to Sarejevo provided a golden opportunity for the Kaiser to enhance his position in Europe on favourable terms and he made every effort to ensure that it did not slip away.

Had Austria been left to deal with the incident without interference from Germany things would probably have been quite different, in the event it was The Kaiser that gave Austria the assurance that whatever action Austria might take against Serbia, the might of the German Army would be behind them. The outcome of that was that the five major powers all mobilised, Germany had set the stage in such a way that war was inevitable.

Following the death of the Grand Duke Austria made certain demands on Serbia who found that these requirements were on the whole acceptable, but Serbia wanted time to consider the implications in some of the detail that related to Serbian sovereignty before it was finalised, Austria however, had demanded a reply within 48 hours. With the request for more time from Serbia, Austria, encouraged by Germany, at once mobilised her army without further notice. Russia had already declared that she would come to Serbia's aid should she be attacked and therefore Russia also mobilised. Germany on the other hand had already mobilised with a view to backing Austria and at this stage declared war on Russia. This of course made Germany the aggressor since Germany was the first to declare war on another nation. France, having signed a treaty with Russia had no choice but to declare war on Germany in support of her ally, and eventually, although there was no such treaty between France and Britain there was a tacit understanding on the part of France that Britain would support her in the event of war. Germany had very cleverly taken advantage of the untimely assassination of the Grand Duke to go to War with at least two of the countries of the 'Triple Entente', i.e. Russia and France, two countries that Germany saw as possible aggressors, and she had done so even though Serbia and Austria were probably at the point of settling their confrontation by each having reached agreement on most of Austria's demands. Nowhere amongst the governments of the five major powers involved was the ability to prevent war against a Germany bent on lighting the fuse.

A Game Of Nap

> I'll go one, said Austria,
> I'll go two, said France.
> I'll go three, said Russia,
> If I get the chance.
>
> I'll go four, said Germany,
> And wipe you off the map.
> But the Kaiser fled,
> When England said,
> Cor' Blimey! I'll go Nap.

Today all those Empires are gone but the struggle for supremacy that led again to WWII continues in the form of the European Union, it is a continuation of that great game where there is a will to be top dog. Being part of the EU however does not mean that Britain is in the running for that. Unlike France and Germany it is something she has never sought, the struggle to be the European leader is a political cat and mouse game played by Germany and France, a follow on from the wars, the traditional enemies. To this point the European union has of course, achieved it's stated goal, and that is to ensure peace in Europe, it is a union of equal status for all members, but some will always be more equal than others. Britain will never ever be accepted on equal terms because the French see themselves as a cut above the rest and will, like Germany, put her interests first, concessions will always be made by the other members whenever confrontations arise with these two because of the power that they wield within the E.U., and of course there is only one top dog between those two, and that is Germany.

4

Germany's Ambitions

Rudyard Kipling said that they were 'Lions led by Donkeys' and there is no doubt that in the Great War human life was wasted on a scale never ever witnessed before, the slaughter, the suffering and misery were of an order difficult to understand for those of today's generation. Generals fought battles on the basis of how many men it would take to achieve an objective, were there sufficient in reserve to replace losses at the front, of course unlike spent shells trained soldiers could not be replaced by simply manufacturing them. For most people the savage, sword slashing hand to hand fighting of an age long gone, would be the worst kind of situation to find themselves, The Crimea or Waterloo would probably be that sort of unimaginable bloody battle scene, the reality is that nothing could ever compare to the death and carnage of the two world wars, and in the end with the Armistice signed in November 1918 all it did was stop an Europes most belligerent nation long enough for it to build up its arms and then start all over again with WWII.

That is probably the crux of the whole matter, Germany in the early 20th century was a nation bent on European domination and had a will to expand to become a colonial power, to have a navy capable of dominating Europe and through those aspirations created great unrest within Europe. Germany had huge armies and had created a massive build up of arms against France, Russia, Belgium and Britain (and eventually the United States) the latter two had very small armies and were ill equipped to fight an extensive land war at the outbreak in August 1914. In August 1914 French morale was high, but although she had a large army and the ability to call on legions from her Colonial territories, was ill prepared for war. Only Germany prepared on an enormous scale and was ready to over run anything that got in the way with the massive force of arms that had been assembled, not for national defence but solely for the purposes of expanding German territory and influence in Europe and beyond, Lebensraum!

Loss of life on a huge scale was inevitable for the Allies if the west was to remain free, but in the end Germany suffered even greater losses in its efforts to dominate Europe; such was the determination of the Kaiser and the German military machine and it took the youth of Britain and the Dominions, France and in the end the Americans to push them back beyond the Rhine from the enormously strong defensive positions that they had taken after the small British regular army was all but wiped out at the 1st battle of Ypres and the French armies had been decimated all the way to the Swiss border. Military commanders are there to lead armies into battle at the command of their governments who decide in the first place whether or not to go to war. It is the military commanders who take the consequences, if they do not do the job then they are relieved of their command by politicians and replaced by someone who will, that is the point where the decision is made that the job has to be done come what may if the matter is to be brought to a successful conclusion, even though the cost may seem unacceptable high at the outset, or any other point on the way.

The job of the armed forces is to ensure the nations defence by whatever means are available and that role devolved, as it always had, to the Royal Navy. But for the B.E.F. fighting a static war where unlike in mobile war there was a need for heavy field guns, the initial shortage of ammunition and the entrenched positions of both sides led to enormous loss of life; the patriotic stance of the British soldier knowing that freedom of European domination meant security for the homeland and that the cause was a just one, enabled the British army to resist German aggression and end the war victorious. Today that rush to arms would be anathema to the young men of this country, the present day mentality is completely different and thankfully war on that sort of scale is now a remote possibility.

The British Government was already gravely concerned about the loss of life as early as autumn of 1914, but the political leaders sat on their hands and had little idea of what was needed by the forces on the western front, mainly because those who were required to meet those needs i.e. the War Office did not inform them. Kitchener had crossed the line from soldier to politician and was now the Secretary of State for War, and as Lloyd George had noted in his memoirs, Kitchener was more concerned with the high level of artillery shells being expended than he was in the number of casualties being inflicted on British troops by the enemy.

The problem of such enormous numbers of dead and injured manifested itself later on in the War when the ranks of the French Army in April 1917 began to mutiny in despair at the task given to them during the 'Nivelle Offensive' a plan fully endorsed by Lloyd George. First one battalion and then others followed in the belief that the task was impossible and that nothing was worth such enormous casualties, this was kept from the British Army Commanders for a very long time and probably because at that same time the Battle of Arras was in progress where some of the severest fighting of the war was going on. It was battle thrust onto the British and Canadian troops that was nothing more than a massive diversion to fool the Germans and enable General Nivelle to carry out his doomed Grand Plan. Following the battle of Verdun the ranks of the French army (the poelus) began to mutiny, first one battalion and then others followed in the belief that 'nothing can be worth such sacrifice', a large number of the French mutineers were rounded up and executed as an example to others and at that point Marshal Petain took over command from the reclusive General Nivelle and said 'no more'. The disastrous loss of life in the French ranks up to that point compelled Petain to look to the Artillery to carry the burden in future.

In the end the war was a very close run thing, after almost four years and all the loss of life on both sides the allies could sense that the end was sight, but then the Germans, just as weary as the allies, almost turned the tables in a massive push, enabled by bringing all their divisions from the Russian Front where the 'August 1917' revolution had put an end to Russia's involvement in the war. It was the British front that the German High Command was determined to break toward the end of March 1918 and it almost succeeded, it would have seen the British crushed, the possibility of Britain evacuating her army as she did in 1940 at Dunkirk would have been unthinkable, in 1918 it was an infinitely larger army, some 1.8 million men in total and evacuation would have been impossible.

The Fifth Army held and denied them the breakthrough that would have ended the war. The German watchword was 'England the Enemy', they knew that if they could beat the British in one big push that the French army would just collapse and the war would be won. The fact is that just a few weeks later the French army did collapse at the Chemin des Dames and allowed the Germans to reach the Marne some fifty miles from Paris, had it not been for the build up of reserve divisions by Foch, largely at the expense of a weakened

British front, that again would have been the end for the Allies.

The main thrust of the German attack at the 2nd battle of the Somme was aimed at the front held by the British Fifth army under General Sir Hubert Gough, who in his book 'The Fifth Army' refers to 'it's great victory in retreat'. It was when the Germans had pushed back the Fifth army and failed to break through that they decided to attack the French and was successful. But Foch held back his reserves until the German lines of communication were overextended and the troops exhausted, then he struck, it was the turning point that allowed the British Army to attack and sweep everything before it. It serves to show how close the Allies came to losing the War even after 4 years of struggle and the enormous increase in armed forces, guns and munitions. Whilst Germany was fighting on two fronts Britain and France could see the end in sight, but Russia's peace agreement with Germany changed all that. The British were having to draft increasingly older men to the front to replace the huge number of casualties, and Foch's huge reserves were gained largely at the expense of the British having to extend the line and relieve French divisions at a time when the British were not only doing all the fighting but doing it against massive odds. Foch's plan placed a huge burden on the B.E.F. and was a cause of great friction at the time, the plan worked and that was all that mattered, but it was mainly thanks to the dogged defence of the British Fifth, Third and Second Armies in those desperate March/April days that prevented the occupation of Amiens or Hazebrouck and total defeat.

Lloyd George begins the first volume of his memoirs with a comment by Lord Rosebery about the 'Entente Cordiale', during a visit to him in 1904 at 'Dalmeny' his home in the Scottish Lowlands, Lloyd

George recalls, His first greeting to me was, "well I suppose you are as pleased as the rest of them with this French agreement?" I assured him that I was delighted that our snarling and scratching relations with France had come to an end at last. Rosebery replied "you are all wrong, it means war with Germany in the end!"

The French army was mobilised to meet her obligations to Russia for no other reason than Russia's support of Serbia, a country that was part of the Austro/Hungarian Empire and with which Britain had little or no interest. Yet Britain was now tied to France, it was the fact that Britain's interest in securing the Channel and avoiding conflict with France over territories in North Africa that paved the way for the Entente Cordiale in 1904. From there it was the increasing co-operation between the British and French military, even though there was no treaty guaranteeing mutual support in the event of war for either country, that brought Britain into a situation that she had always strove to avoid, being drawn into European conflict. Not only was Britain dragged into the war unwillingly by France fulfilling her commitment to Russia, It was to support what had been a few years earlier, a vital enemy. Britain had relinquished her isolation from Europe and has never regained it to this day, and was to pay dearly for that in two world wars and beyond.

The Fly

Buzz fly, gad fly, dragon fly and blue,
When you're in the trenches, come and visit
you.
They revel in your butter dish and riot on your
ham,
Drill upon the army cheese and loot the army
jam.

They're with you in the dusk, and the dawning
and the noon,
They come in close formation, in column and
platoon.
There's never zest like Tommy's zest when
these have got to die,
For Tommy takes his puttees off and strafes the
blooming fly.

***

5

The Opening Moves

For a Month prior to Britain declaring War on Germany in August the1914 the British Govt. had been watching the situation in Europe following the assassination of the Austrian Emperor Franz Ferdinand with only a passing interest, it meant little to a government to whom matters at home, in Ireland and in her far flung Empire were of far greater concern. On the Continent however, things very quickly began to escalate and the players started to show their hands like in a game of 'nap'. Britain was on the sidelines and would only be involved if Belgium neutrality was threatened which, initially seemed highly unlikely, the various attempts at avoiding war by Austria and Russia seemed to be less ambitious than the will to go to war as the countries directly involved took entrenched positions, Austria pushed along by an aggressive Germany, mobilised against Serbia ensuring that that Russia mobilised also.

The opportunity that might have helped to defuse the whole situation was not allowed to appear, the simple reason for that was Germany's interest in keeping things moving toward the cliff edge. Matters were brought sharply into focus for the British Government when, having initially taken a non-committal approach to Germany declaring war on France, herself was plunged headlong into war. The Austro – Hungarian Empire was disintegrating and was taken advantage of by Germany who was bent on dominating Europe and expanding her empire. For one hundred years and more Prussia and the German states had sought to dominate, to be in the same league as Britain and France on the world stage, it was that spark that lit the tinder, the assassination of the Archduke Ferdinand at Sarejevo that came out of the blue. General Sir Hubert Gough recalled[5] that he attended the Court Ball at Buckingham Palace only a matter of a week or two after the assassination and had sensed that conflict was in the offing, but looking back at his then thoughts he wrote 'In the summer of 1914 a man who anticipated the conflicts of 1918 would have been laughed to scorn'. No one could foresee the horrendous consequences of what was to happen.

In August 1914, as far as the larger part of the British cabinet understood, Britain had no agreement to go to war in the defence of any country except Belgium, however since the incident involving the French at Fashoda in the Sudan and later the signing of the Entente Cordiale of 1904, Britain and France had become increasingly friendly. Later, as a result of an incident that occurred in 1905 known as the 'Morocco incident' (In which Germany had made significant demands, the details of which hold no further interest) and a subsequent conference at Algeciras, the British and French military had worked much closer together, the details of the incident Although the British Cabinet generally knew nothing of it they had made plans that would be put into practice in the event of France being invaded by another European power. The French request to the British at that Algeciras conference and the action that followed was what Sir Edward Grey was so much at pains to expand on in his House of Commons speech on August 4th 1914, the day Britain declared War on Germany, and the reason was that this close co-operation between British and French military chiefs had been kept under wraps. Now, what had seemed a most unlikely situation for the British to find themselves in, was unfolding fast.

Field Marshal Sir John French makes reference[6] to

having dinner in London with the French Military Atta-ché Vicomte La Panouse. The attaché said that the French Ambassador was very concerned about the doubts being expressed that the British would enter the war in support of France. Sir John says "I felt perfectly sure that so long as Mr Asquith remained Prime Minister, and Lord Haldane, Sir Edward Grey and Mr Winston Churchill continued to be members of the Cabinet, their voices would guide the destinies of the British Empire, and that we should remain true to our friendly understanding with the Entente Powers". It did seem that all those who needed to know were well informed about the British commitment to France but that everyone else was in the dark. Sir John also makes the comment in his book, It is now within the knowledge of all, that the General Staffs of Great Britain and France had, for a long time held conferences, and that a complete mutual understanding as to combined action in certain eventualities existed. A further indication at the time that Britain had made a prior commitment was the fact that a [7]precautionary period was ordered without prior notice on the 29th of July 1914 (a state of alert in today's terms).

Although well aware of developments on the continent, Britain was not unduly concerned as Austria threatened Serbia who in turn entered into discussions with a protective Russia, there was a distinct feeling that there was little likelihood of British involvement, and as a consequence the British Government did nothing to indicate that Britain would come to the aid of France if she ordered mobilisation. It is a fact that there appears to have been little consultation between Britain and France regarding the visit by the French President, Ms. Poincarre to St. Petersberg on the 21st of July 1914, and what sort of line the French were likely to take as events unfolded, matters that of course would now affect Britain. In fact at that stage France had, in a communiqué to Austria, already made it clear that France would go to war in support of Russia if Austria declared war on Serbia. Britain at that stage was not implicated in these discussions, or so it was thought, and was hoping that she would have a role as mediator to help take the heat of the whole situation. The reality was at that stage that Britain was committed to entering the war in support of France by a tacit agreement but not too many people knew that. Austria, in discussion with the German High Command, was convinced that nothing would be gained by taking up Britain's offer to mediate and Germany reinforced it's offer of support for any action that Austria wished to take against Serbia, irrespective of whether Russia became involved or not, of course Germany knew that Russia had a pact with France and what the consequences of that would be.

The first direct involvement by Britain appears to have been on the 22nd of July 1914 when the Secretary of State suggested, through the British Ambassador, that Serbia accept within reason the Austrian ultimatum which was expected at any time, he added that nothing, more could be said. The British Ambassador to Rome informed the Foreign Secretary, Sir Edward Grey that he had information indicating clearly that the terms of the Austrian ultimatum to be delivered to Serbia were deliberately set out so as to illicit a negative response from Serbia, and that also there was to be a mere 48 hour time limit for a Serbian reply accepting the terms in total. Serbia did in fact accept almost all of the conditions but asked for time to discuss certain points, particularly regarding Serbian sovereignty, at which Austria without more ado ordered a pre mobilisation. Russia immediately responded by mobilising and this was followed by German mobilisation, and as things progressed the French Government ordered mobilisation of its armies against Germany.

At that point Britain found it necessary to ask France, through the U.K. ambassador in Paris, whether or not she would respect Belgian neutrality so long as no other power violated it. This same message in essence was sent to the German Government via the U.K. ambassador in Berlin requesting an assurance that Belgian neutrality would not be violated, but the concern here was that even if Germany were to give assurances to safeguard Belgian neutrality, should France be defeated then without doubt Belgium, Holland and Denmark would all be overrun by Germany, Belgium could not stand alone, neither could Britain go to war with Germany on her behalf with the whole of western Europe under German rule.

France replied that she was agreeable to the terms, however Germany did not reply to the request but that same day declared war on Russia, this made Germany the aggressor and confirmed that from the moment the Archduke was assassinated The Kaiser had manipulated events to ensure war. Of course the Kaiser knew that France would have to declare war on Germany because of the Franco Russian pact and he also knew that the German [8]Schlieffenplan depended on access across Belgium in order to attack France. Britain informed the German Ambassador Count Lichnowski, that should Belgian neutrality be compromised the British public would be greatly concerned. Germany, it seems was prepared to take the chance that Britain would not declare war under such circumstances and at this point Lichnowski asked whether Britain would remain neutral if Germany agreed not to violate Belgian neutrality, or if in fact Britain could formulate terms on which she would be prepared to remain neutral. To this Sir Edward Grey, the British Foreign Secretary, replied that he could not give that assurance, that Britain needed to have her hands free to do whatever she saw fit.

It seems obvious in hindsight that France, although eager for Serbia to accept the Austrian terms and not at all keen to see the matter escalate, (France had withdrawn her troops to 6 miles from the border as an indication of her unwillingness to go to war) was however quite ready to mobilise in support of Russia in the event of war being declared, in fact France had already discussed plans with Russia in their recent meeting. Because of her treaty obligations France had no choice but to support Russia against an aggressor, but at the same time had shown little concern for Britain's position since there had been no discussion with Britain regarding any mutual understanding that both countries were committed to go to war to support of either except in the case of an unprovoked attack by an aggressor. France simply took it for granted that Britain would join with France if she were at war. France mobilised full in the knowledge that France, Britain and Russia would be together at war against Germany and Austria but had carried out no high level talks with Britain as she had with Russia. When it seemed to France that Britain was dragging her feet about entering the war, the French Ambassador, Paul Cambon, who was a signatory to the 'Entente Cordiale', made comments about the British 'code of honour' and created a situation where Britain had no choice but to quickly go to the aid of France and again that gave rise to Lord Grey's explanation to the House about the little understood relationship between Britain and France in the event of war.

On the 4th of August Sir Edward Grey reminded the House of Commons that whilst Britain had no obligation to go to war, France was now a friendly nation, and in a long speech outlining what were essentially Britain's interests he made it clear that 'In his opinion' Britain really had no choice. Well it does seem that Britain had no choice because over several years the Chiefs of staff at the Admiralty and War Office had entered into discussions with the French military about what would happen in the event of an unprovoked attack on France by another power. It would be highly unlikely that any other power but Germany would make an unprovoked attack on France so at least that was clearly understood. Britain could not stand by and see the domination of the Channel ports by Germany, and although the circumstances that France found itself in did not quite fit the existing Entente agreement, it was not in Britain's interest to stand aside. France was not subject to an unprovoked attack by another power but had gone to war in support of Russia with whom Britain had no such arrangement, if we went to war it would primarily be to meet our treaty obligations in preventing Belgium from an aggressor, and to keep the Channel clear of any threat to British shipping, not to save France.

Plans had been made as to how an attack on France by another power would be met; the discussions concerned only plans for how the British Forces would be deployed and identifying in what area of France the British forces might operate in such an emergency. These arrangements were sanctioned by the British Government, on the basis that Britain's hands would not be tied by such talks, and that she would not necessarily have to support France in the event of war. However, if Britain were to see fit, then certain arrangements would then be in place, ready to be acted on. France had originally put feelers out with regard to Britain and France having such talks during the 1906 Algeciras conference, which took place after what was known as The Morocco incident of 1905. France had been keen at that stage to get a firm arrangement with Britain, but such a treaty or alliance was not in Britain's best interests at that time, but on signing the Entente Cordial, France was no doubt thinking ahead and hoping for the opportunity to arise when the subject of some sort of alliance could be mooted. The Entente Cordiale greatly favoured France in that she knew that sooner or later France and Germany would go to war and to have Britain on her side might deter the Germans from any thoughts of attacking France.

Lord Grey told the House on the 4th August 1914 that when the question was raised about the possibility of an Anglo-French accord by the French at the 1906 Algeciras conference the British cabinet were in fact on holiday, it was the summer recess and he was able only to discuss the matter with the Prime Minister, Richard Haldane, the Secretary for War and the Chancellor of the Exchequer. They all agreed that the War Office and the Admiralty should enter talks with France. It does however seem that nobody saw fit to discuss this matter with the rest of the cabinet or Parliament at any time before Grey spoke to the House some 7/8 years later on August 4th 1914, and this also seems to indicate that not only did the four ministers not discuss this matter other than amongst themselves, but the War Office also kept it quiet, had war not broken out then the rest of the cabinet, members of the House of Commons and the general public would never have been aware that Britain and France had been conducting talks on a military level for plans that would be put into practice if and when they both saw fit. The British Military entered the talks sure in the knowledge that Britain would have to come to the aid of France in the event of war with Germany come what may. There was of course no treaty with France but there was quite clearly a gentleman's agreement, however none of this knowledge was in the public domain until August 1914.

The military plan was, that in the event of war the B.E.F. would embark for France and take up positions in the area of Amiens with a view to operating in the area of Maubauge on the Belgian border covering the French left. It was near to the Channel and convenient for the transportation and supplying of British Troops from the UK. This was by all accounts an informal understanding and no agreement was signed, but major changes introduced in the British Army by the then Secretary for War, Richard Haldane, were put in place for the express purpose of supporting France in the event of War. The changes included the formation of The British Expeditionary Force of some six divisions plus a cavalry division, the introduction of the Territorial Army and the establishment of the Officer Training School.

In the event of France going to war Britain would have also gone to war in any case whether or not Belgium was invaded, it was simply a matter of time before the decision would have been made in order to oppose German efforts to occupy Paris and take control of the Channel ports, this was a scenario that Britain had worked hard on for several hundred years and the potential danger was too great for this country to ignore. There had been ample evidence of the bullish attitude of the Germans and their wish not only to be the strongest power in the world militarily but also to have the most powerful navy afloat.   The Germans were working continuously toward that end and the threat to British Naval supremacy along with the possible threat of invasion was of great concern to the British Government and had been for some considerable time. The German economy was also growing at a faster rate than that of Britain; competition between the two countries on foreign markets was becoming fierce and threatening British overseas markets.

In 1911 there was an incident referred to as the 'Agadir incident' in which a German warship, the Panther, was sent into the harbour of the French Morrocan town of Agadir on the Atlantic coast. It was done in response to French Troops occupying the city of Fez and breaching the Terms of the Algeciras conference by so doing. This action was seen as an opportunistic move by Germany to press the French into giving way on German expansionist demands in Africa, perhaps it was also intended to embarrass France, but it was also intended to give warning to the signatories of the 'Triple Entent', France and Russia and France and Britain. The British Government became concerned at the brash attitude of the Germans and sought to quell matters before they escalated further between what were the two leading European belligerent Nations.

Increasingly Germany was committing hostile acts and the 'Agadir incident' could not be ignored, Britain had to get a message across that if Germany went to war with France it would inevitably mean war with Britain, and a hope that Germany would see the futility in making such a move. A communiqué was sent to the German Government expressing concern and at the same time indicating that the British Government was sensitive to German expectations of empire building in Africa, indeed Britain was prepared to work with Germany to peacefully achieve that end. The communiqué was ignored and after almost three weeks David Lloyd George, the then Chancellor of the Exchequer, took it upon himself to clarify the British position in his annual speech to the City at the Mansion House in 1911. He pointed out that whilst the last thing that this country wanted was war, that in the event of war between France and Germany, Britain would enforce the terms of the London Treaty of 1836 guaranteeing Belgian neutrality, in other words Britain would declare war on any country who violated Belgian neutrality.

Germany certainly got the message, because whilst prepared to take on the French who, after having defeated them in the 1870 Franco/Prussian War, were in their view weak and would be unable to resist a German invasion, but they were reluctant to also take on Great Britain. Germany suffered an embarrassing setback and Prince Von Bulow said at the time that the episode had made them (Germany) look ridiculous in the eyes of the world, it also served to sharpen the British attitude toward the growing threat from Germany and confirmed the need for the further strengthening of the North Sea Fleet based at Rosyth which had been formed specifically to counter the German threat.

Germany was itself signatory to the London Treaty of 1836, entered into by the 5 major powers agreeing to uphold Belgian neutrality, to come to her aid and to declare war on any aggressors. But in August 1914 German columns were marching south and massing on the Belgian border. Germany, having given Belgium an ultimatum, and having been refused by the Belgian Government permission to cross Belgian territory in order to attack France, was now threatening to invade Belgium. No one was prepared to accept German assurances, and with good reason, that having advanced through Belgium, the Germans would retreat to within their own borders and also make good for any damage as a consequence.

Prior to the Great War Germany had formulated long standing plans for the whole of Europe, and therefore had the war gone against the Allies the outcome would have seen Belgium a puppet state, Germany would also control access to the coast and Channel ports from Antwerp to Boulogne. The intention was that France should be defeated and required to indemnify Germany with crippling war damages that would prevent her from being in a position to wage war for a generations to come. France would be dominated by Germany and required to open her markets to German goods both at home and in the Empire and at the same time would be required to close her markets for the import of goods from other countries. Luxembourg would become a state of Germany taking parts of Belgium with it and France would be compelled to redraw her borders with Germany in the area of the Vosges. Germany would then form an association with the other continental countries of Europe including Scandinavia and what became after WW2, the Eastern Bloc countries of the Soviet Union

Whilst each country would be free and independent, the German plans for the domination of Europe prior to WW1 included as a major aspect the design for a European Common Market; these plans did not include Britain and her Empire or the Russian Empire, they were specifically excluded. The plan initially was to subdue France and the Low Country's, but the rest of Europe would ultimately be forced into a German dominated bloc. Had Germany been triumphant in the Great War there is no doubt that national boundaries on the continent would have been redrawn and the map of Europe today would be quite different than it was in 1914. Germany is nothing if not consistent, because the aims she had then were little different after two world Wars than that which she strives for today, a united Europe with Germany at the head. An indication of the level of thinking with regard to Germany's aspirations can be gleaned from what Kurt Waldheim the former United Nations Secretary General and President of Austria wrote.

Waldheim was a former Captain in the Deutsche Wermacht during WWII; he served on the Eastern front and was wounded. The well known Nazi hunter Simon Wiesenthal carried out intensive investigations into Waldheim's wartime past and had exposed information that had led to allegations against him and prevented him from becoming Austrian President on his first attempt. During his time in office as Secretary General to the United Nations and later President of Austria, further accusations were laid against him with having been a member of the Nazi youth. He was accused also with being an Intelligence officer alleged to have been fully involved in the transportation of people to Auschwitz and other death camps, and also the mass murders of civilians by shooting. Charges he vehemently denied by giving false information to cover his story of non-involvement in the 'Final Solution', a story that he changed several times on being proved to have lied. He alleged that after being wounded on the Eastern Front in WWII he was given permission to follow his studies and to write a thesis, the content of which was made public in 1986 to a UN committee investigating his wartime past. The thesis was based on 'The Federalist principles of Konstantin Franz'.

In his thesis he refers to the concept of the Reich, which he describes as the 'Calling of Germany', included a statement to the effect that, Europe has fallen through Germany but it is through Germany that it must be resurrected in the glorious collaboration of all the countries of Europe. The Concept of the Reich was of course the German long-term goal of the domination of Europe, but it begs the question, when was this concept first developed in practice, Waldheim was obviously referring to WWI, and the indications seem to be that it was during the Kaisers reign.

6

The precautionary period

The precautionary period was ordered without prior notice on the 29th of July 1914, (a state of alert would be the present day terminology for that same situation) so when mobilisation came things happened very quickly. British troops had not prepared for war and were by no means in a state of readiness for what was to come, but the regular soldier was a fit, well-trained soldier. When the order to mobilize was received by the various regiments there were already thousands of re-servists who had eagerly reported to their depots having mistakenly thought that Royal Proclamations had been put up during the day of the 4th Aug 1914 when in fact they had not. The deadline for the British ultimatum had passed and therefore the Cabinet had made a deci-sion late at night on the 3[rd,] when by eleven pm GMT it was midnight in Berlin. But the army units did not re-ceive their orders for mobilisation until early evening of the following day, the 4th and this was carried out over the next few days by which time the majority of those who were required to report for duty had done so. These territorial battalions would eventually be needed for service other than in the UK but unlike the territori-al battalions in the Second World War that were front line troops and part of the British Expeditionary Force drafted to France in 1939, in the Great War they did not form part of the Expeditionary Force. Eventually the territorial battalions were called on in the Great War, it was to take their place at the front line along with the Regular and Service battalions in the trenches. Such was the extent to which the battalions at the front were depleted through massive losses in successive battles all along the Western Front as the War ground on and on that the Territorial Battalions that were made up of older soldiers were required to go to the front.

CHURCH PARADE

Now a soldiers life on Sunday, is easier than the rest,
He rises up at six o clock, or when he thinks it best.
He does not do much on that day except his church parade,
And even that he tries to dodge with any excuse he's made.

Still and all he goes to church, cursing his blooming luck,
The man who started this parade, him he'd like to duck.
He hears the parson stump about some saint or great apostle,
Or how the Lord above made water run from fossil.

There he sits half sleeping till round comes the blooming plate,
But all that he puts in it is a look of scornful hate.
Then they sing a little hymn, or perhaps a little psalm,
While Tommy growls out something about it being bloody warm.

***

In August 1914 all over Europe huge armies were mobilised and poised ready for war, most of them, having dashed headlong into war for an ill defined purpose, found themselves totally unprepared for what was to come. The Germans were the mightiest army in Europe, indeed the world, and they alone had prepared well for this event. The French on the other hand with a somewhat smaller and poorly equipped army was ill prepared, but they had their tails up at the thought of erasing the humiliation of 1870, here was the chance to recover the provinces of Alsace and Lorraine. It was the French fear of an imminent coming together of the separate German states as the Federal state of Deutschland, that precipitated the Franco-Prussian War of 1870 and the threat of war had always been an abiding factor between these two countries. The French, themselves not prepared for such a massive German onslaught had only allies who, in August 1914 had small armies and were unprepared for war, nevertheless as was later seen, together the allies held out and eventually changed the face of the war.

Some idea of where Britain stood with regard to manpower in relation to the main players can be gleaned from the fact that Germany had a force of some two million men poised to attack on the western front in August 1914. Austro-Hungary was able to mount a similar force of two million, Russia on the other hand could also call on an immediate force of similar size but there was the potential for an army of immense size owing to its population count. In Belgium where the first German attack was aimed at Liege there was a standing army in excess of 205,000 and the French had about one million, mainly part time soldiers who were called up when war was declared. The British Expeditionary force was 160,000 strong, by contrast a miniscule force, however it was perhaps the best trained and most professional army in the world at that time and against massively superior odds proved itself in the first two weeks of the war.

One of the great problems was that The industrial North of France was occupied by Germany and this created supply problems for the French, Britain was unable to redirect manufacturing quickly enough to provide for the Expeditionary Force and could not at that stage assist France in compensating for the loss of its industrial capacity. Russia was desperately short of weapons and ammunition and looked to the vast manufacturing capacity of Britain for supplies. The assault on the Dardanelles was Britain's major attempt to create a supply route to Russia through the Black Sea and was a disastrous setback for the Allies, whether Britain could ever have supplied Russia with its needs was doubtful in any event.

In 1914 whilst Germany with its massive army was well prepared for war, Britain although having a small highly trained army had not prepared for all out conflict. Nothing could have been further from the minds of the British Government, or the nation as a whole, where domestic and Empire matters were far more important issues. Unemployment was rising and the competition from overseas in manufacturing, from Germany in engineering production, from India who was seriously challenging the Lancashire cotton industry, these were increasingly matters for concern. The suffragettes were creating unrest but the all-consuming problem was the demand for Irish home rule.

7

The Curragh Incident

Unlike Canada and Australia in the past, Ireland had refused dominion status and sought to become a republic, but the Government was intent on pushing through a Home Rule Bill, but the six counties of Ulster were having none of it. The thought of coming under Home Rule as a minority by the Catholic south threatened rebellion and possibly civil war. The Ulster Loyalist were not looking to break away from the United Kingdom whatever the south wanted, finding that they may find themselves a pawn in the governments negotiations with the Irish agitators the Loyalist started to prepare for conflict with the south and shipped in 25,000 rifles along with other defensive measures.

In view of the seriousness of the situation, General Paget, the G.O.C. Ireland based at the 'Curragh' main British garrison in Ireland, decided to test the attitude of staff officers to find out where they stood with regard to the potential unrest in the north. He told them that they must be prepared to take action against the north in the event of any rebellion against Home Rule, if they did not they faced dismissal and all loss of pension rights. Sir Hubert Gough, Commanding Officer of the 3rd Cavalry, said that under those circumstances he would resign his post, and some sixty of the officers under him followed suit rather than fight against their countrymen. Gough was of Anglo/Irish stock and was not inclined to go to war against the part of the UK that was his homeland. The matter became known as the 'Curragh Incident', and it had the potential to strike at the very foundations of the British Army. Henry Wilson, the Director of Military Operations, (DMO) at the War Office who had responsibility for all military operations was immediately informed of the threat of resignation by so many officers, General Paget had in fact poked a stick into an hornets nest and Wilson at once saw the potential for the matter to escalate, furthermore, being himself of Anglo/Irish landed gentry, he was fully in accord with the feelings of the officers that had threatened resignation.

He advised Prime Minister Asquith through discussion with Bonar Law that, if not satisfactorily dealt with, the matter could quickly get out of hand to the point where the objection to military intervention against Ulster could ripple right through the British Army. Were that to happen it was a safe bet that quite a significant part of the army would sympathise with the Curragh Officers, not all the officers at The Curragh were Irish or Anglo/Irish, on the other hand quite a significant number of Officers serving outside of Ireland would be of Irish descent, if it spread to the mainland and the army in general supported the Curragh action, it could be construed as mutiny, particularly if having resigned these officers took up arms with the North.

Henry Wilson arranged at once to see CIGS (Chief of the Imperial General Staff) Sir John French who again was of Anglo/Irish descent, but appeared not to display the same enthusiasm for going against the Government when told by Henry Wilson that he was ready to resign in support of the Curragh Officers and against taking military action against Ulster, that in his opinion the Government should back Sir Hubert Gough and make clear in writing that no officer will be called on to take action against the six counties.

Henry Wilson also went to see the Adjutant General to the Secretary of State for War, Sir John Seeley, who later presented a draft document that was, ostenibly, a solution to the problem, it said that the troops would be asked only to be involved in the 'maintenance of law and order', Wilson rejected this on the grounds that assuming that Home Rule became law, the north would have to be forced into accepting its terms and under those circumstances 'maintenance of law and order' would become military action against the North. Seeley and Sir John French then produced an alternative draft at the end of which there was a paragraph that seemed unclear but was read to indicate that troops would not be placed in a situation where they would be required to force Ulster into accepting Home Rule. Hubert Gough spoke with Sir John French about the wording and he said that he also said that he understood it to say that Gough would not be asked to take up arms against his fellow Ulstermen, French then wrote as much at the bottom of the last paragraph and with that assurance Brigadier General Gough returned to Ireland to resume his duties.

In the meantime General Haig had become involved; his Chief of staff, Brigadier General John Gough was the brother of Hubert Gough and had handed in his resignation. Haig, who had been brought back from India to work with Lord Haldane in the reorganisation of the army, saw the danger in the what was occurring and went to see Haldane who in turn addressed the House of Lords with a speech in which he said, ---- "No orders were issued, no orders are likely to be issued, and no orders will be issued for the coercion of Ulster". The ambiguous document given to Hubert Gough by Sir John French and signed by Sir John Seeley had now been made public and Asquith was obliged to repudiate Haldane's statement and say that it was Sir John Seeley who had worded the document given to Gough. The result was that Seeley, French, and the Adjutant General, (Sir John Ewart) all resigned; however none of it happened, Henry Wilson was agitating like mad telling everyone to say nothing, That he and the general Staff were four square behind those involved, that they had the situation in the bag whilst they had the letter from Seeley and that it was up to the Government to make the next move. That happened when Lord Haldane summoned Sir John French, [9] He told French that he had spoken with Asquith and that they had agreed that Sir John French should write to Hubert Gough to tell him privately that the pronouncement made by Lord Haldane the previous week was the final word on the matter. That was an end to the matter.

In his book 'The Fifth Army' General Gough makes no mention of the 'Curragh Incident' when so many officers were guided by their conscience with regard to protestant Ulster and the Catholic South. Gough begins his book by saying that the orders for mobilisation were received by telegram at the Curragh at 5.30am on August 4th 1914, at that point the Irish Question and the demand for Home Rule was set aside for the duration of the War. Gough was transferred to France and went on eventually to command the British Fifth Army. In late 1917 the Fifth army was engaged in the 3rd battle of Ypres (Passchendaele) and then in late March 1918 along with the 3rd army under General Byng, suffered the full onslaught of a German offensive bolstered by reinforcements pulled from the eastern front where peace had broken out. This was the 2nd battle of the Somme; an attack on the 50 miles of British front in an attempt to breakthrough in what was an impossible situation for the British alone against greatly superior odds. Marshall Petain held back his reserve divisions believing that the Fifth Army was a spent force and left the British to take the brunt of the German attack.

In 1914 however the problems at home were as nothing when our small but not insignificant army faced the might of those in Europe, the B.E.F was not half the size of Von Kluck's German 1st army alone at the out break of war, but as the war progressed all that was to change to the extent that the British Forces on the western front in 1918 grew to some 1.8 million. In 1914 of course we had the navy and as things were we could always rest assured that no nation, however large an army they could muster would be able to invade England's shores, but the worrying question was, would that be the case if Germany were to gain victory over France and take control of the channel ports?

Complacency reigned in the British Government, nothing seemed to be very important and even though the academics said that the next war would be a long one and gave very sound reasons why that should be, everyone else thought that it would be over by Christmas. They all rushed in their thousands to volunteer, more than seventy five thousand per week for the first 3 months, however when it was seen that the War was settling into a sort of stalemate there was great shock at the reported losses at the battles of Nueve Chapelle and Festubert etc. that hundreds were being killed, and that the British had no ammunition with which to return the German Artillery fire. These events ensured that the rate of enlistment slowed very considerably.

At the time it led to demands that single men who did not have the married responsibilities of a wife and children should go first, and although there was a strong lobby that married men be exempt, the time came as early as January 1916 when conscription was introduced and they had to go. All these thoughts of being exempt for one reason or another went by the board when the losses at the front at the end of almost four years meant that even the longest serving men and non-combatants were called to the front at the 3rd Battle of Ypres – Passchedaele. It is perhaps ironical that many died at an age when in other circumstances they would have been too old for combat, they had in fact been in non-combatant posts since call up because of their age, but the gaps had to be plugged by whatever was available and that meant old soldiers and even 'B' grades, not only did this apply to old soldiers and non combatants, the list of reserved occupations was revised and many who had considered themselves ineligible for service found themselves in uniform and at the front.

8

August 1914 War is declared

On the 2nd of August 1914 Britain gave Germany an ultimatum that unless an assurance was given by midnight on the 3rd of August 1914 that Belgium would not be invaded, Britain would be at war with Germany. No such message was received and as the evening wore on the chances of getting a positive response became less and less, at 11pm G.M.T (midnight central European time) it was clear that we were at war. At the Foreign Office on the morning of the 3rd of August Lord Grey, emphasising the gravity of the country's situation said "The lamps are going out all over Europe, we shall not see them lit again in our lifetime". German troops, in violation of the London Treaty of 1836 guaranteeing Belgian neutrality, crossed the Belgian border that same day. Huge crowds gathered in London as the public declared their indignation at the German invasion of Belgium. The King and Queen came onto the balcony at Buckingham Palace to see the crowds gathering all along The Mall. There was tremendous excitement among the people at the momentous declaration of War, but the enormity of the situation was not immediately apparent to those ordinary people who had nothing to gauge it against.

The enormous loss of life that was to ensue, the suffering of families as a generation of young men were annihilated, their families condemned to long term suffering and misery, and the colossal debt that the country was to incur, these tragic elements of the war were to be mind numbing for everyone, but these were aspects for the future, for the present the nation was lost in the excitement and cheering as the King and Queen waved from the Palace balcony. The outcome of course was that the country was plunged into massive debt and by the end of the next four years the world would see death, agony and bloodshed on a scale greater than had ever been witnessed throughout history, but these things were not a consideration when weighed against the arrogance of the Kaiser and the German Govt. The British public rallied in their thousands to endorse the Government's decision to go to war, they made it clear that they were eager to support little Belgium and put the German aggressors back where they belonged. Who could have guessed that Britain would go to war in support of France, but it was unlikely to have been seen that way by the working class, rather a matter of stopping a bully and in doing so meeting Britain's commitment to the Treaty of 1836.

The precautionary period had been ordered without prior notice on the 29th of July 1914, so when mobilisation came things happened very quickly. British troops had not prepared for war and were by no means in a state of readiness for what was to come, but the British regular soldier was fit and well-trained to a high standard, probably better trained than the infantryman in the continental armies, and an able match for his opponent on any terms. Capt. Frank Hopkinson[10] records that in July 1914 the orderly room of the 1st Battalion The East Lancashire Regiment in barracks at Colchester received a telephone call out of the blue saying that the 'Precautionary Period' was to come into effect. Under this order the battalion was required to find one company of men at war strength to join a composite battalion and to be ready to move out in two hours. The order was received at 4.00pm and within the allotted time a company of men fully equipped for war was marching to the station to entrain for Felixstowe. This gives some indication of the level of training and preparedness that made the British army such an efficient fighting force. July 29th 1914 was a Wednesday and probably sports afternoon as was always the case in the army, certainly the camp was very quiet at the time the call came, nevertheless a company was found and on its way as ordered.

Capt. Hopkinson[11] also records that in 1913, the year prior to the outbreak of War, he was sitting at the orderly room table as acting Adjutant when the telephone rang, he was told that a large case was being sent to him that was to be deposited unopened in the mobilization store and was to be signed for as 'a case, said to be maps'. The case arrived and was duly deposited in store and remained there until opened in August 1914. That the maps the case was found to contain were those actually required for most of the fighting in 1914, i.e. the positions the B.E.F. were to take up in France etc is some proof of the efficiency of the General staff. Although the battalion often lacked maps for other areas, particularly during the retreat from Le Cateau it was due to circumstances that could hardly have been foreseen, certainly the B.E.F.'s long retreat to the South East of Paris could not have been foreseen.

When the order to mobilize was received by the various regiments there were already thousands of reservists who had eagerly reported to their depots having mistakenly thought that Royal Proclamations had been put up during the day of the 4th Aug 1914 when in fact they had not. The deadline for the British ultimatum had passed and therefore the Cabinet had made a decision late at night on the 3rd, when by eleven pm GMT it was Midnight in Berlin, but the army units did not receive their orders for mobilisation until early evening of the following day, the 4th, and this was carried out over the next few days by which time the majority of those who were required to report for duty had done so. Of course many of the new conscripts had undergone training in the territorial army, but the majority that were to enlist were totally untrained and the job of training them was down to those who had seen service with the colours. These were mainly ex regulars who had served with the colours at home and abroad and then gone onto the reserve for a number of years, they had not been too long out of touch with their training. The men of the territorial battalions also responded and it was their job to take over the duties of the regular battalions in order to free them for active service.

As the war progressed the territorial's became training units and took on the role of training drafts to provide replacement troops for losses at the front, as well as for home defence. Many of the men involved in training were ex regulars who had done their period on reserve and were considered too old at that stage to send to the front, their skill was now invaluable in the training of raw recruits. The call up of the territorial battalions in some cases was simply a matter of them not going home from summer training camps, in some cases even when Summer camp was due to disband and return home, knowing that a proclamation was about to be made they stayed and waited and then made their way to the Regimental Depot.

Many diverted to other accommodation such as school rooms or factory warehouses, whatever was available, and therefore never returned to their families and their jobs; this of course must have caused a great deal of upheaval particularly for the family and must have been a great shock to many. These territorial battalions would eventually be needed for service other than in the UK but unlike the territorial battalions in the Second World War that were front line troops and part of the British Expeditionary Force drafted to France in

1939, in the Great War they did not form part of the Expeditionary Force. Such was the extent to which the regular battalions at the front had depleted that when the territorial battalions were eventually called on in early 1915, it was to take their place at the front line in Belgium and France.

9

The Rush to Arms and the problems it created

Old soldiers, who were in no way required to report for service and were probably unfit for active service anyway, were asked to volunteer and offer their expertise in training the huge influx of raw recruits that were volunteering every day. Some of the new army battalions and territorial battalions were initially commanded by retired officers recalled for short-term service, in order to meet this shortage of expertise. Every effort was made to bring the men to fitness and fighting ability through the regular routine of exercise, forced marches, drill parades, field craft and above all rifle practice. To the infantryman, his rifle is his best friend, he learns how to keep it clean, handling it becomes second nature and in return it does its duty for him.

The British Army is extremely efficient in turning out well-trained soldiers with the right attitude of mind for the job, it did not take long before all of those 'wet behind the ears' having had their spirits broken and undergone rigorous disciplinary training, were fit for transfer to units at the front line. All the bull and time spent on the parade ground instilling the kind of discipline and teamwork that is essential in any good Squaddy proved to be well worth the effort when they were eventually moved to the front.

A SOLDIERS LAMENT

Now a soldier's life is not easy, it's sometimes
very hard,
If not a kit inspection, it's cleaning up for
guard.
Or sloping arms by numbers, perhaps at the ra-
tion stand,
Or doing a blooming route march, to an out of
tune brass band.

No peace you get from anyone, not even in your
bed,
For at 6.00am a gentle voice SHOUTS! Hey
there, show a leg.
Its then you curse the day you took the King's
own shilling,
And promised by the help of God, that you'd be
brave and willing.
Now on parade at 7.00am it nearly breaks your
heart,
We double up, we double down till our feet,
they smart.
Then we get dismissed, its time, fed up, tired
and sore,
And after breakfast, such as it is we do a little
more.

Our breakfast is a dainty dish, eggs or chips or
steak,
But with a hammer and chisel, them you could
not break.
We get a little porridge, its mixed like Irish
stew,
One pint of so cold tea, you could read a paper
through.

For dinner we often get a change, it may be
beef or mutton,
The man that eats it as it's served would have to
be a glutton.
And then comes rice with strawberries, believe
it if you can,
Or it may be sago pudding fried with a shank of
ham.

But with all we do not grouse, what would be
the use?
If you do make a complaint you get nothing but
abuse.
So we sit tight and curse our luck, to pass the
time away,
With visions of a great big boat, roll on that
happy day.

***

At home huge manufacturing and supply systems had
to be set in motion with the output of factories diverted
to the needs of the military, in every area there was a
desperate shortage and probably the most important
was the need for shells, machine guns and rifles. Dur-
ing the pre war period when Lloyd George was the
Chancellor of the Exchequer he had kept a tight hold on
the purse strings and consequently ensured that the War
Office only got what was felt necessary. The allocation
of machine guns was kept at a very low level and it was
not until the war started and the shortages caused such
tragic casualties that he became committed to ensuring
that this matter was addressed.

Not until he became Prime Minister himself did he
ensure that the army was supplied with sufficient needs
in equipment and in so doing was quick to take the

credit, as Prime Minister of course he was aware of the appalling casualties at the front and did not want to be seen as the one responsible for that, heavy artillery and machine guns were the things that would reduce the need for so much loss of life and if they did not have them history would point the finger at Lloyd George, he was canny enough to ensure that did not happen but perhaps he also felt that with the right equipment the war could be brought to a speedy end. The reality in 1914 was however that through his policy of cutting back on defence funding in peacetime, he ensured that when the British Expeditionary Force went to France they had only one machine gun for every four or more of the German Army, neither had they barely enough ammunition to feed the Royal Artillery with no more than four rounds per gun per day whilst the Germans were using 30 to 40 rounds per gun per day in the early stages.

The Boche had long recognised the immense value of the machine gun and were extremely well equipped with them, something in the order of six or even eight per battalion, there were even reports of 16 per battalion, whereas the British Army had two for each Battalion with no provision made for reserve stock if they were lost in action, neither was there provision for training use in the UK. To put that in some sort of perspective, a company would consist of about 220 men and so there would be one machine gun per 440 men, the Germans on the other hand would have at least one machine gun for every 150 men and probably considerably more. The British Tommy was extremely adept with the .303 rifle, but against that, the Germans demonstrated the devastating effects of the machine gun over and over again, a stark example of this was the mowing down of some 400 men of the Kings Own Royal Regiment during the opening minutes of The

Battle of Le Cateau on the high Ground above Haucourt on the third day of fighting in the War, 26th of August 1914.

However, from Oct. 1914 following the battle of the Aisne the war became 'trench warfare' and the machine gun even more became *the* weapon above all else, used to devastating effect by the Germans in countering enemy attacks from defensive positions and when used in conjunction with barbed wire entanglements. Heavy artillery of course was intended to do the most damage by softening up the enemy before and during an attack, the initial artillery bombardment was intended also to cut the wire entanglements leaving the way clear before an attack, but in many cases failed to achieve that. These heavy guns pounded the enemy trenches and the 'no mans land' in-between, the latter was done in the form of a creeping barrage in front of the advancing troops the object was of course to pin the enemy down in their trenches whilst the attacking forces advanced. The problem was that, in Flanders, as soon as the troops went over the top they were confronted by nothing but pounded mud and huge shell craters filled with water from the rains, that in itself was as much an obstacle as the enemy, it was in fact the other enemy and a killer. Men got into the mud one way or another and in many cases found movement difficult, wounded men, if not helped by their comrades simply perished, many drowned in the slippery steep sided shell holes that were permanently filled with rain water, many horses were left to drown since it was impossible to help them.

As equipment goes in WWI, the humble pick and spade must take their place, these pieces of equipment played a massive roll in the war, quite apart from artillery damage in pounding the earth to smithereens, the very ground itself was also under continuous attack from the pick and spade which were in use day and night for 4 years both above and below ground proving to be some of the most vital pieces of equipment of the whole War. Never can there have been so much trenching and tunnelling done as the hundreds of miles dug at the western front and whilst every soldier worked on the trenches to keep them in order and in particular dry, those who had worked in the pit and road building at home were moved into Pioneer companies, and did they show how to make short work of trenching. Each side had 1st, 2nd and 3rd line trenches with access roads between them that zig zagged all the way back to the reserve lines. Many of these were given name and so directions could be given along so and so street etc. One of the really useful jobs that Field Marshal Lord Wavell initiated during his brief time as a Major with the B.E.F. at the First Battle of Ypres was to make accurate maps of the trench systems.

The emphasis in the British army was placed on rapid rifle fire, having learned in the South African War what superb riflemen the Boers were, this was a matter given very serious consideration. It is a fact that the Boers were equipped with the very latest Mauser magazine rifles and this may have accounted for the difference in accuracy and speed of rifle fire, nevertheless the School of Musketry at Hythe laid on courses and rapid rifle fire in the British Army was raised to a very high level of efficiency were 15 rounds per minute with the bolt action Lee Enfield .303 rifle was quoted as par. Having been myself in the British army and trained with the .303 I know that the magazine holds only 10 rounds and bullets were supplied for reload not spare magazines as they are were with say the Sterling, I find it difficult to see how 15 rounds could have been got off when there needed to be a magazine reload. I have no doubt that the rate was 5 rounds per 20 seconds but the stated rate sounded more impressive. As a result of this high rate of fire there is no doubt that in open, moving battle the British rifleman was far superior to the German soldier. This was shown in the opening phases of the war at Mons and Le Cateau where, against vastly superior numbers, the B.E.F. and in particular II corps and the independent 4th Division, inflicted very heavy loss's that left the enemy wondering just how big a force they were up against. Von Kluck said after the war he thought that every British Tommy had a machine gun each.

So good was the Lee Enfield as a bolt-action rifle that they were still used in the British army in the late 1950's and to this day are still in use in other parts of the world, it was also an excellent snipers rifle. In the Great War it was fitted with an 18inch bayonet for use in hand to hand fighting and against cavalry charges, but long before this it had been recognised that as the pattern of warfare had changed, the use of the bayonet had become very limited. With the development of the magazine rifle, machine gun, wire entanglements and heavy guns with recoil mechanisms (rapid fire artillery) battles were fought from a distance and only mopping up was done hand to hand, and in trench warfare the machine gun was infinitely superior to the bolt action rifle.

By the time of the Second World War a smaller bayonet with single edge was fitted and later still what was known as the 'pig sticker' which was in effect a 9/10 spike and proved to be very unpopular, as a result the short bayonet which had been retained only for ceremonial drill was reintroduced.

10

Mobilisation

My paternal grandfather was a territorial and like my maternal great Uncle was with the 4th battalion the East Lancashire Regiment (territorials) when War was declared and later he was with the 8th East Lanc's. My maternal Grandfather was a territorial with the 4th battalion the Kings Own Royal Regiment (Lancaster) and his brother William Clough volunteered for the 1/7th battalion the Lancashire Fusiliers, one of the LF 'New' battalions raised at Salford. My maternal grandmother's older brother Ben, served in the 4th Battalion East Lanc's as did my wife's great Uncle George who was later drafted into the King's Shropshire light infantry and shipped to the front to make up for losses. They all died except George. Brigades were made up of these famous battalions, they in turn made up Divisions, units that stayed and operated together as self supporting units in the line, support and reserve.

Many of these units now no longer exist, the battalions of the New Army were disbanded at the end of the War and as for the rest, many Regiments have amalgamated and many of the older regular army Regiments have also been disbanded, amongst those latter were for instance the York and Lanc's and the Manchester Regt. They were proud and famous regiments of the British

Army that fought throughout the Great War with exceptional courage and selflessness.

It is interesting to look at how these units fit into the order of battle and this example made up of Lancashire regiments is typical of how other battalions formed brigades and divisions at the front.

The 125th Brigade was made up entirely of 'New' army battalions of the Lancashire Fusiliers 1/5th, 1/6th, 1/7th and 1/8th battalions. (You will of course remember Billy Clough and the poem; he was with the 1/7th.)

The 126th brigade comprised 1/4th and 1/5th battalions East Lancashire Regiment along with the 9th (Oldham) and 1/10th (Ashton-Under-Lyne) battalions of the Manchester Regiment.

The 127th comprised the 1/5th, 1/6th, 1/7th, and 1/8th Battalions of the Manchester Regiment.

In 1918 a division was made up of three brigades and the three brigades mentioned here comprised the 42nd or East Lancashire Division. Other Divisions were made up of Battalions from the Kings Own Royal Regiment (Lancaster), The Loyal North Lancashire Regiment, the Kings Liverpool and the South Lancashire Regiment. These divisions fought alongside other county divisions and although they would move from one Corps to another and one Army to another as the General staff required, generally they stayed intact at Brigade and Divisional level.

The First Hundred Thousand

With mobilisation and the massive munitions programme that was put into place, the volunteers left gaps in the workforce that urgently needed to be filled and this of course meant that women had to take on the jobs of the men who went away. An example is the two full companies of workers from the Brunner Mond Chemical factory at Northwich who volunteered for the East Lancashire Regiment; that was a huge loss in manpower for one company that had to be replaced by women workers. (Later, the company name was changed to ICI Mond; ICI was a German company name Before WW1 and later became British along with other brands like 'Persil').

An interesting story about a British involvement in a German company resulting from war is that of one of the world's largest car manufacturers, Volkswagen. At the end of the WWII a team from the Corps of the Royal Electrical and Mechanical Engineers under the command of Major Hirst was commanded to carry out an assessment to see what could be done with the Volkswagen factory At Wolfsberg which was situated on the west side of the Yalta line dividing East and West Germany. The Ferdinand Porsche designed 'Peoples car', the Volkswagen 'Beetle' had never gone into production owing to the outbreak of WWII, instead the factory produced the Kubelwagen on the same chassis for use by the German army as part of the war effort, a sort of jeep like the American Willey's. The REME team successfully organised and set up the production of the VW Beetle car that was boosted to some extent by a huge order from the War Office for use by British army personnel with BAOR. From that early beginning the business was offered to the Rootes group (makers of the Hillman and Humber) as a going concern, they refused to touch it and said that the quirky rear engine car would never sell successfully, in their opinion it had no future. It was offered to other British manufacturers all of which showed no interest.

Major Hirst and his REME team managed and administered the company taking the Beetle from strength to strength. Boosted by the huge order from the War office and with increasing annual sales the company gained a strong reputation for reliability and build quality. Eventually the REME team pulled out when it was handed over to a German consortium and production of that one model far outstripped the production of any British car model. For many, many years Major Hirst was an annual guest of honour at the Volkswagen factory and was often mentioned in the VW monthly magazine 'Safer Motoring' in in the 1960's, articles based on the part he played in managing the company. Even to this day his name is remembered as the person who raised Volkswagen from the ashes and on the road to what it is today, the VW company that took over Rolls Royce motors at Crewe and sold the RR franchise to BMW who now manufacture Rolls Royce cars at Goodwood in Surrey, VW continue to produce Bentley motor cars at Crewe.

Following the 'Call to arms' by Lord Kitchener on posters put up on billboards throughout the country, the recruitment process had a sort of snowball effect, a sense of 'we are all in it together' it was an adventure, and nobody was wanting to be left out, there was a certain amount of cajoling in the factories and pubs aimed at those who where not disposed to volunteering, a practice that took on a more serious and sinister aspect later on as women presented chicken feathers to anyone avoiding call up. The opportunity to be in a man's world, well ordered and disciplined gave rise to a feeling of pride, a sense of doing ones duty to King and Country and of course that is exactly what Kitchener appealed to. Also of course there was the fact that the only opportunity to travel abroad for most men in those days was with the army or navy, an urge that proved irresistible for many men working very long hours in industry. Even in my youth foreign travel was for the well off so the stories that soldiers told of India and the wars, the places they had been and the things that they had done were exciting to listen to.

My own father had been in India, the Sudan and West Africa and an elderly relative of my wife who was in the navy between the wars and during WWII used to tell of visits to the Caribbean, Malta, Singapore, Simonstown Naval base, Rushcutters Bay, Sydney, Freemantle, Shanghai and Kobi. I longed to go to these places and I suspect that the same sense of adventure played as big a part for those who signed on, as did feelings of patriotism. Besides a lot of them had trained in the territorial's and enjoyed the comradeship and training at summer camps, many had families so full time service was not for them. Here was the chance to see a bit of the action, and who could blame them. It might not be what we would think of as a worthwhile break in this day and age but life was vastly different then, the sense of comradeship and patriotism in those days bears no comparison with that shown today where the loyalty is to oneself or perhaps the immediate family, now a culture of greed, individuality and selfishness exists, increasingly relationships exist only through TV, computer, mobile phone or video games.

During a tape recorded interview with my mother in 1983 she talked about the weavers in the mill and the hours that they worked, which served to highlight the dreary hard working lives that many lived in those days. My maternal grandfather was in the 4th Kings Own, he was discharged from the army in March 1919 and arrived home whilst my grandmother was at work in the mill. She herself was a weaver at 'Needle Brig', it was the local name for Gorse St Mill Blackburn that was on the canal by the very narrow Gorse St, bridge. She started work at 6 o'clock in the morning; At 7.30am she went home for breakfast, the mill was on the canal and not 100yds from her house and when she got home on this particular morning there was my grandfather lighting the fire, home from the war with the British occupation forces on the Rhine, there had been no indication that my Grandfather was coming home and his arrival was a total surprise. It was four and a half months after the war had ended and there was great unrest amongst the troops on the Rhine who wanted to get back to Blighty, even threatened mutiny at the long delays. However it may have been that he was in hospital, he suffered gas poisoning toward the end of the war and was never again able to work as a result of that. He died from the effects of gassing a year later in Blackburn Infirmary, his lungs disintegrating and coughing blood as a result of mustard gas poisoning.

This same scenario could be applied to many other working situations throughout the country during the early part of the 20th century, mining, the steel industry, farming etc. The hours were long and arduous with nothing but more work to look forward to, life outside of work revolved around a social life in the vault of the pub on the corner or the local working mens club. There was none of the technological inventions available that we now take for granted, it was a simple hardworking life. Perhaps it is not so surprising that they would want to change the repetitiveness of it all for some short-term excitement, get out of the rut, as it were. In any case it was probably felt that hostilities would not last too long, after all they had no precedent against which to measure it except perhaps the Boer War.

Kings Own

There's a regiment of bantams in a place I can-
not name,
Who for cussedness and courage stand alone,
You'd pass 'em by in Blighty with a look of
mild surprise,
You'd calculate the column was a-wantin'
p'raps in size,
By Glory on the other side you'd hand 'em out
the prize.
King's Own!
When shell and other trifles scream their pas-
sage through the night,
And very lights a'twinkle in our zone,
When snipers pick a penny from your pocket at
their ease,
And enemy machine gunners are cutting life as
cheese,
We ring for reinforcements and we say to Bis-
set, "please,
Kings Own"

And when the units muster in the great review
above,
When God to every Tommy lad is shown,
With picks and packs and Lewis guns you'll
see'em swingin' by,
Just little men, not giants, but their chins are
carried high,
And kindly he'll look down on them and whis-
per, "they are my
Kings Own.
(The Bantams)

***

In 1914 the whole country was behind this race to arms as it was when the troops went off to the Boer War, crowds cheered as they marched through the streets to the place of embarkation, bands were on the quayside and the whole thing was headlines in the local newspapers. The same thing would happen when they arrived home and perhaps this is difficult for people of the present day to imagine, troops marching down the road with the band playing from the barracks in the town to the local railway station, everyone out lining the streets to see them off, marching behind, cheering and singing, wives and sweethearts heartbroken as the men marched away, sons, brothers, husbands they were, so many of them never to come back. They went so willingly to fight for their country, what would they think now?

The response to the call for volunteers for Kitchener's new army was astounding and it grew and grew, so much so that the regimental depots and training camps could not cope with the influx. Many were sent home until they could be accommodated, others were billeted in private homes, parish halls and under canvas. During those early days the shortage of uniforms meant that those that were available had to be issued to those reservists likely to go into active service, new recruits and those that did not have uniform already were issued with whatever was available which was mainly the old blue uniforms of the militia, others were allowed to stay in 'mufti' until uniforms could be provided. The training camps in the south of England and East Anglia witnessed a huge influx of personnel, a great many of whom were under canvas, again a programme was very quickly put in hand to provide wooden billets for the troops and get them from under canvas as the Winter came on.

Unfortunately a lot of troops suffered with gales and

torrential rain in the autumn of 1914 before they could be moved into permanent accommodation in what was one of the worst periods weather wise in years. Not only were there reservists and Territorial battalions to cater for, the recruitment for the New Army (Kitcheners New Army) had also got under way and this further extended the demand for training, equipment and accommodation. Some of the men were billeted in private households, bed and breakfast and suchlike when they were paid a subsistence allowance until there was accommodation in training camps and depots. There was also a desperate need for experienced N.C.O.'s and Officers to train and command these new battalions. Weapons were in very short supply and these units must have resembled the 'Dad's Army' of the Second World War in many ways, using wooden rifles and machine guns for training and becoming proficient by reading handbooks on the subject. This of course presented a daunting task in getting recruits trained and kitted out into something resembling a fighting unit particularly since there was a desperate shortage of small arms and machine guns and an inability on the part of manufacturers on the War Office approved list to meet the increasing demand.

All too quickly those in the territorial's, on being asked, responded at once agreeing to serve in Imperial service, they found themselves undergoing intensive training before eventually going into the front line, the first ones in were at the front in early 1915 just months after war broke out and when eventually they got into France they had a big shock, it was not what they expected. From the early days at Mons and Le Cateau there were heavy casualties, the main body of the regular army had been wiped out by the 1st Ypres and it was something that those who went to the front, and were lucky enough to survive, somehow coped with, and later needed to put the horror of behind them and get on with their lives. The fact that they may have had other strong reasons for wanting to go besides patriotism does not detract from the courage and loyalty of those who went, or indeed to say that they would not have gone had they known what it would be like, of course they would have gone, but it probably was not how they saw it when they volunteered. Although these men of the New Army battalions were relative rookies, they gave a good account of themselves vindicating Kitchener's faith in them.

LETTERS

When 'Stand to' hour is over and we leave the parapet,
And scamper to our dugout to smoke a cigarette,
The post has brought in parcels and letters for us all,
So now we'll light a candle and stick it on the wall.

Dark shadows cringe and cower, on roof and wall and floor,
And little roving breezes come rustling through the door.
We open up the letters of friends across the foam'
And thoughts go back to England, of London and of home.

We've parcels small, and parcels of quite gigantic size,
We've Devon cream and butter, and apples baked in pies.

We'll make a night of feasting, and all will have
their fill,
See our mate Bill has dainties from the maid
that's gone on Bill.

Oh! Kensington for neatness, it packs its par-
cels well,
Though Bow is always bulky it isn't quite as
swell.
But here there's no distinction twix Kensington
and Bow,

We're comrades in the dugout and fight a
common foe.

Here comes the ration party with tins of bully
stew,
'Clear off' you ration party; we have no need of
you.
Machonochie for breakfast, it aint' no blooming
use,
Look here we've something better than 'bully
after Loos.

The post comes trench-ward nightly; we hail it
with glee,
Though now we're not as many as once we
used to be.
For some have done their fighting, packed up
and gone away,
And many boys are sleeping, in their little
homes of clay.

We all have read our letters, but one's un-
touched so far,
An English maidens letter to her sweet heart at

the War,
And when we write in answer, the news for her
to tell,
What can we say to cheer her, except of how he
fell?

We'll write to her tomorrow, and this is what
we'll say,
He breathed her name in dying, in peace he
passed away.
No word about his moaning, his anguish and his
pain,
When slowly, slowly dying, God! Fifteen hours
in dying,
He laid a maimed thing dying, alone upon the
plain.

We often write to mothers, to sweethearts and
to wives,
And tell how those who loved them have given
up their lives.
If we're not always truthful, our lies are always
kind,
Our letters lie to cheer them, the women left
behind.

***

11

THE B.E.F GOES TO FRANCE

The B.E.F. (British expeditionary force), after being addressed by King George V and under the overall Command of Field Marshal Sir John French, was drafted to France in August 1914. At Boulogne the French people on the quayside welcomed them and as the band struck up they marched to their barracks. Sir John French was particularly seen as a good omen, someone at some stage pointed out that the names of Sir John the G.O.C. (General Officer Commanding) of the British Expeditionary force and General Joffre, the G.O.C. French Forces, were intertwined in such a way that it could only bode well for the Allies. When the name Joffre is set above the name French by strange coincidence the first half of both names reads Joffre and the second half French.

JOF FRE
FRE NCH

Sir John French wrote a poignant paragraph in his book '1914' describing the evening of his arrival at on August 14th 1914.[12]

"An unusually cold and miserable day, the hustle and bustle of activity by British and French troops and the excitement of the local people cheering them along, the supply ships being unloaded and the ant like activity on the quayside as the evening sun broke through. Over all towered the monument to the greatest world soldier - the warrior Emperor who, more than a hundred years Before, had from that spot contemplated

invading England. Could he now have revisited 'the glimpses of the moon' would he not have rejoiced at this friendly invasion of France by England's 'good yeomen' who were now offering their lives to save France from possible destruction as a power of first class? It was a wonderful and never to be forgotten scene in the setting sun; and, as I walked around the tents and bivouacs, I could not but think of the many fine fellows around me who had said good-bye to Old England forever".

The British Expeditionary Force consisted of I Corps under the command of General Douglas Haig and II Corps under the command of General Sir James Grierson. Each of the two Corps was made up of two Divisions, a Cavalry Division, engineers, pioneers etc. and some elements of the Royal Flying Corps. The established B.E.F. actually consisted of 6 Divisions but two divisions were held back in England and therefore the force sent to France was a much smaller contingent than had been originally envisaged, it amounted to some 100,000 men in total. Quite apart from not wishing to commit all his available first line troops, Kitchener was all too aware that experienced soldiers were in short supply and their contribution would be invaluable in training recruits of the proposed New Battalions; besides this there was a strong belief amongst many military and political leaders that Germany would try to invade England.

General James (Jimmy) Grierson died of a heart attack in France as he travelled by train to Amiens even Before the B.E.F. became engaged in action with the enemy. At that stage Sir John French requested that General Sir Herbert Plumer be appointed to replace Grierson, a request that would traditionally have been looked on favourably, but Kitchener ignored the request and to Sir John's dismay appointed General Sir

Horace Smith Dorrien who was, like Haig, a veteran of service in India, the Sudan and the South African War and had replaced Sir John French as Chief of the Imperial General Staff on his becoming General Officer Commanding the B.E.F. For whatever reason it was clear that French did not wish to have Smith Dorrien under his command.

Within a week of the outbreak of war scores of Regular battalions left the Channel ports of Folkstone, Southampton etc. for the French Ports of Boulogne, Le Havre, St. Nazaire etc. where for the next 4 years thousands of British troops landed on their way to the front, equally thousands never came back, many of those have no known grave and are commemorated not with a headstone but some on roll of honour, they were never found. Thousands of others were wounded and as a result their lives were shortened or changed forever because of their injuries, needless to say the families of those injured and killed in the war suffered greatly for many years to come.

On arrival in France the B.E.F had no clearly defined role, it was there because of a longstanding agreement between the British and French military chiefs that should France find itself at war the B.E.F would move to French soil in the general area of Amiens with the object of extending the French left. Little was really known about events as they happened except that the Belgian Army was being pushed back to the sea and that France had launched an attack on the provinces of Alsace and Lorraine, her former territories. There was a gap between the French and Belgian Armies along the Belgian Border in the area of Maubauge and historically this had been identified as a suitable area for British forces to operate in, it was close to the channel ports for troop movements and supply lines. Although this had been a long standing plan at a War

Council meeting on the 6th of August, Sir John French put forward alternative plans for the Expeditionary force to operate from Antwerp against the right of the German 1st Army suggesting that this would disrupt the fundamental principal of the Schlieffen plan, a long-standing plan of attack on France designed by the German military strategist Count Von Schlieffen should the occasion arise. Following the Franco Prussian War of 1870 and the annexing of Alsace and Lorraine, Germany always had a fear that France may try to recover her lost territories by force and in the event of any military conflict with France, Germany had to consider that Russia would also be involved because of the treaty between France and Russia.

The meeting of the War Cabinet called by Asquith at Downing St on the 6th of August 1914, (other sources indicate that this meeting was held on the 5th of August) was attended by no less than eighteen representatives of the Government, the War Office, the Admiralty and those of the General Staff immediately involved with command of the Expeditionary force, the latter being some twelve officers. Henry Wilson says in his diary that what Sir John French proposed regarding the B.E.F. going to Antwerp, operating with the Belgians and split from the French was ridiculous. Douglas Haig was equally aghast at the suggestion that the British could operate to advantage with the Belgian and Dutch forces indicating that Sir John was not even aware that the Dutch were, and would remain neutral. In his book '1914', Sir John comments on this meeting and indicates that Douglas Haig was keen to introduce changes to the original plan along with Lord Kitchener's different offering, and that he, Sir John, felt these suggestions inappropriate and possibly disruptive, that he was keen to see the original plan adhered to. Neither does Sir John French's son, Major Gerald French in his biography of his father 'The life of Field Marshal Sir John French First Earl of Ypres' make any mention of Sir John suggestion of Antwerp as an operating base for the B.E.F. at that meeting. Churchill, as First Lord of the Admiralty killed French's idea by stating that the Royal Navy could not guarantee the troops safety over a wide stretch of North Sea.

The fact that Sir John French did not comment on what he thought the British Forces ought to be doing perhaps indicates that he himself felt that he had blundered and had a strong desire to forget about it. Nevertheless Sir John's seemingly outrageous suggestions were commented on in the diaries of Henry Wilson and Douglas Haig, at the time they were left agonising and cringing at the thought of Sir John's proposals and were sure to make some adverse comment. However it is interesting also to note that Lloyd George also drew attention to French's proposals in his memoirs published six years after French's death. At the time of the said War Cabinet meeting Lloyd George was Chancellor of the Exchequer and therefore did not attend the meeting to hear French put forward his plans.

Count Von Schlieffen was charged with the task of drawing up plans to deal with any act of aggression against Germany by France or Russia. An essential element was to deliver a rapid knockout blow to France allowing some 6 weeks for this to be achieved, to then send in occupying forces before turning those same divisions to face the Russians who the Germans thought would be slow to mobilise. The plan involved an attack on France of some 62 Divisions and a token force of some ten or twelve divisions facing the Russsians. The attack on the Western Front meant that the German right therefore had necessarily to be very strong, and once it was on the move had to develop an increasing momentum, pushing the enemy ever south and east in its relentless advance as if pushing on a hinged door. Sir John French's proposed plan on the other hand was that the B.E.F. congregate at a point near Antwerp and join with the Dutch and Belgian armies to form a considerable force that would act on the German right flank. The thought was that if the German 1st Army (Von Kluck's) on the extreme German right were compelled to remove the threat of that combined British, Dutch, Belgian force Before turning south towards Paris as per the Schlieffen plan, they might think twice Before invading Belgium at all. In other words the Schlieffen plan, which took no account of British intervention would be severely disrupted if not rendered inoperable.

French's idea of falling onto the German right flank was to disrupt the Schlieffen plan by tying up German divisions and preventing them from being moved to the Eastern Front where German divisions were thin on the ground. This would buy time for Russia to mobilise and hopefully defeat the Germans on the Eastern Front. The two glaring shortcomings of this idea was that the British would be cut off from the French, a situation that would be most undesirable, and a British/Belgian force may have been to weak and easily defeated by the huge army they would have to face and this is precisely what happened at Mons. Secondly there was a naïve assumption on the part of Sir John that the Dutch would be invaded by Germany or that they would relinquish their neutral status to join the Allies.

Sir John French had no support for this idea, there could be several other reasons for that, one is that the French High Command had already expected the B.E.F. to cover their left and there was little time to now start to renegotiate a different strategy. The second is that it would be difficult for the Royal Navy to move the whole of the B.E.F. safely so far North given the threat of German submarine activity in the channel and North Sea and besides the means of access to Antwerp was through neutral Dutch waters. It would have been interesting to see whether or not that sort of move would have significantly affected the course of the War; one has to feel that it would have taken a powerful force to threaten the German right and the Dutch of course had not at that stage been attacked or drawn into the War. Nevertheless following tactical mistakes made by Von Kluck and the German High Command that is exactly what happened, an opportunity occurred following the battle of Le Cateau when the British and French retreated to the River Seine but that is a matter for a little later.

With regard to the alternative plan to move the B.E.F. to Antwerp put forward by Sir John French, it must be born in mind that the wider French military plan in the event of war with Germany was not made available to the British High Command before war was declared. The French obviously considered it sufficient that the British should be aware simply in general terms just where the B.E.F. might operate in the event of hostilities. The total strategy was of course a French plan designed to protect France and was not done in collaboration with the British. One other important factor became apparent after the retreat from Mons, and that was that the French did not want the British extending their front to coastal towns, they did not trust the British to go home at the end of the war.

On August 20th Sir John French briefed Generals Haig and Smith Dorrien on the plans for the B.E.F. to move beyond Maubeuge, The French Fifth Army under General Lanrezac and operating on the French left (right of the B.E.F. was having a rough time against Von Bulow's Second Army and at the battle of Charleroi Joffre had asked that the B.E.F. move up to extend the French left flank. He was encouraged in this by General Sir Henry Wilson, who had recently been appointed Sir John French's Chief adviser, even though army intelligence and reports from the reliable RFC (Royal Flying Corps) were indicating massive numbers of German troops moving south from Brussels. General Joffre was also aware that these large troop movements were taking place and that the fall of Namur was imminent but Wilson for some obscure reason was convinced that the number of German troops facing the B.E.F. was less than half of those actually there. Reports came in from the R.F.C and General Joffre's G.H.Q., of increasing numbers of German troops on the march along the Belgian border with France, and thousands more marching south west from Brussels, this latter was of course Von Kluck's 1st army and his intention was to find the extent of the French left flank, turn it, roll it up like a carpet and march south to take Paris.

Sir John French ordered the B.E.F. to take up positions between Mons and Charleroi. Their main objective was to support the left flank of the French Fifth Army taken up by the 18th Corps, the Commanding Officer of the Fifth Army, General Lanrezac was keen to have the B.E.F. mount an immediate attack and it was Sir John French's intention to do just that, however word filtered through from the French G.H.Q. that the French Fifth Army was being pushed back by massive German forces. Already the Germans had broken through in the Ardennes and had over run Castelnau's Second Army in Alsace and Lorraine, now the French Fifth Army had been driven back on the right rear of the B.E.F., thus leaving the British right flank in the air.

Even Before the B.E.F. had taken up positions there had been reliable reports from the R.F.C. and Gen Allenby's Cavalry reconnaissance that strong German columns were moving south, information that had been ignored by Gen. Wilson, who for some reason felt that the B.E.F. was well placed to handle any threat. The B.E.F. however was a miniscule force compared to the German forces opposing it and in reality barely constituted a half the size of the French Fifth Army whose left flank it was ostensibly covering but was in fact well to the rear of the B.E.F.

With Von Kluck's 1st Army moving rapidly south seeking the extent of the left of the B.E.F. did not have time to prepare for an attack which is what they had planned, word came from General Joffre that the French Fifth Army was pulling back to the South bank of the Sambre and consequently when the German 1st army did make real contact it was with Smith Dorriens II Corps in the late morning of August 23rd 1914, the French Fifth Army was well to the rear by now. By early evening, fighting fierce rearguard actions, II Corps was pushed further and further back, this was the battle now added to the Colours of those battalions involved, The Battle of Mons and more often referred to as the Retreat from Mons.

During the evening of the 23rd Gen. Smith Dorrien continued his retreat and withdrew to positions in the area of Maubauge, I Corps took up new positions on his right and late that evening, Sir John French ordered a withdrawal to positions yet to be determined but was estimated this should be achieved within two days. Even though the French Fifth Army had left I Corps exposed it had little problem as it withdrew being on the right of II Corps and away from Von Kluck's attacking forces. II Corps was being very badly handled and late into the night was fighting running battles, trying to disengage as it withdrew, until eventually the weary troops passed through Solesmes supported by the arrival of the Independent 4th Division, and on to the area of Le Cateau.

The rearguard of II Corps, found by the 1st Cheshires and the 1st Norfolks were between Bavay and Solesmes when the main body of II Corps managed to disengage, unfortunately the rearguard never got out for the reason that they never received the order to retreat and, so both Battalions were taken prisoners. The 24th of August is now a second Regimental day for the Cheshire Regiment on account of the heroic stand made by these two battalions which did so much to ensure that II Corps withdrew successfully. The independent 4th Division, one of the divisions of the B.E.F. that had been held back in England had been shipped over to France and was now in the area covering the left flank of II Corps as it withdrew through Solesmes to Le Cateau.

I Corps under the command of General Douglas Haig had little contact with the enemy as they retreated from Mons although they could hear the shells and the sound of gunfire in the distance, they withdrew virtually unscathed seeing little or non of the action, for the B.E.F. the War at this stage was being fought against the German 1st Army by II Corps in a series of fierce defensive actions whilst retreating in front of a rapidly advancing enemy. I Corps instead of maintaining contact with and covering II Corp's right flank made its way in a more southerly direction virtually without incident south through the Forest of Mormal to the banks of the Sambre, and then headed toward the area of Landrecies where they arrived in the afternoon of the 25th. By this time they had completely lost contact with II Corps. There is no doubt that the men of I Corps were exhausted following the long forced march in hot dry weather but otherwise they were intact and clear of the main German advance on the other side of the forest. Sir John French was of the opinion that I Corps came under great pressure as they made their way through the forest, it is clear however that the main thrust of Von Kluck's Army was along the North side of the Forest on the same line as II Corps, Bavay and Solesmes a detachment that had advanced as far as Landrecies where they were easily dealt with by the Guards Brigade of 1 Corps.

DeJa Vous

In August 1914 the B.E.F found itself in the valley of the Sambre, an area where in 1695 a little way to the east the 4th and 30th foot (under Cardwell's County regiment system, The Kings Own and the East Lancashire Regt. respectively) had fought and captured Namur, the very town that the Belgian army were currently being driven from. The armies of Prince William had been opposed to those of Louis XIV who still supported the deposed King James against William of Orange. Amongst the officers and men of the B.E.F. there must have been a strong recognition of the fact that only one hundred years before in 1815 between the Sambre and the Roman Road a mile or two North, Napoleon had made contact with and routed Blucher and his army who were on their way to join an allied army under the Command of the Duke of Wellington the day before the battle of Waterloo. Napoleon was on his way North to confront Wellington, when he had news of Bluchers army marching from Namur to Sombreffe, He decided to attack Blucher before he could join with Wellington and in doing so leave his way clear to deal with a much reduced allied army at Bruxelles. Wellingtons force had similarly been attacked by French troops at Quatra Bras but easily fought them off.

Napoleon crossed the Sambre between Charleroi and Namur and scattered Bluchers Divisions in a hard fought battle, it was about 7/8pm in the evening and in the normal course of events Napoleon could have expected to decimate Bluchers army in retreat. However a French Cavalry patrol brought news of a huge army advancing from Fleurus where Napoleon had Headquartered the previous night, he cut off his engagement with Blucher and turned to meet this new threat that turned out in fact to be one of Napoleon's own reserve divisions, D'Erlon's advancing from an unexpected direction as a result of bad communications.

That evening Blucher managed to make contact with Wellington who asked what his plans might be, to which Wellington, replied that if after the routing by Napoleon Blucher could raise a token force and support him the next day, he would withdraw to St Jean and there would do battle with Napoleon. Blucher promised that he would do his best and would be there; the battle of Waterloo took place the next day. On the morning of the battle Napoleon stopped on the hill at La Belle Alliance and there made his headquarters across the vale from St. Jean, between the two armies down in the vale was the village of La Hay Saint.

Wellington, at the end, made no bones about the fact that the battle was a close run thing and said that he would never want that experience again, he said that had Napoleon chosen his Generals more carefully it is highly unlikely that Wellington would have been the victor. But at 4.30pm on the day of the battle Wellington felt he had won and exclaimed 'the day is mine'. There are those who feel that Blucher was the victor and had he not been there the battle would have been lost. The fact is that Blucher was always part of the allied force in the confrontation with Napoleon, the fact that he happened to turn up and save the day was not by chance, he turned up alright but he got there late when the battle had already been all but won. It was late afternoon/early evening when Blucher joined the battle having taken most of the day to get his men to the area and then under cover through Park Wood to the East of La Hay Saint, a small but dense coppice that due to mud and thicket was almost impossible to get through. Blucher at aged 72, was himself quite badly injured from the previous day when he was brought from his horse and it came down on top of him, nevertheless he was concerned that he had made Wellington a promise and not wanting to be seen as a liar he urged his men on.

It was whilst Napoleon's army, defeated and retreating in disarray that Wellington met Blucher at La Belle Alliance, the place that Napoleon had chosen to make his stand. With Wellington's army all but spent they agreed that Blucher should continue to push Napoleon and his men back to Quatra Bra and there fall on the rear of his army as it crossed the River Nive. The tables were turned and Blucher was now able to enjoy the task of chasing Napoleon in retreat and of course he had a clear field in that the enemy was on the run. Wellington, having taken the day, rested his men before following on; the two armies met at Fontainbleu and on the 7th of July 1815 marched into Paris.

Napoleon no longer believing that he could regain the confidence of the French people, resigned as Emperor of France and when the coalition forces entered Paris he had gone to stay with his stepdaughter, Hortense De Beauharnais at Malmaison. There he made plans to go to America and had two frigates standing by at Rochefort, they were prevented from leaving port with Napoleon and eventually when Napolean was ordered to leave Paris he surrendered himself to Captain Maitland of HMS Belleraphon and was transported to Plymouth. Since Napoleon himself to be regarded as an evil tyrant by the British people his first choice was to settle in America, failing that, and having shown that he admired the English, he was prepared to reside in the UK in obscurity and hoped to live under a nom de plume. The name he would take was of a Colonel Muiron who had died saving Napoleons life. However having breached the terms that had been agreed when he was exiled to Elba, and having rallied the French again during the 'Hundred Days' it was felt that incarceration on the remote South Atlantic island of St Helena would be a more appropriate solution. He was considered far too dangerous a person to be allowed to settle in Britain or even America.

Napoleon was transferred to the 74 guns HMS Northumberland, the Belleraphon being an older vessel and considered unsuitable for the long sea voyage. Admiral Sir George Cockburn was given Command as a suitably senior naval officer to accompany Napoleon and he remained as Governor of St Helena and Station Commander of the South Africa Station after arriving at the Island. Sir George Cockburn had recently returned from a successful tour patrolling in American waters and causing havoc to American ships and harbours, he was also the person responsible for the burning down of the White House at the battle of Bladensberg. Napoleon spent the last six years of his life on St Helena, mainly at Longwood. He was buried there but later his body was taken to Paris. During the latter part of his life on St Helena the Garrison Battalion was the 1st battalion The XXth, later with the naming of the County Regiments, introduced under the Cardwell system, the XXth became the 1st Battalion The Lancashire Fusiliers.

I am proud to say that it was with the 1st Battalion The Lancashire Fusiliers that I served as a REME technician for 18months after transferring from Reme Workshops in Dortmund to the battalion at Iserlohn at the start of the Suez crisis in 1956. I joined them on the

6th November 1956 the day the war started and on the 7th the battalion travelled by train to Rotterdam and boarded the SS Dunera for Southhampton and on for re-kitting at Strensall, the KOYLI's depot at York. As we entered Southampton roads we sailed very close to the Empire Ken, the decks lined with squaddies all bound for Suez, there we were, jumping up and down, cheering and shouting across to each other as we passed, eventually we managed to make out what they were shouting, 'Your going the wrong F------ way'! Thanks to the anti Colonial John Foster Dulles and his extreme dislike of the British, Suez was a 10day affair. The LF's were diverted to Cyprus, to the EOKA terrorist campaign. Omnia Audax.

The Old Contemptibles

The original long standing German plan (the Schlieffen Plan) had been an outflanking drive west to the sea and the Channel ports Before wheeling south to roll up the allied armies in a drive to Paris. The B.E.F. having been charged with the task of protecting the left flank of the French Fifth Army under General Lanrezac were pushed back, I Corps to Landrecies and II corps to Le Cateau. Lanrezac had consistently warned of the danger of being outflanked by Von Kluck's 1st Army and he was proved right, having extended the French left it was now the B.E.F. that was outflanked with the consequent threat of annihilation. The deployment of the independent 4th division that arrived too late for the Battle of Mons probably saved that from happening by covering the retreat of Smith Dorrien's II Corps and making a stand in the area of Haucourt.

I Corps had suffered a small attack at Landrecies that was quickly dealt with by the Guards Brigade, General Haig however felt that it was the precursor to a full scale attack so he decided with all haste to retreat to St Quentin with his HQ staff and left the rest of I Corps to move out as and when they were ready. This need to be positioned well behind the front line by the General Staff and Corps commanders was to be a feature of the High Command of the BEF throughout the war. Haig having departed with his senior staff now saw I Corps withdrawing from their positions on the Sambre and retreating further still from II Corps who despite having no support were managing to hold out. At this time General Haig, far from going to the aid of II Corps was in fact offering to cover Lanrezac's left flank, a move objected to and over ruled by Sir John French. The following day after fierce fighting along the front covered by II Corps and 4th Division, Smith Dorrien's made a successful staged withdrawal ending what became known as the Battle of Le Cateau were. The Expeditionary Force was not driven out; they left in good order and were of course right in their belief that they had never been beaten. The furthest extent the B.E.F. had retreated was to a small town to the south west of Paris, Brie Comte Robert. It was here on Christmas Day 1914 that Field Marshal Sir John French split the B.E.F. and from the existing Corps formed two Armies; they would grow tremendously in size and were the first of what became 5 British armies on the western front in France and Belgium during WWI.

When I first become aware of this I found it interesting to recall that in 1966 my wife along with our daughter, had travelled through France to Switzerland and Italy in our new Volkswagen Devon campervan. I recall stopping in the lovely little town of Brie Comte Robert and having a meal in a quaint little café before going on to Belfort for the night. Little did I know at the time that I had visited a place of some historical British military significance on route to Switzerland,

Brie Comte Robert was the place where the B.E.F. re-grouped and I would have been proud to look around me to realise that I had, as it were, billeted in that same area. Belfort itself was a place of such significance to the French that it was heavily defended during the 1870/71 War with Germany, and with the start of the Great War was one of two important objectives identi-fied by the German Chief of Staff General Falkenhayn that if attacked on a narrow front would bring the French army to its knees. One was Belfort and the other Verdun; Falkenhayn chose Verdun a name that is writ large in French military history.

Under the Schlieffen plan Germany had allowed for a token force to join with Austria in holding the osten-sibly slow to mobilise Russians, the main force of the German Army was to rapidly over run France before releasing those armies to fight on the Eastern Front. The battle of Tannenberg, although an eventual out-standing victory for the German Army, showed just how vulnerable the German plan was by having so few divisions deployed against Russia. The expectation was that it would take Russia some time to mobilise it's ar-mies and move them to front, but the rapid movement of the two Russian Armies from the East and from the South caught the Prussians with their pants down at Tannenberg.

The Russians had attacked in a brilliant offensive but unfortunately without making the necessary backup preparations, the German General Staff turned their armies to face the Russians to the South and in despera-tion moved divisions from the Western Front, and con-trary to long established plans weakened their offen-sive. Whilst moving troops from the west enabled the Germans to defeat the Russians and push them back, it in turn led to the Germans suffering a crushing defeat on the Marne. The Battles of The Marne and Aisne had very far-reaching consequences, not only for that moment, but also as a defining point in European history. Already the war on the Russian front was compelling Germany to transfer troops away from the Western Front before it had the opportunity to conclusively defeat the French army and occupy France,

The lynchpin of German strategy was lost and would never be regained. Following the battles of the Marne and the Aisne and having lost the initiative the Germans started to dig in creating the front line in the trench warfare of WWI, they now made a massive attack at Ypres (1st Ypres) on the 20th October 1914 in an attempt to outflank the allied armies and strike for the coast, in this they almost succeeded, but having failed in that offensive the war changed from mobile warfare to trench warfare and the long stand off began. The outflanking push made by the Germans at Ypres was generally thought to be a push to the Channel to dominate the Channel Ports and provide facilities for the German Navy, that of course would make a great deal of sense if the war was to continue, but in fact the real objective was to drive down to Paris and to roll up the French armies towards the German Swiss borders, had that happened the urgent need for control of the channel ports would have taken on a more long term significance.

Had France fallen then so would have Russia, Germany along with Austria would have dominated the whole of Europe. But unlike the war of 1870 when, in defeating the French who at the time stood alone, Germany annexed Alsace and Lorraine, France now had a treaty with Russia which meant that Germany was threatened from both sides. Not only that, if Germany violated Belgian neutrality there was also the British Empire to cope with, that should have been deterrent enough for Germany not to have declared war for although Britain had but a small army, the potential was there to raise a large army. The Expeditionary Force was very small in 1914 and the British army reserves also small in numbers, but it very quickly grew from the two Corps of the Expeditionary Force to five Armies in France and more than two million men in total, but in 1914 Britain had a small and badly equipped army, miniscule in comparison to the Germans, French and Russians.

An interesting comparison was made by Winston Churchill in his book 'My early years'. He commented that when he was a young subaltern with the 4th Queens Hussars he recalled a time when he was an observer at Aldershot at what we now call 'war games', i.e. manoeuvres. On the field was a Cavalry division, the only British Cavalry division, Churchill referred to it as our 'Darling Cavalry Division', which by comparison the Germans could muster twenty cavalry divisions to our one. Britain had the most powerful Navy in the world but was being severely challenged by Germany's growing High Seas Fleet; and Germany was also the most powerful military nation in the world.

Regardless of what happened in Europe, even had France fallen and the British army gone with it, Britain would still have Her Empire and the Navy with which she ruled the seas. Germany however, had for a long time been building her High Seas Fleet to a size that could threaten the Royal Navy. At the start of WW1 there was no comparison in size between the two navies and in the long run one of Germany's fatal mistakes was to go to war with Britain without the understanding that whilst the Royal Navy was intact Germany could never win. Neither did France fully comprehend the value of the Royal Navy to the Allied effort and even said that it was worth nothing to the France in the WWI conflict.

An article published in The Times by The Times War correspondent, Colonel Repington, pointed to the fact that the Royal Navy was worth 500 guns to France in the war and it created ill feeling in France. General Foch is reported to have exclaimed that The Royal Navy was not worth even one gun to France's war effort. Foch may have been a reasonably good army commander, but he failed completely to see that increasingly everything France needed, troops, munitions, railway track and rolling stock etc all arrived in France courtesy of the Royal Navy which ran the gauntlet of German U boats day in and day out carrying troops and equipment. It was perhaps insensitive for The Times to publish such a comment when the allies were allies only in name and in fact were partners only to satisfy their own interests. But it was with a severe lack of understanding and even more so churlish of Foch to pass off the Royal Navy as worthless.

Britain would have continued in isolation and taken any opportunity to prevent German expansion as she did with the coalitions against Napoleon in his efforts to dominate Europe. Whatever Germany might achieve militarily, in the end it was never able to conquer the Allied forces that fought to prevent them from dominating Europe. The British intelligence services had intercepted a German coded telegram to the German Ambassador in Mexico outlining how Germany intended to ally itself to Mexico and help them recover there lost lands, Arizona, New Mexico, Texas etc. in return for supporting Germany. In the final analysis with the sinking of the Lusitania, the submarine blockade of American southern ports and the attempts by Germany to influence Mexico into a mutual alliance, the US declared war on Germany, even the South American countries declared war.

The Saviour in all this was the British Navy without

which the British would have been starved into submission and the lines of communication to her forces overseas and those of France and Russia to some extent would have been decimated in both world wars. In 1914 Britain, as the smaller partner, had a job to do alongside France, but her share of the burden would increase continually as the war progressed until in 1918 Britain was taking the brunt of it, the Royal Navy had a very major part to play in that, so much so that without the Royal Navy the British Front would have been starved of all that it needed to carry on the war, the major part of industrial France was in German hands and Britain had a huge part to play in maintaining supplies across the Atlantic and the Channel.

Not only had it been a hundred years since British troops had been on the continent, Britain was now going to war in aid of her traditional enemy, France, they were also operating to a French plan, not a British one. Britain was supporting France against the German aggression, but France, having badly lost the opening battles all along the front, the war raged on and Britain was now compelled to commit itself until one or other side was victorious and the outcome of that was a further four years of war in the trenches. Throughout English history there had been conflict with France, at Cressy and Agincourt, in the Low Countries, The peninsular wars in Spain and Portugal, the West Indies and with 'Clive of India', on the Nile, Wolfe at Quebec and in America Before and during the American War of independence, what was happening now was a massive volte face in fighting for French Freedom. Britain joined with France and fought in the Crimea against Russia in 1854 but not as an ally; that was Britain again simply protecting her interests and helping to prevent Russian expansion into areas of British interest, Mesopotamia, Afghanistan and India, part of which is now

Pakistan. Neither was Britain going to the aid of Turkey on whom Russia had declared war, Britain was joining with France, Austria and Turkey to put Russia in her place within Europe and at that time Prussia was small and did not count for much.

In fighting alongside France, Britain was doing what she had always done, and that was to seek to prevent any one nation dominating Europe. Of course this is the European history that we should not mention today but it is interesting to note that Britain eventually found it convenient to hop into bed with a willing France, no doubt the German threat compelled both Britain and France in the interests of national security to put aside their animosity toward each other, the outcome of which was the Entente Cordiale, a mutually beneficial alliance. It would allow Britain to safeguard her interests by curbing German expansion and by ensuring the Channel ports remained free. France, who had been badly defeated by Germany in 1870 suffering the loss of Alsace and Lorraine, sought to increase national security and now had Russia and Britain as her allies, she had good reason to feel much more confident since having Britain on her side was infinitely more important than her pact with Russia. That confidence however would be sorely tested in the Great War.

12

The Retreat from Mons

The retreat from Mons was an outstanding feat for the B.E.F. and particularly for II Corps under General Horace Smith-Dorrien assisted to no small extent by the of the Independent 4th Division. The Ind. 4th had landed at Boulogne and arrived at Solesmes in time to cover the retreat of II Corps Via Bavay and Solesmes to Le Cateau, they then fought alongside II corps when they turned and gave the advancing Germans a bloody nose at Le Cateau before continuing their withdrawal south to St Quentin. Sir John French had ordered Gen. Smith Dorrien to continue with the retreat south but Smith Dorrien felt that to do so would have risked the annihilation of II Corps by allowing the Germans to fall on their rear and scatter them. Sir John French seems to have been adamant that to continue the retreat was the right course of action but said nothing when Smith Dorrien decided to do what he thought was best. In the event Smith Dorrien's action was proved right and he was further vindicated by the fact that II Corps not only managed to hold off the attack of the German 1st Army, they managed to completely fool Von Kluck's pursuing army into thinking that they had withdrawn west, to the Channel coast. Later Sir John French said that he felt that since The II Corps Commander was on the spot, he was better placed to make a decision as to whether he ought to continue the retreat or turn and make a stand, but at the time it would appear that Smith Dorrien had countermanded French's orders, or at best ignored it.

The Kaiser had demanded that all the battalions of the B.E.F. should be exterminated. His order was the

143

"extermination of the treacherous English, and Field Marshal Sir John French's contemptible little army". Against Von Kluck's 1st Army the British expeditionary force faced vastly different odds in a very different kind of War, still, the British showed the same spirit that they had at Namur, Minden, Waterloo, Badajoz, Talavera, Salamanca, San Sebastian and so many other great battles, the Kaiser should have known better than to speak of them with such contempt. By comparison with the German army it was indeed a very small army, but Von Kluck himself could testify to the contempt that his large army was held in by "The Old Contemptible's and indeed he was moved to say as much after the War was over. He referred to the severe losses his army suffered as they forced the B.E.F to pull back by sheer weight of numbers, and the Kaiser unwittingly gave a lasting name 'The Old Contemptible's' to those of I and II Corps of the B.E.F. at Mons and the term is now part of military history.

The B.E.F. moved up and took up positions to the east of Mons on a front astride the Charleroi canal on the left of the French Fifth Army under General Lanrezac. General Allenby's cavalry division had on the 22nd made contact with the enemy but had not reported any immediate great danger confronting the B.E.F. and the Royal Flying Corps had also indicated that the Germans were now facing them. On the evening of the 22nd Lieutenant Spears, British liaison officer with the French Fifth Army, told Sir John French That Lanrezac was in great difficulties at Charleroi and that the B.E.F. risked being cut off. At the outbreak of hostilities I Corps under Haig was positioned to the left of and in contact with the French 19th Division, on its right in contact with Smith Dorriens II Corps. There appears to have been a general lack of co-operation between General Lanrezac and Sir John French, Lanrezac pressing

Sir John French to move up into the attack and Sir John pointing out that not only was he not ready to attack but he would not do so until he (Lanrezac) gave the order for the French Fifth Army to move up and attack from their positions which were well to the rear of the B.E.F.

The German 1st army opened its bombardment on II Corps in the evening of the 23rd Aug. and under heavy fire II Corps retreated some three miles or so during that evening. In the early hours of the next morning the B.E.F. was ordered to withdraw, I Corps had little difficulty in getting away at once but II Corps found difficulty in breaking off and withdrawing due to heavy enemy activity. I Corps under General Haig had been ordered to withdraw whilst covering the right flank of II Corps, but in fact I Corps found itself retreating further to the south of the line they were intended to take and far from covering the II Corps right flank they lost contact. Instead of retreating along the line Bavay, Le Quesnoy, Solesmes, they turned south into the Great Forest of Mormal and headed for Landrecies and the River Sambra

This highlights the fact that having lost contact with II Corps he had no idea what pressure they were under. It begs the question as to whether Haig ever knew at any stage how badly II Corps was being handled, did he just accept the order From HQ to retreat and hastily carry that out? II Corps was under heavy pressure from the evening of the 23rd and even as they regrouped and turned to fight at Le Cateau they were shelled from the high ground across the small river Selle on their right flank. No real reason seems to have been put forward as to why I Corps veered so far south into the forest and away from II Corps, whose right flank it was supposed to have been protecting, it cannot have been a matter of retreating in disarray since at that stage they were not under heavy attack, II Corps on the other hand were under severe attack and again taking up positions to confront the enemy.

Sir Henry Wilson, who was the deputy at GHQ was convinced that the BEF was faced by something in the order of a German Army Corps, but by now Sir John French was beginning to understand the size of the forces that he was up against and it does seem that the concerns of General Smith Dorrien having been played down by Sir John French on the 23rd were in fact soundly based. I Corps continued to move away to the south from the advancing German army and away from II Corps right; the direction taken was dictated by the need to ensure that the corps managed to avoid contact with the advancing force but at the cost of exposing I corps flank and eventually losing contact. Comments made by Officers of the East Lancashire Regt. part of the 4th Division covering the withdrawal of II Corps at Solesmes, indicated that the troops straggling back had been in severe fighting and were exhausted. The roads were blocked by civilians fleeing the advancing German army and this in itself created delays for II Corps. The Germans had no compunction in clearing the way by force but the nature of the British Tommy was far more compassionate.

Just as the battle opened at Mons on the 23rd of August the British army 4th Division (operating independently at the time) was landing in France, the various battalions of the Division landing at different ports. They proceeded by rail to Le Cateau and Bertry and took up positions in a triangle, firstly marching north to Viesly. The east of the triangle base was Le Cateau, the west at Caudry and at the apex at Solesmes located on the line II Corps was withdrawing along to Le Cateau. The task of 4th Div. was to cover the withdrawal of II Corps and to prevent the Germans turning their flank. By midday of the 25th the first men of II Corps (3rd

Div.) were arriving in the Solesmes area, the men weary and bedraggled after the hard fighting and long hot march were slowed by the number of refugees on the road with hand-carts, prams, wheelbarrows, anything to carry their belongings in their bid to flee the Germans. The state of the men retreating did not go unnoticed by the men of the 4th Division and they wondered what they had been up against, could this be a rout and were the B.E.F. a beaten army? The Germans were in very hot pursuit and an order was received from G.H.Q. that the B.E.F. would continue the retreat on the 26th.

DUG-OUT PROVERB

Here are the old sweats sayings, he tells the tale of his trade,
Gleanings from trench and dugout, battle fatigue and parade.

Tis' said the Bosch has pluck, of this I have no doubt,
But see him in the darkest light until you've knocked him out.

Your dugout took you hours to build, got broken in a minute,
A rotten shame! Be thankful son, your carcass wasn't in it.

And if one shelters you a night, tend it roof and rafter,
And make it better than it was, for those who follow after.

The trench is calm you say, my son? The Bosch is keeping quiet,

Then keep your rifle close at hand; we soon
shall have a riot.

A soldier's life is risky; it may end damn quick,
well let it,
Since we get five francs every week, we'll bust
it when we get it.

You may cough and sneeze in your dugout, but
you can't go anywhere
There's little health around the house, the dead
are lying there.

You may dig as deep as spade can dig, but the
Bosch's eyes can tell,
Where the khaki moles have plied their trade,
and the beggars' burrow well.

Pray to God when the dirt (shells) flies over,
and the country flops about,
But stick to your dugout all the same, until
you're ordered out.

When guns are going large a bit, and sending
gifts from Krupp,
You've got to keep your napper low, but keep
your spirits up.

These are the dugout maxims, that the old
sweats fling about,
For the better education of the 'Rooky' newly
out.

***

148

There was now quite some distance between the two Corps of the B.E.F. Haig eventually made camp at Landrecies some 11/12 kilometres East of II Corps cut off at Le Cateau. II Corps was fighting a severe rearguard actions as it withdrew along the planned line of retreat of Solesmes and Le Cateau and Smith Dorrien was quite rightly fully expecting Haigs I Corps to cover his right flank. Haig however saw things differently and asked HQ to direct II Corps to come to his aid, even though he had put the River L'Oise between himself and the Germans he felt that he was sufficiently under pressure to warrant help from II Corps.

Sir John French in his book '1914' says that II Corps managed to withdraw at the arranged time but that I Corps was delayed for several hours, this does seem to be questionable since it was II Corps that was taking the brunt of the fighting, and in view of what happened at Landrecies it begs the question as to whether Haig, being convinced that he was about to be overwhelmed simply made another rapid retreat to St. Quentin leaving the bulk of I Corps to follow on, as and when they were able. It would appear that the German force that attacked at Landrecies was a brigade sized detachment from the main German thrust that had moved South West along the edge of the Mormal Forest on the Le Quesnoy/Landrecies road. This skirmish that Haig had felt so threatening by now had been quelled and he, along with his staff had moved back to St. Quentin. Meanwhile, as II Corps was being very roughly handled, Haig was suggesting to Sir John French that his I Corps should offer support to the French Fifth Army, an offer Sir John French flatly refused to consider.

At this stage the men of II Corps were in such an exhausted state that the Corps Commander Gen. Smith Dorrien felt that to continue with the retreat beyond Le

Cateau would be foolhardy and probably lead to the annihilation of his troops. He looked to I Corps, some 11/12 kilometres east by now, to move up and stand alongside him on his right, but Haig the Commander of I Corps had his own worries, more imagined than real and non existent when compared to Smith Dorrien's. It was by the late evening of the 24th that Haig had moved out from Landrecies and on the 25th Sir John French moved his HQ from Le Cateau to St Quentin. A phone call received at GHQ was answered by Henry Wilson (Deputy Chief of Staff) who, since the Chief of Staff, General Sir Archibald Murray was sleeping took S.D's message to Sir John French. The message from S.D. stated his intentions that having consulted the Cavalry Commander General Allenby, he was as yet undecided as to whether he should ignore French's order to retreat and instead turn to strike a hard blow at the enemy in order to allow the corps to slip away.

Wilson felt that French did not understand what was happening but agreed to S.D's plan and to this Wilson comments in his diary, 'this will lead to disaster, or ought to'. With that he went of to St Quentin railway station to the only telephone line on which II Corps HQ could be contacted at Bertry. Smith Dorrien later mentions that telephone conversation,[13] "Henry Wilson asked what I thought of chance of success, and I replied that I was fully confident and hopeful of giving the enemy a smashing blow and slipping away before he could recover." Wilson replied, "good-luck to you, yours is the first cheerful voice I have heard in these three days." "With these pleasing words in my ears, which I will never forget, I returned to my headquarters." S.D. Made a further request that the Ind. 4th Division be put under his command and this request was sanctioned. Haig, now having taken himself and his staff south to St. Quentin, well away from the action rather than to the west, and having been refused permission to go to the support of Lanrezac there was little for 1 Corps but to view events from a distance, the coming onslaught that II Corps faced in what became 'The Battle of Le Cateau'.

Sir John French records in his book '1914'; "I Corps had been hounded through the Forest of Mormal by a mechanised infantry brigade and at Landrecies the enemy moved into the town in a column filling the streets", He goes on to quote from a letter that he sent to Lord Kitchener on August 27th 1914: -

"The 4th Brigade (1 Corps) were fighting in the early morning in the streets of Landrecies, a German infantry column, 'about the strength of a brigade, emerged from the wood north of the town and advanced south in the closest order, filling up the narrow street. "Two or three of our machine guns were brought to bear on this magnificent target from the other end of the town. The head of the column was checked and stopped; frightful panic ensued, and it is estimated that, in a very few minutes, no less than 800/900 dead and wounded Germans were lying in the streets". French was never so glowing with regard to Smith Dorrien's actions in his book.

Haig had already been ordered to retreat by GHQ just as II Corps had, and being in a totally different situation than II Corps he was able to carry out the order without interference from the enemy, of course Haig had already moved out on the night of the 24th with his staff and left the retreat to be organised by others, a matter that brought criticism of Haig's actions. II Corps was left unsupported, other than by the independent 4th division who were operating on Smith Dorriens left, to face a far superior German force, better equipped with troops and artillery, and occupying high ground on the right across the valley of the Selle from which they could rain down fire. Smith-Dorrien's stark choices was either to retreat and face II Corps being wiped out, or stand and give the enemy a hard blow so as to give his men the chance to continue their withdrawal in an orderly fashion and without harassment. He asked GHQ to arrange for I Corps to move up on his right flank and was in utter despair when Wilson replied that Haig was actually asking that II Corps should move South East the 10 or 12 kilometres to support I Corps.

Smith-Dorrien issued orders on the afternoon of the 25th for II Corps and the Ind. 4th Division (having been placed under his command) to move to their new positions on a line from Le Cateau to the high ground west of Haucourt. The battalions of the 4th Division were providing cover for the retreating 3rd Division at the time these orders were issued but the retreating troops were slow to get through, the number of refugees on the road meant that the troops were not in marching order but split up and consequently held up. As a result many of the 4th Div. Battalions in rearguard positions did not manage to get away until late at night, they in turn were held up by the refugees as they fled from the Germans through Caudry and Ligny.[14] An officer of the Lancashire Fusiliers moving back down that road from Viesly recalled the scene.

The withdrawal of the 3rd Division had been seriously delayed by congestion in and near Solesmes, owing partly to the converging march of the 19th Infantry Brigade and partly to the ever- increasing number of refugees. The latter were much more of a problem to the kind hearted British, who could not bring themselves to thrust these poor folk and their few belongings piled on carts into the ditch, than they were to the pursuing Germans who had no such scruples. As a result, it was not until 9~3O pm that the battalion started from Viesly to march about five miles back to a position a little to the north-west of Ligny amidst rain and mud.

13

Ind. 4Th DIV. AT THE BATTLE OF LE CATEAU

Whilst I Corp of the B.E.F. was making its withdrawal from Landrecies, II Corps under General Smith Dorrien was taking up positions in order to confront the German Ist Army on a front stretching from the high ground above Haucourt to Le Cateau and the River Selle. The independent 4th Division that had covered the left flank of II Corps on the Solesmes area during its withdrawal under heavy fire had itself retreated to Haucourt and the Warnelle ravine. General Smith Dorrien, who had requested that the 4th Div. be placed under his command in order to prevent Von Kluck's divisions outflanking him, had positioned the 4th Div well to his left. The idea was that II Corps would turn and give the Germans a sharp shock and retreat as quickly as circumstances would allow. 4th Division's job was to hold that flank and enable II Corps to break of contact with the enemy and withdraw in good order after giving the enemy a bloody nose. The enemy attack took the form of heavy artillery fire from across from River Selle into II Corps right flank, and from the direction of Solesmes. The Germans had also raced ahead beyond the left flank of II Corps and were able to surprise the brigades of the 4th Division by attacking from the direction of Cattaniere that lay to the west of the high ground at Haucourt.

It is not my intention to write a full account of the battle of Le Cateau, I would however like to briefly add something about the part played by the 4th Ind. Division and particularly the Lancashire Regiments, the ones that my family have been involved with since the Boer War. What happened is typical of the what all of the battalions of the B.E.F. faced at one stage or another, Le Cateau was an integral part of that first period of the Great War ending with the long march of the B.E.F., including The Ind 4th Division, to the east of Paris.

The first battalions of 4th Division to arrive in the area of the Warnelle Ravine started to dig in at 3.30am on the early morning of the 26th of August. According to records the East Lancs arrived at in the area around midnight and they bivouacked in a field near to Fontaine au Pire until first light, they then they took up their positions close by. Their actions seem to give some indication that they felt that the German advance was some considerable distance behind in the direction of Solesmes, at this stage the Brigade Commanders of the 4th Division understood their job to be that of covering the left flank of II Corps whilst it withdrew and were not aware that there was to be an offensive. These men were probably issued with 24 hour rations when they set out for Viesly on the 23rd in support of the B.E.F. and would have been fed again probably on the 24th and 25th, but it is unlikely that they would have anything else unless they had been issued with 24 hour ration packs on leaving the field in which they had bivvied on the night of the 25th. Each man had a 'Poncho' a rather peculiar shaped waterproof cape that tailed down one side to a point; it was made from a sort of rubberised 'Macintosh' or trench coat material with large press-studs for fasteners. It was short at one side and long at the other tapering to a point about half way down the calf of the leg. It served a dual purpose in that two of these fastened together with the studs made a reasonably waterproof bivouac for two men, a sort of small ridge tent in which the ends were closed against the weather (but there seems to be no record of it having been used for that purpose). It was rather a peculiar thing to wear especially around the neck were it seemed to bunch. This is what the men would have used if the weather were bad as it was on that particular night. These Ponchos were still standard army issue in the 1950's.

The position that Smith Dorrien found himself in was an unenviable one, it would appear that he was undecided whether or not to stand and give the enemy a hard knock, even though he had been in telegraphic contact with H.Q. to request permission to have 4th Division placed under his command and to make a stand, he decided that he would consult fully with his divisional commanders and to leave his final decision until the last minute, the fact that the G.O.C. had given the order to retreat made his decision that much harder. It may well have been that the decision was made for him when the Germans took the high ground to the east of Le Cateau on the banks of the Selle River and attacked the exposed right flank of II Corps in the early hours of 26th, this was part of an attack along the whole front from Le Cateau to Beauvais and the high ground above Haucourt. By 2.00pm the 14th Brigade, having been heavily shelled from across the valley, where overwhelmed by the Germans attacking from across the river into the valley below them, what was left of them were taken prisoner. Further to the west and along to the area of Haucourt the 3rd and 4th Division were holding up well. When Smith Dorrien ordered the retreat the 5th Division who were under the greatest pressure were moved first, then 3rd Division and finally the 4th Division. The 5th and 3rd Divisions had already fought a fierce battle at Mons and also some very hard rearguard actions as they withdrew on the 24th and 25th, for the 4th Division Le Cateau was their baptism of fire.

The Lancashire Fusiliers were in position by Longsart farm and digging in by 3.30 am, it was 2 hours later at 5.30am when the Kings Own arrived at their allotted positions, only half an hour Before the first German attack. They had been the pulled back covered by the Inniskilling Dragoon Guards, all of these regiments plus the 2nd Essex made up the 12th Brigade, and had been held up by refugees and French Cavalry as the night turned to mist and rain. The Lancashire Fusiliers had been ordered to dig trenches for the company of Kings Own that would take up positions to their right and had succeeded in digging shallow trenches by the time the first German attack came. What followed was to earn those battalions involved the Battle Honour, 'Le Cateau' a battle overshadowed by others to come in the trenches later in the War, nonetheless 'Le Cateau' was an honour proudly won by tired, exhausted men fighting against vastly superior odds.

At this same time the French Fifth army commanded by General Lanrezac was having a hard time being pushed back by the German Second Army under Von Bulow. Sir John French had decided that he would hold out for no longer than 24 hours and was in no position to offer support to Lanrezac. At that stage General Joffre made several decisions to try to stem the German steamroller and if possible turn it back, he had been working on forming the new Sixth Army and he also created a new 9th army under General Foch whose XXth Corps had just been defeated at Morhange. He fired Lanrezac and started to plan for the two new armies to move into the line either side of the French Fifth Army with Franchet D'Esperay as the new Commander. These two new armies were in the early stages of being formed but they would very soon play a crucial part in stemming the headlong German advance.

The 1st Kings Own marched from Haucourt along the Cattinieres road as the dawn broke and the sun came out, the little terrier that the battalion had been given before leaving England trotted along with them in the Union Jack coat they had made for it. They went down towards the Warnelle Brook and up the other side to the top of the brow where they entered a field on the left. The transport was on the road with the horses still in the shafts, the men had been stood down and their rifles stacked along with their packs before having breakfast.

The KORR. C.O. Colonel Dykes was still on horseback and two officers; Capt. Higgins and Capt. Nixon were intently watching some movement in the distance that concerned them. All at once a troop of French Dragoons that the men had been watching turned and raced for the cover of the Warnelle Ravine. Before the Colonel could have the men 'stand to' there was a terrific burst of machine gun fire opened up, Colonel Dykes was killed outright and also his horse. The men tried to turn the transports but in the confusion the horses bolted and others were killed where they stood along with the little terrier. The machine gun Jackets were riddled with holes that rendered them useless and as the Company commanders tried to get their men back out of the field and into the cover of the Ravine they had severe losses.

The enemy had found their range and with shells bursting immediately in front of them the whole battalion went headlong over the lip of the ravine with the dead and dying left over the top in the ranks as they were hit. The Machine gun fire was concentrated to the left where the Lancashire Fusiliers were positioned and they had started to receive enfilade fire from their left where the 1st Essex should have been. Capt. Roffey, Second in Command of the Lancashire Fusiliers set off to locate the right of the 2nd Essex and found that they had moved back, the Germans had outflanked them and they also were receiving enfilade fire from the left, as they moved back so the Germans found the LF's exposed. Roffey was badly wounded in the mouth and neck and Capt.Vandelour (B Coy) 2nd Essex with whom Capt. Roffey was liasing, was killed.

After several attempts to push back the enemy the brigade were unable to hold the position and the order to withdraw to the main road was given at about 8.45am when shallow dugouts were hastily prepared along the main road either side of Haucourt. Capt. Roffey lay badly wounded in a trench and whilst there he received further injuries when a German crept up to the trench and aimed his pistol at point blank and shot him twice. Even after this he managed to crawl away to some corn stooks in the field where he was later rescued by the adjutant of the Lancashire Fusiliers and some men from the 2nd Essex regiment. A great number of officers and men of the 4th Division were killed and wounded in this way, trying to find cover or going back to help wounded comrades. Capt. Sidebottom who had taken over 'D' Coy of the LF's tried to gather as many men as he could and take cover by a hedge but was badly wounded, Privates Banister and Hanson tried to recover his body but were also badly wounded. Second Lieutenant Humphrey was moving back the only remaining machine gun when he stopped to help an injured comrade, in doing so he himself was fatally wounded and leaving the battalion without machine guns.

The Kings Own suffered the worst casualties by far in the 4th Division having been the first hit and taken unawares, they had more than 400 men killed, wounded or missing in the first stages of the battle, a level of casualties never again exceeded by the battalion throughout the War. The Kings Own Medical Officer had set up aid posts in the Church and a local café in

Haucourt where the wounded were taken from the 12th Brigade, the walking wounded making their own way although many with severe wounds continued to fight. At about lunchtime the German attacks seemed to subside and the actions mounted by some of the remaining officers and men of the Division were managing to hold the situation. At this time volunteers were sought from all the units in the Division to go out and bring in the wounded and they managed recover a great number of them along with one Uhlan prisoner (Prussian Cavalry) Before enemy machine gun fire compelled them to withdraw. These men were all taken to the aid post where the priest was giving absolution to those who were very badly wounded but unfortunately those still injured and lying out on the field had to be left for the Germans to take prisoner and care for.

The Long March

The order for II Corps to retreat was given at about 2.00pm and the first to withdraw were the 5th Division whose right flank held by the 14th Brigade had suffered the heaviest attacks; the 3rd Division followed these whilst the 4th Division covered their withdrawal on the left flank

The 11th brigade were still holding out by the quarry and the railway cutting but eventually received the order to pull out after receiving heavy enfilade fire from the direction of Caudry where the 3rd Division had withdrawn, they were also heavily attacked on the left through the railway cutting and at a point where there was a gap between the 1st East Lancashire Regiment on the left of 11th brigade and the 1st Kings Own. One Company of the East Lancashire Regiment and one Company of the Rifle Brigade did not receive the order to withdraw and were very hard pressed particularly on the left held by 'C' Company East Lancs. By around 5pm their ammunition was almost spent, they were in a salient with the enemy on both flanks when their Commanding Officers decided it was time to withdraw.

They fired their last rounds in one great burst and retreated, this gave them a hundred yard start but the next two hundred yards was swept by enemy fire up to the edge of the Warnelle ravine where they formed up and marched towards Ligny. The Enemy came to the edge of the ravine but were met by withering artillery gunfire and beat a hasty retreat. The extreme left and right of the Kings Own positions, which extended several hundred yards either side of the village, did not receive the order to move and at about 8.30pm they were instructed to report to the Village where Major Parker, now commanding the battalion, was getting together as many men as possible to move out. Near the aid post Capt. Clutterbuck asked what was going on thinking that he could hear French being spoken, it was in fact German and at that moment the Church door opened casting a beam of light across the road, there the Germans had taken some of the Kings Own prisoners. Capt. Clutterbuck was called on to surrender but refused; he was killed along with two others as he tried to jump over a wall, the rest bolted in the half-light with the Germans firing at them as they fled.

By about 11.00pm that night a group of about 50 had gathered together with Major Parker, they were danger of being cut off from the main body of II Corp and decided that they had to move out and leaving the wounded and injured behind at the aid post, they had no choice if the group were to have any chance of successfully rejoining the rest of II Corp. Other senior officers gathered their men together and the main body set off, at about midnight Major Parker and his group left, skirting round villages that were occupied by Germans and later billeted at a farm. The retreating men of II Corps and the 4th Div. followed the two prongs of a 'Y' until they reached Hancourt where they managed to join up together. The long retreat continued until eventually 12 days later they arrived at a small town to the east of Paris, Brie Comte Robert.

II Corps had inflicted such heavy losses on the Von Klucks 1st army, that they lost their appetite for battle and having driven out the B.E.F. failed to follow it up. The withdrawal had been conducted for the most part in broad daylight but the Germans could not locate the B.E.F. and it was later said that they felt that they were up against a much larger force, well they were, they were up against the 'Old Contemptables'

By not adhereing to the agreed line of retreat and covering II Corp's right, Haig had left a vacuum into which the Germans had charged briefly making contact with I Corps at Landrecies before finding the exposed right flank of two Corps across the valley of the Selle River. 14th Brigade took the full brunt of a flank attack that would never have occurred had I Corps been in position to extend Smith Dorrien's right. Haig had been ordered to retreat early in the morning and it was later in the day when he offered to provide support to cover II Corps right flank, the offer was not acted upon but even if it had it would be difficult to see how he could turn around his retreating Divisions and effectively help II Corps. The exposed II corps right flank created the greatest danger, all along the centre and left the British troops were dealing very effectively with Klucks Divisions, in other words the damage had been done and Haigs help could not recover that. It is clear that Sir John French took the decision not to support Smith Dorrien by committing I Corps; neither was he making any attempt to reunite the two Corps of the B.E.F into a fighting unit and in that he left himself open to the suggestion that he was unsuited to the command of the B.E.F. He reinforced this in the early days of September when the French 5th and 6th Armies positioned either side of the B.E.F made a spirited attack on the German 1st and 2nd Armies, but Sir John French held back the B.E.F. until General Joffre took it upon himself to visit Sir John French at GHQ on the eve of Sept 5th to persuade French that he must attack on his allotted front between the French 9th and 6th armies At the Marne. There probably was good reason for Sir John French's reluctance however, the B.E.F. had just completely a 10-day retreat, they were still a force but they were exhausted and desperately short of supplies.

Fortunately Smith Dorrien handled Mons and Le Cateau brilliantly to the obvious annoyance of Sir John French who had not wanted Smith Dorrien on his staff. He achieved what he set out to do at Le Cateau and proved his worth as an army commander; the object was to hit the enemy hard and for two Corps to slip away whilst the Germans recovered. Being outflanked on the right was a situation he could not avoid and in the circumstances II Corps deserved great praise for the way they fought. The Germans suffered very heavy losses and were reluctant to continue when II Corps slipped away. There were significant losses on the British side also but they pulled off a very daring and successful action against some three German Army Corps with far superior artillery fire and made an orderly withdrawal in full daylight leaving the enemy duped.

The B.E.F. was now in full retreat to the south in two completely separate columns with the French Fifth army on it's right being roughly handled by the German Second Army under Von Bulow, but the numbers were still very low. The newly formed French sixth Army under General Manoury, operating on the Fifth Army's left, was still grossly under strength whilst waiting for troop transfers from General Castelnau's Army in Lorraine. The B.E.F. was by now in total disarray and a full days march behind (or ahead in retreat) of the two retreating French armies. By the 1st of September The B.E.F. had safely crossed the River Marne and looked to a short period in which the various units could rest and regroup.

Haig wrote in his diary that he thought French, to whom he was Chief of Staff in South Africa, was not up to the job of G.O.C. and of course French proved that to be correct. Haig also noted in his diary that he had said as much during a meeting with King George the V, neither did he think French's chief of staff, Sir Archibald Murray, had enough backbone for the job in hand. Haig said he was honoured to command I Corps and relished the thought of proving himself in battle but he had made little effort up to this point, he had seen almost no contact with the enemy at Mons and was not involved at Le Cateau. II Corps on the other hand, throughout the Battle of Mons and the retreat, and again at the retreat from Le Cateau had taken a hammering but held out and disengaged in such a way that left the Germans with a sharp poke in the eye and baffled as to their whereabouts. Added to this Sir John French did not like Smith Dorrien, a veteran of Islawandana in the South African War, who was said to be given to uncontrollable outbursts and never to have personally addressed the soldiers under his command. It was rather unfortunate for both Smith Dorrien and Sir John French that Kitchener made that appointment.

Haig had been Sir John French's Chief of staff in South Africa and I suppose one could be forgiven for feeling that French's reports regarding I Corps were somewhat biased. In the event SD found himself as an old soldier fighting two glorious battles whereas Haig, who was looking for that very opportunity, was relegated to the sidelines to watch with envy as Smith Dorrien, not having sought it, stole the limelight. Had Haig maintained the line of retreat on the right and in contact with II Corps and been involved in the fighting, that would have been to his credit, but he did not, there does not appear to be any record of what Smith Dorrien thought of that, however, even though Haig failed to do so, his star was in the ascendance. By sheer coincidence Foch's early periods of the war were marred by defeat or lack of success, but like Haig, his time came later.

The official historian, Sir James Edmunds is recorded saying, "The Retreat from Mons" was in every way honourable to the Army. The troops suffered under every disadvantage. The number of reservists in the ranks was on an average over one-half of the full strength, and owing to the force of circumstances the units were hurried away to the area of concentration Before all ranks could resume acquaintance with their officers and comrades, and relearn their business as soldiers. Arrived there, they were hastened forward by forced marches to battle, confronted with greatly superior numbers of the most renowned army in Europe, and condemned at the very outset to undergo the severest ordeal which can be imposed upon an army, they were short of food and sleep when they began their retreat, they continued it, always short of food and sleep, for thirteen days; and at the end of the retreat they were still an army, and a formidable army. They were never demoralized, for they rightly judged that they had never been beaten."

Several months after Le Cateau news filtered through about the wounded and injured at Warnelle Ravine and the aid posts when the 4th Division was driven out. The injured, not receiving any food from the Germans, were compelled to return to the battlefield to gather what food they could from the transports and packs left behind. The Germans said that the French people would feed them but also gave a clear indication of what would happen to any Frenchman who did; in making this stipulation the Germans breached the terms of the Geneve Convention. They arrested the old priest who had given absolution to the wounded at the aid post and accused him of not only assisting the wounded but also giving help to all allied soldiers. He was taken out and shot; after the Armistice the people of the village erected a memorial in his memory. How many more would suffer that same fate Before the Armistice was signed in November 1918.

THE OPEN DOOR

It was after the fight, one autumn night, in the
province of old Lorraine,
When two of our wounded English lads
emerged from a village lane.
They had forced their way through the German
lines, into the village street.
Where no one would offer shelter, or a morsel
of food to eat.

For death was the penalty that old 'Von Kluck'
had promised to any of those,
Who would dare to shelter an Englishman, or
one of the allied foes.
As our lads limped painfully along, they came
to a village store,
They stood for a while as their eyes caught
sight of a house with an open door.

They went inside and an old priest came, he of-
fered each lad a seat
He gave them food and saw to their wounds,

and bathed their tired feet.
Then they spoke of the fight, the terrible plight,
and how many comrades
had died.
The old priest looked at his rosary, "War is a
terrible thing", he cried.

Men must fight for wrong or right whilst wom-
en are left to weep,
He gave up his bed for the English lads and sat
on a chair to sleep.
At the break of dawn the Prussians came, with
clinking swords and spurs,
One of the Uhlan officers said, "You have been
sheltering British curs".

"I shelter all" the old priest cried, his pale lips
moving in prayer,
They seized him roughly and led him out, to be
shot on the village square.
"I don't mind dying", the old priest cried, like
those who have gone before,
"But heaven forgive the man; who closed my
house, the house with the open
door".

On the morn a volley rang out and the old
priests day was done,
To the terrible list of the enemy crimes, they
added another one.
There's a lord to be met by the Warlord yet,
when he answers for Reims and
Lorraine,
For outraged women, the lured priest, and the
little babes that have been slain.

For on that day he'll be kneeling down, and for
mercy beg and pray,
I would not give much for the Kaisers chance,
on the Kaisers judgement day.

***

Praise and appreciation was given to the B.E.F. for
their gallant effort, Brigadier General Hunter Weston
who had commanded the 11th brigade said, "they had
always been reliable; they had died but they had never
given way, and they had acted up to the highest tradi-
tions of the British army, there could be no higher
praise". Marshal Von Kluck, German 1st Army G.O.C.
in conversation with a British General for the first time
after the War said; "in the whole history of the world
there is in my opinion no military feat, which has ever
been excelled or equalled by that accomplished by the
British army in 1914. My admiration for that army is
greater than I can express".

In his book, Spectamur Agendo, Lt. Hopkinson re-
fers to an appreciative comment on the stubborn fight
put up by the British Army "this day appears in the
memoirs of Von Kluck's Chief of Staff: One cannot
refuse to recognize the bold attitude of the British
troops who succeeded, even at the price of heavy loss-
es, in carrying out their withdrawal in the middle of the
fight".'

It has to be recognized that this was not a humiliat-
ing defeat for the B.E.F., but an extremely well execut-
ed withdrawal by a small but efficient force, which,
whilst opposed by infinitely superior enemy forces was
at the same time exposed on the right flank and out-
flanked on the left by Von Kluck's First Army.

In the one hundred years since the British had

fought on the continent, there had been involvement in very few conflicts of any consequence other than the Crimean War and the South African War, and things had changed little since the latter. There were no armoured or mechanised divisions then, the cavalry were still very much in existence although as a result of the Haldane recommendations (as the Secretary for War he introduce the changes described earlier i.e. the B.E.F. and the Territorial Army) the cavalry were now trained to use a rifle and fight as demounted soldiers. The first battles of the Great War were the traditional encounters involving mobile Warfare but after the battle of the Aisne both sides dug in and it became a war of attrition.

Later machine guns and heavy artillery, guns and howitzers of enormous size ensured a solid defence of whatever the enemy won and the breaking down of fortress strongholds as in the case of Verdun. The Germans and the French were from the beginning using heavy guns with high explosive shells whereas the British Army still believed that shrapnel was sufficient when in fact it was a little use against the trench positions and barbed wire, they had to learn that lesson.

In the stalemate of the trenches, attacks were preceded by huge artillery bombardments of the enemy positions before the attack took place. Later when the troops went over the top they were instructed to walk at a steady pace and the reason for this was that a system had been developed by the Royal Artillery that was known as the creeping barrage, a barrage of HE that preceded the rows of attacking infantry at a pace determined by the estimated progress of the forward line, those at the leading edge of the attack would signal back by any means available (and often that was by runner), to the Artillery gunnery officer. The R.F.A. were excellent at their job, but this was not a precise art and so there were times when the shells fell amongst our own troops. The ground was continually churned into a mass of mud and water-filled shell holes, almost impossible for troops to attack across and when they did they were exposed to withering machine gun fire and the possibility of wire entanglements, that should have been cut by the opening gunfire, still being intact. On one occasion during an attack at Langemarck the Lancashire Fusiliers found the wire, supposedly cut, still completely intact, consequently the German machine gunners wiped out a whole company as they became more and more entangled in the barbed wire.

Certainly it was not possible to move heavy guns over such terrain and it was for this reason that the machine gun became the dominant weapon of the German defence against infantry attacks, cavalry charges were also completely ineffective until later when tanks were introduced and were designated as the 'heavy machine gun section'. Yet heavy artillery alone could not win the War, men had to get in there and occupy the ground just as they had to after tanks had advanced, and this of course led to massive loss of life. Just as the infantryman would gauge how much ammunition he had used and how much he had left, so the General Staff calculated their needs in terms of men, how many used and how many left, how many more recruits would be needed, would they get through the men they had before the newly trained recruits came to replace them, human life was very expendable.

The Germans had for their part, developed the use of snipers just as the Boers did in the South African War. These were courageous individuals who acted alone, often in darkness, and would position themselves in shell holes to lie up for long periods in a position where if possible they could see into the British trenches. In this way many senior officers, Generals, and other ranks succumbed to German sniper fire by briefly exposing themselves in the trenches, (my great uncle is counted amongst those who died in this way), later the British developed this as a speciality. Precision sniping rifles were manufactured and housed in special wooden boxes, strapped in to prevent them being knocked, the rangefinder/sight would be calibrated for the use of a particular individual, a battalion sharpshooter who had shown consistently that he was a crack marksman, what they called 'the battalion shot'. Many of the skills developed were learned from the Gillies who worked on the estates in Scotland where they stalked the deer, these people were sought out and brought aside to teach their skills to others so they could not only pick off the men and particularly their commanders but also the German sniper.

THE SUPER SNIPER

Hermann Schwein was a sniper fine, of the famous Prussian guard,
He soaked his toes in oil of cloves and he rubbed his nose with lard.
Despite the cold, this sniper bold, lay out both day and night,
With a Mauser of the latest and a telescopic sight.

Snipe, snipe, snipe said Hermann, enthusiastic Hun,
in my crump hole snug I'm as warm as a rug, or a 'blanket, G.S.1' one.
Now Major Breen was an Officer keen of the 'Royal Artillery',
He'd four big guns to strafe the Huns, and very hot stuff was he.

He'd made their parapets hop like flies; he gave their emplacements hell,
When a sniper fired it made him tired, so he sniped with Lyddite shell.
Strafe, strafe, strafe said the major, "whether it rains or blows,
"I don't mind chaff" and by God I'll strafe till there's nothing to shoot but crows.

With a thirst for blood he stood in the mud of the sandbagged firing line,
To observe the burst, as he did his worst, to the men from across the Rhine
His head he'd pop o'er a sand bag top in a very unhealthy spot',
Our Hermann saw the Major rise, so he ripped the bag with a shot.

Impudent son of a sweep, said the Major, grabbing the telephone wire,
then he called with a grunt "Action front" and likewise "Battery fire"!
There's a vacant space where the trenches face, called the 'no man's land
And a yawning pit in the midst of it that could hold a German band.

And all around queer things are found, more human than divine,
With chalk and stones and Frenchmen's bones, but there's nought of Hermann Schwein.
Weep, weep, weep for Hermann, but what could a poor Bosch do?
'Gaist Major Breen, that officer keen, who snipes with a nine point two.

14

The Battles of the Marne And Aisne
Sept. 1914

The commander of the French Fifth Army, General Lanrezac was relieved of his command By Joffre after being overwhelmed by Von Bulow's Second Army, probably the worst thing that can happen to a commander in the field. In his place Franchot D'Esperaz was appointed, nicknamed by the British as 'Desperate Franky'. He was ordered to renew the attack against the German Second Army with vigour in order to relieve the pressure on the Expeditionary Force. He was successful to some extent in what was known as the Battle of the Guise, and the German Second Army was now in retreat.

The French High Command had been unable to understand the rapid gains made by the Germans on all fronts and the overwhelming defeats suffered by the French army in these early stages a situation leaving the French troops demoralised, especially at Verdun where later they would mutiny on a large scale. The 'gospel' Attaquez! Attaquez! as preached by the French General Foch, later Marshal and Supreme Allied Commander, was that only by all out attack could France succeed in overcoming the Germans. Foch, an old style French soldier of the Napoleonic school who had taught as a Professor was later Commandant of the French War College, The Ecole Superieure De Guerre. He had already commanded the XXth Corps in Castelnau's Second Army and been defeated by a far more prepared and better equipped German Army at Morhange. The main thrust of the German offensive was in the north, the French 2nd Army under Castelnau had been given the task of retaking Lorraine, lost to Germany in the 1870 war and a matter of national pride that it be retaken. It was a difficult task; the Germans had defence in depth and the rivers Sarre and Moselle posed obstacles to the French. Foch commanded the XXth Corps and suffered a huge defeat, now, unlike Lanrezac who had also been forced to retreat under the heavy German onslaught and then relieved of his command, Foch was given command of the newly formed 9th Army, one created by Joffre to fill the long, weak front between the French 5th and 4th Armies that opposed Von Bulow's Second Army

A situation now occurred as a result of General Joffre having pushed the French Fifth Army into a renewed attack, Von Bulow, having released divisions to go to the Russian front, was finding the going a lot harder and sought support from Von Kluck's 1st Army on his right. Von Kluck had lost contact with the B.E.F, he chased west across through Albert and on toward Amiens in an effort to locate them in their long retreat, it was the direction he naturally supposed they would take toward the channel ports. But by extending himself so far he had allowed a dangerous gap to open between the German First and Second armies, perhaps that was of little concern to him in the knowledge that there was no force in the field that could take advantage of that at the time, and perhaps the possibility of annihilating II Corps led him too far east. The B.E.F. had in fact withdrawn to the south-west from Le Cateau towards St Quentin, and Von Kluck, at last having lost them decided to break off the chase. He was aware that the Second Army was under great pressure and had already responded to Von Bulow by detaching two of his Corps to join with him. Having given up on contacting the Expeditionary Force Von Kluck wheeled his force east to close the gap and support Von Bulow, in doing so he exposed his flank to attack, this of course did not go unnoticed and was swiftly acted on when General Joffre quickly moved up the newly formed 6th and 9th armies. The celebrated military historian J.F.C. Fuller[15] identified the Battle of the Marne as one of the decisive battles of history.

Henry Wilson says in his diaries that on the 4th of September the Germans were observed moving from west to east across the front of the British lines, he recognised at once the opportunity that had opened up for a flank attack and went off post haste to see Franchet d'Esperay at his Fifth Army HQ. They agreed that the Fifth Army should fall back the next day in line with the British and wheel to the east with the Sixth Army covering their left. He makes no mention of the part played by Joffre in this but clearly it was Joffre that made it happen, and played the major role in recognising the opportunity and planning its execution. Had Joffre not created the two armies 6th and 9th there would have been no battle of the Marne. Nevertheless it is highly likely that Henry Wilson could have been a prime mover in the instigation of the battle, but then again, reading the contents of Wilson's diaries he leaves the reader in no doubt that he is the original 'thinker'. Sir John French comments in his book 1914, "I believe that the name of Marshal Joffre will descend into posterity with that battle as one of the greatest military commanders in history".

On his return to HQ Wilson found that Sir John French had ordered a retirement of all his troops and had informed the mayor of Paris that he intended to stay on the Seine and support the French Fifth Army in whatever way he could. Henry Wilson felt the decision was 'heartbreaking'. In wheeling his Army, Von Kluck had committed a cardinal error in exposing is right flank, Joffre, quick to recognize this had grasped the opportunity and made hasty plans to attack, whilst Sir John French rested his men at Brie Comte Robert.

General Joffre the French G.O.C. had, since taking overall command of the French forces, been very much concerned about the French left flank and particularly about the Expeditionary Force being in that covering position over which he had no direct control. Joffre had planned to change that situation by forming a new army that was to operate on the extreme left of the allied line between the B.E.F. and the Ourq, it seems that although he may have discussed his plans within the French GHQ, the British knew nothing of it until the battle of the Marne. This new army was formed from divisions in the Lorraine area and had already been ordered back to the area of Paris in reserve under General Manoury. Joffre cleverly drew a plan that would involve all of these armies in an attacking front from the Ourq to Verdun. General Joffre became annoyed and disillusioned by Sir John French's reluctance to respond to this audacious plan, for General Joffre this was a heaven sent moment that had to be acted on post haste, and he decided to visit the British HQ at Compiegne to discuss Sir John's intentions. Matters were cleared up through an interpreter and the attack was to proceed when Sir John French said that he would give Joffre all the support that he could. The British would take up positions between the French 6th and the French 5th to attack the German right flank. On the 6th of September the bulk of Gen. Manoury's Sixth Army was still at Paris and in order to get his men up to the Marne at once it was necessary that more than 1000 Paris taxis were requisitioned by the French Govt. these and buses and all other means of available transport were used to shuttle reserves to the front. The outcome of this French counter attack was a magnificent victory for the

Allies in which the B.E.F. played a significant role, it stopped the enemy advance and pushed them back in what became the Battles of the Marne, the German Schlieffen plan had been thwarted, they had been triumphantly on the way to entering Paris but they were stopped, their push fizzled out and 'the tables turned' the German initiative was lost to an astounding Allied victory.

German military planner Count Alfred Von Schleiffen had devised the 'Schlieffen plan' at the request of the Kaiser, it was devised to enable Germany to fight on two fronts in the event of war with France and Russia, this was later modified by Von Moltke the Secretary of State for War when he took over. It was intended to achieve a rapid defeat of France in the event of war and thus relieve divisions to turn eastward to the Russian front and was used to devastating effect, so much so that the allies were completely over run and driven back on Paris. The plan can be likened to a door placed along the French border with Germany and Belgium, the hinges at Switzerland and the handle at the Belgian coast. The plan was to push the door into France and drive everything like a rug behind it down towards Paris and back to the Swiss border as it swung right round. The German Armies positioned toward the Belgium end (German right) would be highly mobile and carry a massive punch whilst the armies further along the front towards Switzerland would be dug into strong defensive positions with heavy artillery and mortars awaiting the fleeing French armies. Montgomery used the same sort of plan when he strove to take Caen after the D-day landings, Caen being the hinge on which the attack pivoted.

The significance of 'the Marne' was that it was later to be recognised for what it was, one of the decisive battles of world history. The situation changed from the

German steamroller crushing everything before it, to itself being pushed back 65 miles from the Seine to the Marne and then beyond to the Aisne. It was a crushing defeat for an army that had during the second half of August swept everything before it. The Allies were frantically preparing defences on the Seine when they dropped everything and were whisked to the front to take advantage of this totally unexpected opportunity; it was to be a success as much for the bad planning of the enemy, as it was the hard fought gains of the Allied armies. From that point the Germans were pushed back across the Aisne and the B.E.F. again took a significant part in that battle, on the Aisne the lines were drawn and stayed rooted for the next four years in an immobile trench War. Whatever the magnificent victory the Allies had won, credit must also be given to the fact that the opportunity was presented to the Allies largely because of the failures of the German High Command and Von Kluck in particular.

With the Germans retreating the allied advance continued on the 7th and 8th with hard fighting on the part of the French 5th and 6th Armies, the Expeditionary Force was under somewhat less pressure and although they took severe casualties they also captured large numbers of prisoners and equipment. They crossed the Marne on the 9th and continued the push reaching the Aisne on the 12th. The enemy had already retreated beyond the Aisne and at that stage plans were drawn up for the next phase of the attack, it was felt that the enemy were now split into two groups and that Allied left should pursue the enemy to the North east whilst the Allied right should attempt to outflank the enemy to the east. There was a sense of ultimate victory in the air, Gen. Wilson states in his diaries that he guessed that the Allies might be over the German border in one month's time and that General Berthalot felt that they would be at Elsenborn inside the German border within 3 weeks. It seems however that the Germans had different ideas and started to dig in on the East bank of the Aisne, after lunching all out attacks and severe fighting the Allies were brought to a complete halt all along the Aisne.

Considering the fact that Germany was infinitely more prepared and equipped for War than the allies the battle was an enormous victory. They routed the German army and pushed it back 65 miles, a German army led by a King who was also Emperor and civil leader who could command whatever was needed for his army without question. The Kaiser wanted to rule Europe and there were no votes to oppose him or to prevent supplies to the army as there would be against the Govt. in England or France, the latter two had to fight for every bit of equipment, in Germany the Kaiser made sure the army had all it needed, 'Guns Before butter' was the watchword even then.

The 6th Division had been moved over from Ireland to the UK and arrived at the front on the 15th September, it went straight into action against the German front on the Aisne to try to crush the enemy resistance, at GHQ the thought was that they were up against nothing more than a staunch enemy rearguard and that the main body was hastily pulling back in retreat. However that was not the case, the enemy were digging in and although the front units of the Expeditionary Force did get across the Aisne the positions were eventually taken over by the French when later the B.E.F. moved to the North in the Ypres area. The French later withdrew to positions on the opposite bank of the river where they stayed for the rest of the War. The battle of the Aisne saw the allies suffer heavy losses for no gain against an enemy with superior artillery and having been brought to a standstill the lines remained as they were for the duration of the War.

General Joffre decided to change tactics and moved troops to reinforce the left in an attempt to outflank the Germans by crossing the Aisne further north, he gave command of this task force to General Castelnau but there was little progress and the whole front was again brought to a standstill as the armies faced each other across the Aisne, neither force able to gain ground in a stalemate situation. Although there were many battles throughout the duration of the War it would not be until four years later at the 2nd battle of the Somme that the Kaiser would be able to repeat an all out attack such as that which almost annihilated the allies in August 1914.

Wilson arrived at the conclusion that the possibility of pushing the enemy further back was a forlorn hope unless a new approach could be planned, he visited Castelnau and as he returned to GHQ he says that he had the idea of moving the B.E.F. further to the left of the line. He put this idea to Sir John French who made no comment but said he would think about it overnight, when no response was forthcoming Wilson broached the subject again but French said that he was reluctant to consider it for fear of a repeat of Mons and Le Cateau. Wilson argued that the Germans were not the force that the B.E.F. faced then and that his plan presented a chance of a breaking the stalemate. By all accounts Sir John French warmed a little to the idea and agreed that Henry Wilson should go to see the French Commander in Chief General Joffre and discuss his plan.

In his book 1914 Sir John French writes that on the 29th of September he wrote to the French Commander in Chief a note that was delivered by Henry Wilson. He says that ever since the position of the Expeditionary force was altered by the advance of General Manoury's Sixth Army into the line he had been anxious to regain his position on the left of the French Army and pointed out that the positions of the Expeditionary force on both banks of the Aisne, having been entrenched from end to end were ready for occupation by French troops. Sir John was of the opinion that in line with the original plan, the B.E.F. could operate more effectively with better supplies and communications in the north by opening Boulogne as the main supply port, this had been transferred to Le Havre as a security measure.

The newly formed 7th and 8th Divisions plus a cavalry division were due out from England to bolster the small British Force; there were also two Indian Divisions and an Indian Cavalry Division on their way from India. Although Joffre was fully receptive and supportive of French's plan, he felt however that he sensed a weakening of the German effort and was interested in a concerted allied push along the whole front 'to see what was in front of them'. Joffre however did agree that the Expeditionary Force move to the north would be undertaken as soon as it was possible but in any event it had to be planned in stages. Although Marshal French was thinking in terms of a straight influx of French troops to man the existing British front so that the B.E.F. would remain as one contingent and not become a divided force, there were problems that would prevent that. The movement of such large numbers of troops by rail needed careful planning to ensure that units were available to cover those moving out to holding situations where they would wait their turn to be transported by rail to the station nearest to their new positions. The delays caused by waiting for transportation behind the lines meant a thinning out of existing French divisions, they were taking over a wider front by extending the flanks of the French 5th and 6th armies. The conduct of the War became a series of side steps by the Allies and the Germans, each attempting to outflank the other as they moved further north seeking a breakthrough that never materialized for either side.

About this time Major General Snow the commander of the 4th division had a serious fall from his horse and was taken to a Paris hospital, and on the 4th of September Sir John French sent for Major General Henry Rawlinson from England as his replacement. Rawlinson had, only a few months previously relinquished command of the 3rd Division as his tour of duty ended. His wife had been ill and he had taken her to French North Africa to convalesce whilst he waited his next posting and during this time he listened to the rumblings of War. When War broke out he was painfully hurt to see another commander take his beloved 3rd Division over to France. He was also bitter to find that he was not found a place with the B.E.F. He said 'I can only attribute it to the fact that Sir John French was displeased with my handling of the 3rd Division at manoeuvres last year'. It would seem however that his assumption was wide of the mark and the issue more to do with finding a suitable command for a senior Major General at a time in the British Army when movement was extremely slow. He had little choice but to accept a post at home.

Rawlinson accepted the Director of Recruitment at the War Office and was very much aligned with the ideas of Field Marshal Kitchener in the development of a New Army, (the opposite thinking to that of Sir Henry Wilson) Kitchener had little time for the Territorials and the New Army made up of raw recruits was his pet. When Rawlinson arrived at the Expeditionary Force GHQ he found the general staff excited by the possibility that the War could be over in a few months, a widely held opinion both at home and at the front and contrary to Kitchener's thinking, the general staff at GHQ greatly resented the withholding of regulars soldiers and officers in England for training purposes where they formed the core of the New Army. The feeling was that these men were badly needed and could make a very real contribution to a speedy end to the War. Rawlinson was in the Kitchener camp regarding the prospects of an early end to the War and contrary to the thoughts of the general staff he believed that the regular officers were needed to train recruits for the new army. This War of attrition was likely to be a long drawn out affair of years rather than months but Henry Wilson objected to Kitchener's idea of a new Army and he made plain his thoughts about that to Rawlinson.

He also commented in his diary about Kitchener's New Army "His ridiculous and preposterous army of 25 Corps is the laughing stock of every soldier in Europe. It took the Germans 40 years of incessant work to make an army of 25 Corps with the aid of conscription; it will take us all eternity to do the same by voluntary effort.

The very next day Winston Churchill visited GHQ and the comments made by Wilson were mentioned to him; presumably by Rawlinson, Churchill was of course of the same opinion as Lord Kitchener, that the War would be a long drawn out affair and it is assumed that Churchill discussed Wilson's thoughts with Kitchener when he returned to London. Sir John French had promised Wilson the post of Chief of Staff; a vacancy for the post was in the offing due to the retirement of the present C.O.S. General Sir James Murray. Sir John French was called to London and was told by the P.M. Lord Asquith that both he and Lord Kitchener opposed the appointment of Henry Wilson. On his return to GHQ Sir John French spoke to Wilson and tried to put it to him in the kindest way possible, to try to have him understand the reasoning behind the opposition to his being appointed C-of-S, and also to cover his own embarrassing situation at having been overruled in what was his appointment as G.O.C. Lord Asquith said that in view of Henry Wilson's leading role in the Curragh uprising and his lack of support for the government (Asquith had at the time branded him 'a dangerous man') it would be totally in appropriate for him to be offered that appointment. Kitchener on the other hand of course would find great difficulty in working with a Chief of staff to the G.O.C who so vehemently opposed Kitcheners proposed plans for the New Army. Had it been only Lord Asquith opposing the appointment there might have been grounds to appeal since the army is outside of the realm of politics and that Asquith's objection was a political one.

Wilson was beside himself with rage; his understanding was that the post was his and quite rightly felt that he had been very badly treated. The post was in the gift of the G.O.C. but Lord Kitchener had told Sir John French that he was not to make that appointment even though Sir John was in total command of the British Expeditionary Force and Kitchener was now, to all intents and purposes a politician. French thought highly of Wilson who had accompanied him to France as his Sub Chief of staff and when his Chief of staff became ill and had to relinquish his post, French had offered it to Henry Wilson, now he was in a very difficult spot. Of course Wilson was extremely disappointed, not only in not being appointed to the post of Chief of Staff but also in the fact that Sir John French had not fought his corner against Kitchener. Henry Wilson then offered Sir John a way to save face by him offering the post to Wilson and he immediately refusing it, that would leave Sir John free to appoint someone else without the belittling effect of orders from London, Sir John French declined Wilson's proposal. The post was offered to Sir William Robertson who later became Chief of the Imperial General Staff at the War Office, Henry Wilson was promoted to Lieutenant General with the position of Principal liaison officer between GHQ and the French GHQ at Chantilly, he was an ardent Francophile and was over the moon at his new appointment that he felt moved him into a more powerful and influential position.

The 4th Division was positioned on the left of the B.E.F. and on both banks of the Aisne, this part of the line was reasonably quiet and what action took place were mainly German Recce parties seeking information on the situation re the B.E.F. The news from Antwerp was dire; The Germans were actively involving themselves in achieving the same objectives as those that Sir John French had put to General Joffre. Massive troop movements were closing in on Antwerp and the largest howitzers in the world at that time were trained on the city pounding it daily. The Royal Navy had moved some 7/8000 Marines into Antwerp and now the War Office was making arrangements for the newly formed 7th Division and 3rd Cavalry division to be diverted from joining the Expeditionary Force in order to land at Zeebrugge in support of Belgian troops at Antwerp.

The first units of the B.E.F. started to move north to the La Bassee – Ypres section of the line on the 1st of October 1914, the 4th division was in the process of moving on the 4th of October when a message arrived ordering Rawlinson to GHQ. He says that he dined with Sir John French who told him that 'K' had selected him to try to save Antwerp. The 7th Division and the 3rd Cavalry Division under Byng were to land at Zeebrugge were to proceed directly to Antwerp as soon as they were ashore. Rawlinson was to be under the command of Lord Kitchener and not Sir John French. Kitchener of course was not with the War office but a Govt. Minister, a politician!

French was understandably annoyed at this; he was after all the Commander in Chief of British Forces in France, Kitchener was a minister of the Govt. and therefore not even in the army at the time. Added to this Sir John did not see eye to eye with what Kitchener was trying to achieve, he was of the opinion that these extra divisions would be better employed acting with the main body of the B.E.F. in turning the German left and easing the pressure on Antwerp, rather than trying to repulse a German siege attempt from within the City. But Sir John French had found his authority undermined on other occasions by Lord Kitchener when he had liaised directly with General Joffre regarding movements and actions of the B.E.F. There was also the occasion after Le Cateau when Kitchener, not happy with the interchange of messages with Sir John, crossed the channel at short notice and summoned Marshal French to Paris. When they met Kitchener had donned his full Field Marshal uniform and was intent on placing himself as Sir John's superior officer. Sir John French was having none of it and pointed out to Kitchener a few salient facts about their respective positions, and in front of the French President Poincare Kitchener backed down. One gets the feeling French was trying to do a good job with a very small and badly equipped army and that Lord Kitchener was trying to run matters from London. He was of course a giant amongst generals and was treated almost like a god in England; the problem for him was that he had not been placed in overall command of British Forces in France; and he was now a politician.

Before Rawlinson was able to take any action with regard to Antwerp the Germans were in the city and that was the end of that, he had tried hard to convince the King that he should move south to Le Havre and that the Belgian army should move into France, eventually King Leopold saw the sense in moving out before he was taken prisoner by the Germans, sad and reluctant to leave his people and in the hope that there would be a quick end to the War. Kitchener now placed the 7th Division and the 3rd Cavalry under the command of Sir John French. On the 13th of October Rawlinson received a message from GHQ, 'C-in-C wishes you to move on Ypres tomorrow. On the 14th the first troops marched into Ypres where the British stayed for the next four years. II Corps under Smith Dorrien, III Corps under General Pulteney and the Cavalry Corps were currently covering a line of 35 miles, I Corps under Douglas Haig was still on the Aisne but moved up to join the main force on the 20th October.

15

1st Battle of Ypres –
October – November 1914

Sir John French, Haig and Rawlinson met at Haig's HQ where Sir John decided that Rawlinson should go back to England and bring out the 8th division, there had been a small amount of ill feeling for Rawlinson since Sir John had ordered him to attack Menin and he had not done so, preferring to err on the side of caution and attack the next day. Rawlinson writes in his diary that he had also made a comment in a message to GHQ that Sir John took exception to, Rawlinson had said that things would be easier when we get the 8th Division over from England and Sir John thought that impudent of him and had cut Rawlinson off during a visit to GHQ. The matter had been smoothed over in an exchange of messages and now to show there was no ill feelings Sir John was giving him the task of bringing the 8th Division over to France. In the meantime the 4th Corps was to be temporarily split, the 7th Corps being placed under Haig in 1st Corps and the 3rd Cavalry under General Allenby. The 8th was the last regular division to join the B.E.F. and consisted of battalions that had been serving abroad in the Empire when war broke out and had now been brought back to form the 8th Division. While in England Rawlinson received news of the intense fighting in the Ypres area, the line extended from Nieuport on the Belgian coast to Bethune. From the coastal town of Nieuport to Dixmude the Belgian army held the line and from the Ypres area to La Bassee canal the line was held by the BEF.

On November 6th Rawlinson was back at GHQ, now

based at St Omer and was there to meet the remnants of his 7th Division that had been relieved on the Ypres. The people back in England were getting no news of what was going on at the British front and Rawlinson wrote to Col. Fitzgerald[16] to ask if Kitchener could be persuaded to release more details and make the public more aware of the fighting and the gallantry of the B.E.F. He goes on to say, my 22nd Brigade returned to me from the front line yesterday to join the 7th Division; it consists of Brigadier General Lawson[17] four regimental officers and seven hundred and nine men. All the brigade staff, and all the regimental officers except four have been either killed or wounded for there are very few missing. The fighting has been of the bitterest. The debacle was, I understand, saved by regimental officers who behaved like heroes, and after the last reserves had been thrown in without stemming the tide, managed to rally their men and turn on an astonished foe. They succeeded in driving back the Germans to their positions; not because they were helped by artillery, or by fresh men, but simply because they refused to acknowledge that they were beaten. It would be the greatest incentive to recruiting. I have got Amery here who could write a really strong account and with the approval of Sir John I could send it to you.

On taking up positions on the Belgian border on the left of the Allied line, Sir John French had met with General Foch the commander of the French forces operating on the right of the B.E.F., at that meeting they had agreed a strategy for an all out attack to clear the Germans back over the border but before that plan could be put into operation news started to come through of massive German troop movements from The area of Antwerp. The main thrust of the German attack at the first battle of Ypres started on the 15th of October and lasted for eleven days; the Germans were intent on breaking through to dominate the channel ports. Success in breaking through would give the control of the English Channel and the North Sea, it would also provide the facilities for building and operating the submarine fleet that would eventually isolate Britain and bring it to submission. There was another more distant objective and that was the invasion of Britain, a goal that could not be attained without control of the French channel coastline.

The Expeditionary Force, although insufficiently strong enough to maintain the variable length of front line[18] that it was covering and also the lack of artillery cover, gave a good account of itself, during the whole period there was incessant heavy German attacks by both troops and artillery fire, the fight was continuous day and night, there were no long lines of trenches that were later seen as the war progressed, the water table in these water meadows was so high in places that it was not possible to dig anything other than short shallow trenches and breast works had to be constructed. By the 26th the Expeditionary Force, now some twice the number of men that crossed to France in the middle of August, were thoroughly exhausted. Sir John French, in his forward planning was thinking in terms of an entrenched camp at Boulogne, an indication perhaps that he felt that the heavy German attacks all along the front could not be held and retreat was inevitable at some stage. When Sir John put forward his request to General Joffre he was refused point blank to allow the digging in of an entrenched position that would take the whole of the B.E.F.. General Wilson now chief British/French liaison officer and General Rawlinson the commander of the IV Division were both critical of the way that Sir John was conducting operations and felt that more divisions and artillery support were desperately needed to enable a more robust approach in dealing with the German advance.

Although they had not won an outright victory, the British and French forces at Ypres and along the banks of the Yser had again brought the German advance to a halt and saved the Channel ports from enemy occupation. They had brought to nothing the long term German Grand Plan designed by Count Von Schleiffen. Foch refers to the battles of Ypres as the Battle of Flanders[19] and he takes exception to the British claiming that that Ypres was their battle: Sir John French himself took the title 'First Earl of Ypres'. Although Ypres and Menin were actually the British front line, the battle waged by the Germans for the channel ports was from La Bassee to the coast, the whole line was under great pressure and although the B.E.F. took very heavy losses in the most desperate fighting, the French also where battered and even when there was no hope of making further progress Foch persisted with his attaquez! attaquez! in the forlorn hope of a break through.

Massive German reinforcements started to arrive all along the line La Bassee to the Coast, the intention being to mount a savage all out attack that was intended to crush the B.E.F; to once and for all end this race for power by leapfrogging each other in a desperate effort to turn the others flank. The German High Command demanded a crushing breakthrough paralysing the allied forces and claiming a lasting victory for Germany that would see them the masters of all Europe.

The Kaiser was reported to have visited his troops in the hope of seeing such a breakthrough as the allies were pulverised, for they far outnumbered the British and French and they were far superior in artillery. The B.E.F. had only 26 large field guns and although the French had more 75's, they were very short of ammunition, the Germans however, not only had some 250 field guns, they were also larger calibre. One could say that they had not counted on being up against the 'contemptible little army', but they were, something they found to their heavy cost. There was also gallant fighting to come from the French and the Belgians who also fought bravely to hold the line but like the Expeditionary Force were pushed back mercilessly. On the 28th of October II Corps under General Smith Dorrien was driven out of Neuve Chapelle and for the next two days there was fierce fighting with ground lost and gained and lost again, the French and British forces intermingled as the French sent battalions in to support the positions held by the B.E.F. that were under heavy attack.

The Official History records that the situation on the 31st October and 1st of November was the most critical period of the War to that date and brought the British Empire to the point of great danger, that the channel ports and the French coast were within an ace of falling into German hands. Sir Hubert Gough writes in his memoirs 'The Fifth Army'. I had hardly finished a late meal in Kemmel when the whole of the line from Messines to Wytschaete seemed to wake up and burst into one continuous roar of musketry------ The Cavalry, especially the Household Regiments, were big men, and though probably using the bayonet in earnest for the first time, were using it with vigour which must have surprised the Germans. ------- Our line was falling back, the Germans pressing through Messines and were already on the outskirts of Wytschaete, I had no reserves but it was important to hold up, or at least delay the Germans ------ I knew that two battalions with their Brigadier, Fred Shaw, had arrived in Kemmel that evening. I went over about midnight and raided Shaw's billet. He never hesitated, he told me to employ them as I thought best. They were sent up each side of the Kemmel – Wytschaete road, The Lincolns on the right, the Northumberland Fusiliers on the left. ----- They must have burst on the Germans about 3am. Though greatly outnumbered, and soon more or less outflanked in the dark, they shook the German attack, inflicted heavy losses and prevented any further advance that night, though in their turn they had to fall back, mauled and decimated. But it was a gallant feat and one of the greatest tactical values. ------ By dawn Greenly and I were on our horses and rode up to the scene, the first thing I came across was a group of London Scottish, 20 or thirty men under an officer in their cloaks, mostly hatless, their dishevelled heads caked with mud.

I spoke to the officer and heard from him a brief account of their terrific fight. He did not know where was the rest of his battalion, or indeed if there was any 'rest'. I patted him on the shoulder, told him that he had done splendidly, all that was asked of them. He looked at me with surprise and a half smile of relief came over his young face, and he said, 'I thought it was an awful disaster. 'Disaster be damned', I said to him, 'you have done splendidly. I then got another officer nearby to get them some rations and then moved on ----- A few hundred yards up the road I next met one of my senior officers pacing the road. The strain had been great, and the tears were visible on his cheeks though he was quite sensibly issuing the necessary orders. -----The London Scottish that afternoon lost 400 out of 700 men. They fought magnificently and deserved the greatest praise. Their first action, and untried, untrained troops!

The soldiers of the regular army were fast being killed and wounded and the volunteers of the Kitcheners New Army, The First Hundred thousand were being drafted in to take their place, and how they proved themselves to be equal to the task. The book 'The First Hundred Thousand by Ian Hay published in 1915, tells of the day to day life of raw recruits from all walks of life drafted into a whole new experience and just as quickly fighting at the front and dying. It tells in graphic detail the rapid transition of the first Hundred Thousand, the nitty-gritty of army life through basic training to the front line.

"K. (1)." [20]

We do not deem ourselves A1
We have no past: we cut no dash;
Nor hope when launched against the Hun,
To raise a more than moderate splash.

But yesterday we said farewell
To plough; to pit; to dock; to mill,
For glory, drop it! Why? Oh well---
Have a slap at Kaiser Bill.

And now today has come along,
With rifle, haversack and pack,
We're off a hundred thousand strong,
And --- some of us will not come back.

But all we ask, if that befall,
Is this, within your hearts be writ
This single line memorial: -
He did his duty—and his bit.

***

The 8th Division was the only body of regular soldiers in the country and 'Rawly' had returned from Ypres to take them to Belgium and the front line, the battle of Ypres saw all but the whole strength of the regular army wiped out. The territorials, having already proved themselves at the First Ypres, and the New Army (Kitcheners, 'your country needs you') would be the ones to take the fight forward. Towards the middle of November the weather was bitterly cold, there was no hope of digging trenches of any depth without hitting water and at this stage there were no communication trenches to the rear, everyone was cold, exposed and suffering trench feet. There was little hope of launching any major attack, the lack of ammunition and the reliance on the new battalions coming out from England meant that Spring would be the earliest that there could be any movement. The Germans were also unable to make any headway, they had lost the youth of a generation at Ypres and although they had been preparing for this for years they still did not have the wherewithal to make a breakthrough. January saw the worst rainfall for years and life in the trenches was utter misery. General Rawlinson wrote to Lord Derby, "our little British Army loses about 200 to 300 per day'--- so long as we can maintain our general line we have nothing to fear". The morale in the trenches was very good but being confined to trenches in wet muddy conditions without physical exercise did not prepare men for heavy fighting. If as expected, the Germans were planning to mount another all out attack to break through to the coast there would be a need for new battalions, for fresh troops out from England.

French had been contemplating the news of successes coming in from the Russian front and perhaps comparing it with the lack of movement on the whole western front. He arrived at the conclusion that there ought to be a surprise attack mounted with the intention of regaining Nueve Chapelle and pushing the allied front as far as possible to the east. This was at odds with the thinking of Lord Kitchener who felt it sufficient to hold the line against further German gains, and to transfer their efforts to fighting in the Middle East. With that in mind Sir John French intended not to discuss his intentions with any one as plans were drawn up for an attack by the Expeditionary force, alone and without the support of the French or Belgians. He wrote to Joffre and explained why he was unable to relieve the French and outlining his plans for the recapture of Nueve Chapelle. Joffre replied by saying that he wished him well in the venture, adding that since the B.E.F. had not relieved his 9th and 10th Corps he would be unable to proceed with the planned offensive at Arras.

On the 10th of March 1915 the attack on Neuve Chapelle was opened by General Rawlinson's 4th Corps and by the end of that day the Germans were driven out and the village retaken along with several hundred German prisoners. The 10th and 11th saw heavy counter attacks by the enemy but their the advance was stalled with very heavy losses. The elation at victory on the first day quickly turned to acrimony with French, Wilson, and Rawlinson noting what went wrong and looking for answers as why not enough was done, French pointing the finger at Smith Dorrien and Rawlinson, whilst Wilson was disillusioned by the whole venture. Towards the end of March Kitchener made a visit to see Joffre at The French Command HQ, Sir John French and Henry Wilson were to be at that meeting and on the day Before Wilson went to see Joffre and presented him with a list of things that he should bring up with Kitchener on behalf of Sir John French.

On seeing the list, Joffre was quite astounded at the allocation of ammunition per gun supplied to the B.E.F. and agreed to raise the points with Kitchener. Some time before the battle of Nueve Chapelle, Joffre had shown Wilson a letter which he took back with him to GHQ; it was a request to Sir John French that the Expeditionary Force find relief for the French 9th and 10th

corps at the end of April, a matter that was put in hand after Wilson discussed it with Sir John French. It would seem however that Joffre was feeling rather constrained by having to make such requests and felt that he should have overall command in the France/Belgium theatre, he mentioned this to Henry Wilson and said he intended to bring the matter up with Lord Kitchener when they met the next day. At once Wilson managed to put the matter in perspective by pointing out that were Joffre to be given Command of all Allied Forces he would also be empowered to relieve any officer who in his opinion was not up to the job, and that of course was a none starter as far as the British forces were concerned. The matter was not discussed at that meeting but it is interesting to note that in 1918 the French General Foch was in fact made Commander in Chief of all allied Forces at the 3rd Battle of the Somme.

The meeting was attended by Generals Joffre, Huguet, Pelle, and Graziani the French Chief of the General Staff; Lord Kitchener the Secretary of State for War, Sir John French and Henry Wilson. Kitchener talked about the possibility of making Holland the main theatre of War if Germany declared against them, he also felt that the Allies main thrust should be through the Dardanelles, the Generals felt that Kitchener's thinking was wide of the mark and Joffre pointed instead to a concentrated attack by the 1st of May that would break the German line. Sir John said he would relieve the two French Corps by the 20th of April and Kitchener promised two more territorial divisions within the next three weeks. He also spoke of the labour problems in the factories saying that Lloyd George's speech to the workers of the North did not have any real effect, that the answer must be conscription.

The initial rush to volunteer had slackened off and the Kitchener posters 'Your country needs you' were in evidence throughout the country, the belief that there would be a quick end to the War was seen to be a myth, those at home in the UK were not given the full facts about casualties but could see for themselves huge numbers of killed and injured. They saw the trains coming in to local stations bringing the severely wounded troops to wherever there were available hospital beds in the towns and cities. At Neuve Chapelle alone the casualties were more than 12,000, of those in excess of 4000 were dead or missing. A person who died on the battlefield was classed as KIA, 'killed in action' if they could be identified they were eventually buried in a War grave and the full details were engraved on the headstone, otherwise they were 'Known only to God'. Those classed as 'missing presumed dead' whose bodies were never found were recognised by having their name on a roll of honour on one of the dozens of British War Graves Commission cemeteries in Belgium and France such as Tyne Cot, The Somme, Faubourg D'Amiens etc. by now the male population were no longer so eager to enlist and it is safe to assume that those who had volunteered and were in for the duration were wondering what it was that possessed them to go so willingly.

Kitchener was all for conscription and openly said that he was only waiting for a fall in recruitment to press for it to be passed by the House of Commons. This was a subject that had been talked about for years, to have compulsory service as they did on the continent, but it was seen as a poison chalice by those in government and had been pushed aside even though it was inevitable that it would have to come. There was doubt whether such a law would be passed by parliament, in 1915 the labour situation in Britain was critical and could only be made worse by conscription. The popular view was that single men without family responsibilities should be encouraged to enlist and that even if conscription were introduced, that married men with families should be exempt.

The 2nd Battle of Ypres. April –May. 1915.

On the 22nd of April 1915 General Smith Dorrien became aware of white puffs of smoke towards the German lines, it took the form of vaporous clouds of varying colours, brownish green and yellow blown by the wind towards the allied positions. It reached the French lines in the late afternoon/early evening before it was realised that the Germans were introducing the use of mustard gas used for the first time in the War. The French Algerian troops were the first hit and started to cough and choke, some appeared to fall to the ground and other vomiting or fleeing the trenches. The troops were totally unprepared for it and had little more than handkerchiefs to cover their faces, in the French lines there was utter panic causing the troops to vacate their trenches in the area affected by gassing, the Canadians too were badly affected but stood their ground.

The attack continued on the 23rd. and Sir John French was keenly aware of the dangerous situation that the B.E.F found itself in as a result of the shortages of ammunition, and he had constantly brought the fact to the attention of everyone that might be in a position to influence the Government on the matter. He tried to bring home the fact that no advance could be made by the B.E.F. and that there would be unacceptable loss of life unless sufficient ammunition and men could be provided to enable the Expeditionary Force to meet the enemy on equal terms. Prime Minister Asquith rebuffed the efforts of Sir John about this time in a speech that he made at Newcastle when he said that the army had all the ammunition it required. Sir John French later recorded[21] "When I read this speech, after all my public and private appeals, I lost any hope that I had entertained of receiving help from the Government as it was constituted". The abysmal figures regarding the supply of H.E. (High explosive) as opposed to shrapnel are published in detail elsewhere in numerous books and clearly outline the predicament that the B.E.F. found itself in, but Asquith obviously thought differently.

AN AWFUL PREDICAMENT

A house can stand without a roof'
A ship without a sail.
But the most uncomfortable thing
In the world,
Is a shirt without a tail.

***

Battle of Festubert 1915

On the 9th of May 1915 the Allied spring offensive opened with a French artillery barrage of 1200 guns, a spectacle never before seen. The B.E.F. moved on a front, which became known as the Battle of Festubert and was led by General Haig's 3rd Corps. The British and French armies were to attack either side of La Bassee and were intended to relieve the pressure on forces defending Ypres. On that first day the losses for the Expeditionary Force were extremely heavy. Sir John French says in his autobiography how for several hours he observed the battle from the tower of a ruined church and saw first hand how unequal the battle was. The German artillery fire against the British fire was far more rapid and sustained. After all his heckling for more guns and ammunition they were only able to lay down fire for 40 minutes Before the battle and only 8% of what they had for the battle was HE (high explosive), the most effective type of shell. The lack of artillery support meant that men were being wiped out at a wholly disproportionate rate and it was this that determined French that he needed to take drastic action.

La Bassee Road

You'll see from the La Bassee Road, on any
summer day,
The children herding nanny goats; the women
making hay.

You'll see the soldiers Khaki clad, in column
and platoon,
Come swinging up the road, from Billets in Bethune.

There's hay to save and corn to cut, but harder
work by far,
Awaits the soldier boys who reap the fields of
War.

You'll see them swinging up the road where
women work at hay
The straight long road, La Bassee road on any
summer day
The night breeze sweeps La Bassee road, the
night dews wet the Hay,
The boys are coming back again; a straggling
crowd are they.

The column lines are broken; there are gaps in
the platoon,
They'll not need many billets now for the sol-
diers in Bethune.
For many boys, good lusty boys, who marched
away so fine,
Have now got little homes of clay, beside the
firing line.

Good luck to them, God speed to them, the
boys who marched Away,
A' singing up La Bassee Road, each sunny,
summer day'.

***

On his return to GHQ there was a telegram waiting for
Sir John from the Secretary of State for War, it was a
directive ordering him to send 20 percent of his meagre
ammunition supply to the Dardanelles. For him it was
the last straw and he at once ordered a release of evi-
dence showing how the lack of H.E. had prevented the
Expeditionary Force from succeeding on that day. The
Times military correspondent, Col. Repington was pre-
sent at GHQ at the time and he was provided with full
access to all the correspondence between Sir John and
the Government on the subject of Ammunition shortag-
es. In his own words he says, I immediately gave in-
structions that evidence should be furnished to Col.
Repington, military correspondent of 'The Times', who
happened to be then at Headquarters, that the vital need
of high-explosive shells had been a fatal bar to our ar-
my success on that day. French also sent his personal
secretary Brindsley Fitzgerald and one of his A.D.C's
Captain Frederick Guest to England with instructions

that the same material should be placed Before Lloyd George, Bonar Law and Arthur Balfour. They had all three, when visiting France, expressed a sympathetic understanding of the ammunition deficiencies that Sir John felt, and left him with the understanding that they would take the necessary action to remedy the situation.

Sir John French's action brought on a political crisis that quickly brought the Government down to be replaced by a Coalition Government. According to Henry Rawlinson, Commander Fourth Army, this led to a virulent attack on Lord Kitchener. Rawlinson wrote in furious indignation to Col. Fitzgerald, Sir John's personal secretary, [22]"---- "This attack on K. is perfectly monstrous, and has raised us out here to a pitch of fury. It is a diabolical plot, the in's and out of which you probably know much better than I do, but what I least like about it is that it should come on top of Repington's visit out here, and his article about the H.E. shell. The true cause of our failure is that our tactics have been faulty, and we have misconceived the strength and resisting power of the enemy. To turn round and say that the casualties have been for the want of H.E. shells for the 18 Pounders is a perversion of the truth. It is a shortage of heavy guns and howitzers, rather than a lack of H.E. shells for the 18 Pounders, that we suffer from. Most of the casualties have occurred, not in taking the first trenches, but assaulting the keeps behind the front line, where the Germans have been dug in with their machine guns cunningly concealed". As the war progressed and whenever things looked grim, the incident became a byword and the men would always describe it as, 'it was as bad as the 9th'.

Sir Henry Wilson on the other hand takes a more circumspect view when he records in his diary with regard to the 20.000 rounds that Sir John was required to send to the Dardanelles. [23]"As it happened, the

20,000 rounds were replaced within 24 hours. But there can be no doubt that insufficiency of ammunition had contributed largely to Haig's lack of success on the first day, and that it most gravely hampered the British offensive on subsequent days. Henry Rawlinson says that the attack on K. has brought us here to a pitch of fury but it is anyone's guess whom might be taking such exception; there is no record of Haig or Smith Dorrien expressing that sort of opinion. He is also quick to dispel Sir John French's concerns about the lack of ammunition but he had made no recorded comment in support or otherwise, about Sir John's consistent complaints to politicians and journalist over the last several months, perhaps Rawlinsons concern for his old friend Kitchener took preference over bringing to light the plight of the troops as a result of the ammunition shortages". The fact that Sir John French had put himself in such an unfavourable position seems to have been of little concern and of course there was no love lost between Rawlinson and Sir John French, although that attitude seemed to have emanated from Rawlinson rather than French. It is quite obvious that Sir John was on one side of a fence, on the other was Kitchener, Haig and Rawlinson.

When the Government was brought down and replaced by a coalition, Asquith, the Liberal Prime Minister took the first opportunity to replace Sir John French, this happened at the Battle of Loos (or Lens). At the outbreak of war Kitchener was the Consul General in Egypt and the Sudan, he had coveted the post of Viceroy of India and had even lobbied the King, but his efforts were scotched by John Morley, 1st Viscount Morley of Blackburn, the then Secretary of State for India. It was not seen as appropriate for a serving army officer to be appointed to the top political post in India. However, when John Seeley, the Secretary of State for War resigned following the Curragh Incident, Asquith curiously replaced him with Kitchener who was still a serving officer. Lord Kitchener and Sir John French had served together in South Africa and were old friends, but the War had placed each in a situation where such comradeship had to be set aside and as a result friction grew between them. On the one hand Sir John French was desperate to have the B.E.F provision of artillery match that of the Germans, this was a war that was different than any other, a war that depended on big guns pounding away at each other across an immovable line, those with the biggest guns made the most impact. In his army career Lord Kitchener had experienced conflict in altogether smaller mobile campaign wars, more importantly he was not in command, Sir John French was and he had to learn new methods of confronting the enemy. In this war the old tactics of charging the enemy with fixed bayonets had to be supplemented by massive artillery bombardments if the casualty rate was to be controlled at all, perhaps Kitchener did understand this but was in no position to do anything about it. Both men were doing their level best for the war effort but Kitchener was unable to supply ammunition because of problems with production, he therefore applied himself to recruiting and supplying men. At the same time Churchill was demanding men and supplies to divert to the Dardanelles whilst Sir John French was struggling to conduct a campaign without the wherewithal to succeed. The Expeditionary Force was in fact rapidly increasing in size and May 1915 saw the first units of the New Army in France, even so the Germans were still far superior in numbers.

There was a lull in the fighting during which time the Germans took the opportunity to draft in labour and dig more permanent and serviceable trenches. Kitchener was now reconciled to the fact that the allies could not mount a major offensive until more men and ammunition had been supplied and as a consequence the Governments attention was turned to a breakthrough at the Dardanelles. An attempt to break through had already been made by warships of the Royal navy on the 25th of April without success, neither had there been any success by ground troops in taking the bluffs that confronted them on landing, but it was thought there might be a chance of capturing them if more men could be made available. As a result five divisions of Indian and British troops were sent from India and Egypt totalling 15,000 men. Field Marshal French considered the whole business of a breakthrough at the Dardenelles to be complete madness.

The Second Battle of Festubert. June 1915

On the 7th & 8th of June 1915 the Fourth Division took over trenches on the extreme left of the extended British line which now included the whole of the Ypres Salient, IV Corps, in a move to relieve pressure on the French on the extreme right of the British line, were ordered to mount an attack in conjunction with the French starting 15th of June at Festubert. Early on the morning of the 15th the artillery opened with a bombardment that lasted some 45 minutes and at 6.00am the attack proper was launched. Although the enemy trenches were breached at several points the Germans had dug in very deep and the going was extremely difficult, there were severe casualties and the assault battalions, 1/4 Loyals, 1/6 Cameronians, 1/4 Kings Own and the Liverpool Irish were cut off from the main support group by enemy crossfire that prevented them crossing no-mans-land. The fighting continued all day and well into the early hours of the morning, around midnight the Germans counter attacked and drove the

British forces back until around 4 am when support units were able to move up as relief. The fighting continued on the 16th but the situation remained much the same, heavy casualties for no gain and the situation was once again at stalemate.

The whole front now entered into a quite period through the summer into a glorious September, work was carried out on the trenches with a more permanent outlook. Trenches were traditionally not much more that scratchings in the ground where a soldier could be out of view of the enemy during a phase in a mobile battle. This war was vastly different in that new ways had to be devised for conducting the war and for survival when the enemy was at times merely feet away in his dugout. They set about making the trenches a system of below ground level walkways out of sight of the enemy, these trenches would be entered from a long way behind the front line by a system of communication trenches. They designed them in a special zigzag configuration so that if the trench was breached the enemy could not easily overrun the troops in there but would have to fight at every corner, They also made some provision for social aspects of life in the trenches like brewing tea and taking a nap rather than simply having to crouch on the firestep.

When they were in the line the men suffered badly from the poor conditions of life in the trenches, unlike the officers who fared much better as this comment by a young officer with the East Lancashire Regiment, he was[24] not a Lancashire lad but a Southener. ---- "For the first tour of the trenches I was given this Job. I remember one thing only about it. I had taken our party up the line, and a long tiring job it was. But on the second night I was free. We (officers) of HQ Company had a hut with wire mesh bunks for beds, and chimneys and great glowing braziers. The cold outside was intense. I got to bed in my upper bunk and was given a drink and watched the red glow of the brazier. I was beatifically content. Some other poor bastard had got the job of going up the line and here was I as cosy as a bug in a rug. In fact rather like one". Somewhat different than those five squaddies in the photo taking advantage of a break in the bombardment, they knew nothing about it.

A SOLDIERS LETTER

I've lost my rifle and bayonet,
I've lost my pull through, too.
I've lost the socks that you sent me,
That lasted the whole winter through.
I've lost the razor that shaved me,
I've lost my four by two.
I've lost my holdall,
And now I've got damn all'
Since I've lost you!

***

The 'pull through' was a lanyard with a small weight at one end and a loop at the other. The 'four by two' was a piece of cotton fent, literally four inches by two just slipped through the pull through loop. The weighted end was dropped through the Rifle barrel and then pulled through to clean out the rifling. Both these items were housed in the rifle butt along with a brass screw top oil bottle.

The Battle of Loos - September – October 1915

During the late spring and summer supplies to the B.E.F. were greatly increased with such things as Mills grenades and trench mortars that had up to that point been almost non-existent, these were now coming in as the munitions programme gathered pace. Machine guns had been very scarce but now each battalion was becoming much better equipped so that besides a machine gun section of four guns there was also a Lewis gun section. Activity during this relatively quiet period was mainly raiding/bombing parties by small parties at night, a dangerous business and often they would bump into an enemy raiding party as they headed towards the each others lines. On one occasion the sentry at the listening post with the 1/4 Kings Own heard German voices and kept his head down until they came up to the post, he then popped up and challenged them, told them to drop their weapons and took four prisoners including one officer. Throughout this period the French were pushing for an all out offensive, an attempt to make a breakthrough and plans were developed for the launch of an offensive in the Lens area during September 1915.

General Joffre had pressed for a commitment to an all out attack by the British alongside the French 10th Army, Sir John French however was reluctant to go along with Joffre's plan, he considered that the front Joffre had chosen to attack on was a bad one and was exceptionally well defended. French was unhappy and was looking for ways to release him from a serious commitment of British troops on the legitimate basis that they were not ready for such a large push and the fact that casualties would inevitably be very heavy. General Haig was of the opinion that there was little point in an attack on Loos until Lens had been taken. Lens was an industrial town of closely packed houses, factories and mines etc. about midway between Ypres and the Somme and was infiltrated by Germans. Joffre on the other hand was not interested in changing his plan and Sir John French, although he did not agree with the plan, felt that he had no choice but to offer his support. He passed the planning of the British effort to General Haig to sort out who in turn, based on his brief from Sir John French, proposed a compromise. The British artillery would take care of the German artillery and also hold back any enemy ground attack along the British front, thereby avoiding the commitment of troops and the inevitability of severe casualties.

Joffre dismissed Haig's proposal out of hand and wrote a stiff letter to Sir John French saying that full effect cannot be given to the plan without an all out powerful attack along the whole front, British and French. The Chief of the Imperial General Staff General (CIGS) Sir William Robertson had also weighed in by writing to Haig expressing the opinion that the whole plan was very unsatisfactory, Kitchener crossed the Channel and met with Joffre, the matter was already resolved when Kitchener met with Sir John French at GHQ. He pointed out that the Russians had been badly battered by the Germans and were probably at breaking point, although Kitchener had been an advocat of a defensive war up to then, the present situation in Russia had swung him round to the opinion that there was a need to take the pressure of them, therefore the attack must go head irrespective of the inevitably high rate of casualties. Haig was particularly unhappy about the choice of Lens area but in the interests of allied cooperation he committed himself to it. This was a mining area dotted with winding gear, mining villages and slag heaps where the Germans had constructed extremely defensive positions and all out of sight and well below ground. Even though supplies were coming through in a greater volume, Haig was concerned that these supplies had yet to reach a stage were they matched the enemy who were dug into extensive, complex fortifications each bristling with Machine guns.

THE STAR SHELL

A star shell holds the sky beyond,
Shell shivered Loos and drops.
In million sparkles on a front,
That lies by Hullock copse.

A moment's brightness in the sky,
To vanish at a breath.
And die away as soldiers die,
The wastes of death.

***

The Bombardment opened up on the 21st of September and the Battle of Loos commenced on the 25th with the British 1st and 4th Corps attacking on a front from the village of Grenay to the La Bassee Canal where the French 10th Army was on the B.E.F.'s right. Haig had decided that in view of the shortage of artillery that gas would be used in the opening attack, and during the days before the battle opened there was a constant stream of carrying parties moving cylinders along the long communication trenches up to the front in readiness. Although there was only a very slight wind to carry it into the enemy trenches the gas was turned on at 5.50am. Haig had great anxieties about the success in using gas because of the wind direction, in reply to query as to whether the battle could proceed General Gough had said that it was too late to postpone now.

Smoke candles were lit to provide a covering smoke screen for the advance and the gas containers opened, the gas drifted very slowly toward the enemy lines and then the infantry started to go over the top, they were hindered by the smoke screen that seemed to hang persistently over the British trenches, and by now the

Germans, having seen the gas and smoke, opened with everything they had, a hail of machine gun and rifle bullet sweeping the fog in 'no mans land' and the parapets beyond as the infantry moved forward. Very quickly the wind changed and the gas started to blow back towards the British troops of the second division who in fact had probably been prepared for that, the wind had been so slight and unpredictable at the outset that many had in fact worn their gas helmets when the gas was released. Nevertheless great progress was made on that first day all along the line but mainly in the centre, Progress was made however at the expense of considerable casualties. The French on the other hand had made little progress and that may have urged the enemy to move reinforcements to halt the British advance.

On that 1st day some of the units of the 1st Army had broken through to the German 2nd line on a considerable stretch of the front, and there was a realization that the Germans had no reserves, in fact they were moving the administration and cooking staff into the line to prevent a breakthrough. Haig had made it clear to Sir John French Before the commencement of the battle that it was essential that two divisions be held in reserve and under his command that he could call on quickly if the need arose. Sir John French ordered General Smith Dorrien the Commander of Second Army to have two divisions stand by, but the fact is that they were not put under Haigs command and that they were held too far behind the front line rather than on hand close up to the line. This consequence of this was that at the end of a long march the young New Army recruits were exhausted and as a result of the delay they were too late to hold back the massive German counter attack carried out with reinforcements transferred from the French front. Loos had already been held and there was nothing to stop Haig going on to push the Germans right back and making it a turning point in the War, but because of the delay Haig no longer had faith in French as the General Officer Commanding and believed that he, French, should resign his post as unfit to command the British forces in France. There is no doubt that Sir John French tried to conduct the war from GHQ some 25 miles behind the front line, and rather than provide Haig with the two divisions placed under his command by moving them up close by and in doing so allowing General Haig the means to do the job, he held them back. Many at home as well as with the Army in France felt that French had blundered and that he should go.

On the 26th the heavy counter attacks mounted by the Germans pushed British back regaining the strategic points that they had lost in the previous days fighting. The battle continued until the on the 13th of October when the last attack was launched and by the 15th the battle of loos was all but at an end. During that time they had gained ground and lost it, suffered heavy losses in terrible conditions of rain and mud and at the end the feeling amongst the troops was one of utter dejection. [25]---"The predominant feeling of all ranks after the battle was one of profound disappointment that all their efforts appear to have been wasted. Weary and broken troops had clung heroically to impossible positions", immense expenditure of men and material had resulted in negligible gain. Yet Lord Kitchener, in his congratulatory telegram described it as a "substantial success". Over 3000 prisoners were taken, of who more than fifty were officers; twenty-six field guns, forty machine guns and quantities of other war material had been captured. It was indeed the first large-scale operation since trench warfare began; artillery had shown brilliant competence, subsidiary services were good, and the fighting spirit of the men was magnificent. Whatever else had failed it was not the British soldier.

Before the battle Major General Charteris, Head of GHQ Intelligence commented 'whatever the issue of the battle, the casualty list will be huge. There were some 2500 officers and 60,000 men lost.

At a military debate in the House of Lords on November 8th 1915 the general attitude was one of dissatisfaction at the job carried out by the army from the start of the War. Lord Milner was of the opinion that Neuve Chapelle and the Battle of Loos were in effect defeats and in this Lord Courtney backed him. As a result of the exposure of ammunition shortages Sir John French had an arch enemy in Prime Minister Asquith who would have no qualms about seeing Sir John replaced if the right grounds were presented to him, French had shown up inertia within the Liberal Govt. regarding shortages and that was a grounds for revengeful punishment. The relationship between French and Kitchener was also now at low ebb, although they had been long term very close friends their respective posts set them at odds to each other, French felt that he never had Kitcheners support and recognition of the fact that he alone was the General Officer Commanding the British Army in France. Sir John had relieved six senior officers of their posts and shipped back to England, Kitchener saw that they all had senior posts in the UK and one was actually promoted. It was in French's opinion, an affront to his authority as G.O.C. in France. It may well have been that Kitchener had an acute need for trained senior Officers in a situation where trained men generally were thin on the ground and desperately needed to train the hundreds of thousands of new recruits. Perhaps he saw their contribution to the effort at home somewhat differently compared to how they might perform in a war zone, and that seems fair. Nevertheless Kitchener was unhelpful to French in other ways, and probably helped French in no small measure to come to a firm decision about what he should do regarding the shortages. After a long interview with Asquith on the 29th of November, French submitted his resignation of Command of the British Forces in France and on December 15th 1915 the War office announced that 'General Sir Douglas Haig has been appointed to succeed Field-Marshal Sir John French in command of the army in France and Flanders'

It seems without doubt that Sir John French was not given the support that he needed in a war that was conducted on an unprecedented scale, he may well have been accustomed to High Command but this was a new kind of war and every commanding officer was on a steep learning curve. Not everyone could be expected to make the right decisions faced with the difficulties of War on the western Front, nor did they, but Lord Bertie, the British Ambassador to France wrote in his diary, had it not been for the Daily Mail and Times revelations about the absence of high explosive shells, The cries of Sir John French and his officers would have been unheard and there would not have been a Ministry of Munitions to put matters on a better footing. In the Times appeared an article in which Sir John French was praised, an extract from it said, 'there is deep and general appreciation of the very great services he has rendered since the outbreak of war, and the Viscounty now conferred upon him by the King is a fitting reward. It may be said of Sir John that, while he has faced many difficult situations with invariable courage and calmness, and with unfailing patience, he has the distinction, unusual in war, of having made no conspicuous mistake. In the retreat from Mons he underwent perhaps the severest trial any British Commander in Chief has ever had to face, and he emerged from it with credit'.

Before leaving GHQ at St Omer he wrote a personal

message to be circulated as 'Order of the day' to all the members of the British armed forces in France expressing deep appreciation of the loyalty and courage they had shown during his period in command. He also received numerous messages of sadness and regret at his having been compelled to relinquish his post, one in particular from General Joffre with whom he had shared the task of confronting the German Army and had become a great friend of. In early 1916 Sir John took up his post as Commander-in-Chief of Home Forces in Great Britain and Ireland with his HQ at Horse Guards.

General Haig was now G.O.C. and it is hard to see who else could have been appointed in place of Sir John French. General Horace Smith Dorrien, the Commander of the Second Army had since the war started, given an outstanding account of himself as a commander and leader, at the same time he was a figure that stood largely in the background, where others were well connected with the government, the King and the French General Staff, one hears little of Smith Dorrien and Henry Wilson makes little mention of him, when Sir John French created the 1st and 2nd Armies on Christmas Day 1914 the commanders of the B.E.F 1 and II corps, Haig and Smith Dorrien were appointed to the respective Army Commands, but it is a well-known fact that Sir John French did not like Smith Dorrien but had no grounds on which to have him replaced, he was doing a good job. Relations between French and Smith Dorrien were never good and now to cap it all he was being relieved of his command by Haig so soon after he was appointed G.O.C.

Haig now had the post that he coveted and without doubt he had worked hard to get to that position, not least by lobbying The King, Lord Kitchener and Lord Haldane and regaling them of Sir John French's shortcomings with regard to the nature of things at the front.

16

The effects of ammunition shortages

At the front Sir John French had spent a disproportion-
ate amount of his time daily in sending request after
request for shells to increase the ludicrous daily alloca-
tion for each gun. He had written to Kitchener pointing
out that it was impossible for him to reply to the inten-
sive artillery fire of the enemy or to mount attacks
without the loss of life being at an unacceptable level, if
shells were not available to soften up the enemy and cut
the wire then inevitably there would be massive casual-
ties where troops were required to go in without that
support. Meanwhile his troops were in the soul-
destroying situation of having to kneel in trenches
whilst the enemy pounded them continuously with high
explosive shells. Kitchener was of the opinion that what
was to Sir John French a matter of huge concern,
should in no way hinder the attempts by the British
Army to push the Germans back and 'casualties were
the price that had to be paid'. The lack of artillery
shells should be no excuse for not mounting an attack,
there would of course be loss of life, but the level of
casualties was of little consequence provided the over-
all allied plans were carried out and hopefully their ob-
jectives met. In most cases the latter was more hoped
for than real for whilst the British troops fought hard
and in most cases achieved their objectives, they were
unable to hold off the heavy counter attacks that imme-
diately followed and therefore little or nothing was
gained.

The Germans were using HE (high explosive) this
was extremely effective in blasting the trenches and

bringing them in on the troops that were in them, whereas the British army continued to put its faith in shrapnel, which in mobile warfare is a deadly weapon, but it had little affect on the German Machine gunners. The Germans dug very deep and clear of the shrapnel only to come back up with their machine guns, when the pathetically few shells (5 per gun per day) had been fired from the British Guns, they then cut the British soldiers down as the they advanced to the wire exhausted by the soft mud.

As early as autumn 1914 the French Army had decided not to produce any more shrapnel rounds having recognised that HE was far more efficient in this type of warfare, and of course the Germans were already showing the way with continuous bombardments of HE. It is clear that the British Imperial general Staff were slow to recognize the requirements of the B.E.F. and in particular the need for HE shells, at the same time they were unsympathetic to the demands of Sir John French in asking for shells of any kind at the rate that he required them. He was told in no uncertain terms by Lord Kitchener that even with maximum production, the Woolwich Arsenal would be unable to meet his demands. In fact the B.E.F's stock of shells of any sort at any time were dangerously low in 1914 and that situation did not start to change much until the early part of 1916.

The reality was that the British troops were pinned down in their trenches by enemy shellfire and were unable to return that fire, for every British shell Germany sent over thirty and if the troops threw hand grenades the Germans would reply with mortar fire, the pitifully few mortars available to the British were relics from the Boer War and quite ineffective against the huge numbers that the Germans deployed. The whole situation for British troops was thoroughly demoralising and although this was all being reported back to the national newspapers from a variety of sources they were not allowed, because of censorship to print it. It was not until Sir John gave Col. Repington the full details that The Times decided to 'publish and be damned'.

In France they had a different approach altogether and had made contingency plans in peace time, every factory with the potential to help the war effort was assessed and when war broke out those plans were put into immediate operation with all manufacturing brought under government control. In anticipation of war the French had set up certain bodies to identify the needs of the military in particular. It was also recognised that there was need to harness the manufacturing capacity of the country and channel the ability of certain sectors in time of war. Of course the French had a great need to consider these things, they had a common border with Germany who in 1870 had defeated the French and the expectation was that the Germans, at some time, would attack again, Britain had no such need. Had Sir Henry Wilson picked up on that in all the years of co-operation with the French whilst making plans for a British Expeditionary Force then Britain also might have been better prepared. As it was the C.I.D. (Committee of Imperial Defence) had taken no such action in Britain, that whole issue was seen as secondary to other issues that the C.I.D. needed to consider. France on the other hand was at the cutting edge and stood to be defeated and occupied by Germany, therefore needed to be prepared. It is very unfortunate that at the time, Britain did not know more of the plans that France had laid down so that they could have worked more closely together in the event of war. That of course would never have been possible, the French Generals did not trust the British at any stage and thought the British might decide to occupy the Channel ports when the Germans had been defeated, hence the reason the French were so keen to have a French army between the British and the coast.

At home the larger manufacturers who had the capacity to produce the required military supplies appointed a delegate to approach the British government with a view to getting involved in the War effort, they had two major concerns and the first was that with the massive response to Kitcheners call to arms, the manufacturing industry was losing an excessive number of valuable skilled workers whose expertise was far more urgently required at home than at the front. In future it would be necessary for the recruiting staff to ensure that any skilled workers were filtered out and returned to essential work for the War effort. Also it was imperative that those people who had already enlisted should be located, and where possible be returned to their civilian employment; that would be no simple task since some were already at the front and others maybe already killed in action, the plan was to have them returned to these reserved occupations essential to the War effort but it would be impossible to compel anyone to return to Civvy St. this was especially so if the army, having trained them, encouraged them to stay. Back in Civvy St. there may be uncomfortable questions asked and they certainly would not want to desert their pals with whom they had enlisted, besides this there was always the chance that ladies carrying white feathers would accost them and enquire as to why they were not at the front, that would of course be a terrible blow to a mans pride.

The second main concern was that all the efforts made by the manufacturing companies to turn their manufacturing capacity over to the war effort had been completely ignored and yet it was clearly shown that the present manufacturing capacity was totally inadequate. The War Office was in fact of the opinion that those manufacturers offering there services were simply taking advantage of the current situation to expand their turnover when business was being eroded by foreign competition. The W. O. was quite happy to allow large shipments to be sought from American companies for the arms that were desperately required, whilst at the same time considering British manufacturers to be opportunistic in offering to retool and change production to meet Government requirements purely for there own ends, they were therefore, not encouraged to apply for approved status. The attitude of the War Office was blatantly obvious to members of the House and members of the Government and as a result efforts were made to change matters so that the immense industrial capacity of the nation could be channelled into the War effort.

The Government along with the military leaders, and Lloyd George in particular, were very concerned at the intransigence of the War Office, however, it was the W. O, that ran the arms procurement programme and they held the reins tightly, they knew what was needed and they were not having anyone meddling in their affairs. The W. O decided to appoint a liaison officer to head a committee charged with vetting and approving all applications from manufacturers not on the approved list. If they were accepted then they would be eligible to become subcontractors to the contractors that were on the approved list. In reality since these outside firms were generally much larger companies than those on the approved list, they quite rightly resented the subservient role into which they were being slotted, with the result that the leaders of industry lobbied hard for change and a new Ministry was set up specifically concerned with the manufacture and procurement of munitions.

Men were enlisting in their thousands and to meet their training needs some of the older regulars, men who having been on the reserve and no were no longer eligible for enlistment were asked to volunteer and offer their expertise. Some of the New Battalions and Territorial battalions were initially commanded by retired officers recalled for short-term service, in order to meet this shortage of expertise. These new recruits were quickly brought to a high standard of fitness through the regular routine of exercise, forced marches, drill parades, field craft and above all rifle practice. To the infantryman, his rifle is his best friend, he learns how to keep it clean, handling it becomes second nature and in return it does its duty for him. The British Army is, if nothing else, extremely efficient in turning out well-trained soldiers with the right attitude of mind for the job, it did not take long before all of those 'wet behind the ears' had undergone rigorous training and were fit for transfer to units at the front line. All the bull and time spent on the parade ground instilling the kind of discipline and teamwork that is essential in any good Squaddy proved to be invaluable when they went to the front.

ON ACTIVE SERVICE

For the bloke on active service when 'e' goes across the sea,
He's sure to stand in terror of the things 'e' doesn't see.
An 'and grenade or mortar as it leaves the other side,
You can see an' 'ear it comin' so you simply step aside.
The aeroplane above you may go droppin' bombs a bit,

But laying in your dugout your unlucky if your
hit.

When the breeze fills your trenches with
'hasfixiation' gas,
You puts your respirator on, and allows the
stuff to pass.
When you're against a fellow with a bayonet
long and keen,
Just have purchase of your weapon and you'll
drill the beggar clean.
When man and 'oss is chargin' you, upon your
knees you kneel,
And catch the 'oss's breastbone with an inch or
two of steel.

It's sure to end its canter, and as the creature
stops,
The rider pitches forward and you catch 'im as
he drops.
It's when he see's his danger and knows his
way about,
That a bloke is damned unlucky, if 'e's knocked
completely out.
But out on active service there are dangers eve-
rywhere,
The shrapnel and the bullet that come on you
unaware.

The saucy little rifle is a perky little maid,
An' when you've got her message, you have
done your last parade.
The four point five will seek you from some
distant leafy wood,
An' tap you on the napper an' your out of step
for good.

From the gun within a spinney, to the sniper up a tree,
There are terrors waiting Tommy in the things he doesn't see.

***

17

A Ministry for Munitions

This new Ministry had wide ranging powers authorizing it to take over any factory or warehouse with all its workforce and machinery and to make any changes consistent with the needs of the war effort. It could move the whole of production and the workforce to another site if that was thought appropriate, it could make any changes it thought fit, it had the power invested in it to identify need and to make provision to meet that need without the consent of parliament or the War Office. The new Ministry of munitions was known as the Ministry of Supply during WWII, but everyone still referred to 'munitions' when discussing what the various factories did in the Second World War. All production in factories was liable to be taken over to produce goods for the 'War effort', as well as building shadow factories all over the country, the Ministry of Munitions became an enormous enterprise with very far reaching influence and powers over such things as design and production, transportation as well as peripherals needs such as the welfare of workers, housing, diet, plus a hundred and one other things.

Bills were passed in parliament under the 'Defence of The Realm Act' giving the Minister of Munitions extensive powers to make changes without continually referring to Parliament and therefore speed things along, as things progressed other new Bills were passed in parliament and amendments to the Defence of the Realm Act giving the Ministry of Munitions increased powers.

Where previously all 'munitions' had been the responsibility of the master General of Ordnance at the War Office (at the time General Von Donop), there was now a Minister for Munitions appointed. The immediate object was the increased supply of munitions commensurate with the urgent needs of those already at the front. The ministry would also be responsible for the acquisition of everything that would be required for the large numbers being recruited to the New Army, as well as the growing needs of the Navy. The Royal Ordnance factory at Enfield was tooled up to produce rifles for the army as it existed in 1914, but with the huge increase in the number of battalions it was unable to produce anything like the number of weapons required. The War office had turned to the American arms industry but even they were unable to produce weapons on the scale that was needed without expanding output and that of course would take time. The engineering manufacturers in Britain had the skills to produce anything that was required, the problem was that they did not have the machinery and could not retool to meet these needs in the short term. It would take the American manufacturers equally as long to produce enough weapons as it would for British factories to do the same, i.e. manufacture the machines to make the rifles. Meanwhile the numbers of those enlisting astounded even the most optimistic, the response was unprecedented and to replace them women had to be trained in what were traditionally men's jobs, and so the problem was compounded.

The growing number of casualties and the continuing shell shortages were creating great concern amongst the opposition and the general public, the general image of the government was that they neither understood the seriousness of the situation that the nation was in, nor had they the wherewithal to save the country from the possible defeat by a far more powerful enemy. Churchill was a firm advocate of his plan for a second front, some say he had demanded that the landing at Gallipoli should go ahead against the wishes of his staff and cabinet colleagues, already Britain had lost two battleships and France had lost three all in one day on the 18th of March 1915, sunk by Turkish shore Batteries in trying to force a passage through the Dardanelle's.

The First Sea Lord, Lord Louis of Battenberg was asked to resign on the basis that his German name might be objectionable to the public, Lord Fisher came out of retirement to replace him. He was not in favour of Winston Churchill's proposed offensive in the Dardanelle's and at a late stage before the plan had been put into operation he resigned, and although most of the senior Officers at the Admiralty who were involved also were not fully in favour it was too late to change course. The Royal Navy bombarded the coast in January and February 1915 and there were troop landings in April. There were many brave actions by British and commonwealth troops during the nine months that it lasted, but the first in on 'W' beach was the 1st Battalion the Lancashire Fusiliers.

The 1st Battalion the Lancashire Fusiliers boarded landing craft from the Royal Navy cruiser HMS Euryalus early on the morning of April 25th 1915 and stormed onto 'W' beach. This was the morning that the L.F.s won their six V.C.'s before breakfast. The G.O.C. Sir Ian Hamilton ordered that 'W' beach be renamed 'Lancashire landing', and it was as much an award to the battalion as the V.C.s. It is part of the history of the Gallipoli campaign as recorded in the British Army and Regimental annals, however the War Office insisted on referring to it as 'The landing at Helles' in the citation, which is not what the Sir Ian Hamilton had intended. The whole battalion merited the V.C. award but that was not appropriate, the Divisional Commander General Hunter Weston therefore asked the Brigade Commander to give him six names from the battalion.

The whole campaign was a disaster and by December, and January 1916, the whole offensive was called off and the troops withdrawn. Lord Fisher had opposed the plan and resigned when it was not abandoned, as a result Winston Churchill was sacked from the Cabinet and spent the rest of the war on the backbenches in what he later called his 'wilderness years'.

These events coupled with the governments evident lack of understanding of the serious situation that the nation was in, and a general 'lassez faire' attitude toward the desperate shortage of shells had brought the government to the point of collapse. Churchill, unlike Kitchener, had been of the opinion, along with a bullish Sir Henry Wilson that the war would be a short affair; that a concerted thrust on the western front would defeat Germany's aims and claim victory for the allies, no one, save perhaps Kitchener was able to foresee the crushing defeat the Germans were to mete out in the opening weeks of the war, and yet Kitchener himself could not see the need for a massive increase in munitions production. Asquith fully realised that the cabinet was out of step with public opinion; the bombs scandal had brought matters to a head and he found that he had no choice but to create a coalition government. As a direct result of the Gallipoli fiasco and at the insistence of the Conservatives, Churchill lost his job as First Lord of the Admiralty. He had told Russia that he would give them The Dardanelle's.

Even had Britain managed to open up the Dardanelle's it would have been to little avail, with the attitude of the War Office in resisting the offers coming from Britain's manufacturers to support the manufacture of guns and ammunition, Britain found herself struggling to provide enough for her own military and admiralty needs let alone send supplies to Russia which would be have been the main objective of opening the Black sea route through the Dardanelles. The only other route to Russia was by the North Cape to Murmansk or further still to Archangel, a Russian port in the White Sea that was closed by ice for four months of the year. In any event it would make little difference to the level of supplies available for a poorly equipped Russia in the short term. The situation led to ill feeling on the part of the Russians who expected Britain would use her huge manufacturing capacity for the benefit of Russia and France. The main industrial towns of France of course, were in the northern area that was now under German occupation and there again it had been expected that a large part of the burden for supplies for France would fall on Britain and as the War progressed that in fact was the case, But in the first two years of the War, although Britain was the foremost manufacturing nation, what she produced was not munitions and that perhaps, was not readily appreciated by France and Russia.

When the new Ministry of Munitions was set up the post of Minister for Munitions was offered to Lloyd George who resigned from his post as Chancellor of the Exchequer. The prime mover in Lloyd George being offered the post was the great amount of correspondence that he had received from the front during his period as Chancellor of the Exchequer concerning the shortage of shells, he had made effort to bring this serious matter to the attention of the Prime Minister in order that the needs of the military could be satisfactorily met. He had made visits to France to see at first hand the plans that they had made in peacetime for the supply of munitions in the event of war and he had used the information that he obtained there to strengthen his argument against the woefully inadequate provisions set up by the War Office. France had expected that war was inevitable, as had Germany, France had prepared defensively whilst Germany had prepared aggressively, but Britain had made no such arrangements, there being no reason why she should even though there was an awareness of the level of French nervousness. It was clear to Asquith that since Lloyd George had got this whole thing rolling that he should be the one to head the new Ministry. He made the quantum move from keeping a stringent hold on the Nations purse strings to a level of unsurpassed spending on armaments equipment that was to increase continually for the next four years. As things progressed even the smallest businesses were drawn into the manufacture of goods for the War effort. An example would be the ancient smithy in the village where I live, it has been in the same family for the last three generations and during the Great War it was working full blast producing horseshoes, these were packed in wooden boxes and taken to the jetty on the Conwy river and shipped on to the Western Front.

Lloyd George realised that it was essential that he got the support of the trade unions to the demands that were likely to be made. He went out to the major cities and put it to the Manufacturers and the workers alike that it would be necessary, in the interests of the nation as a whole, to apply themselves to a work ethic that would ensure that those at the front had their whole-hearted support. The level of agitation amongst the workers would have to be measured against the needs of those at the front and not the factory workers until the war was over. The troops at the front were laying down their lives to secure the country's security, soldiers could not choose to work more hours to earn more money, neither could he choose to work less hours that he was ordered to do and there was no earthly reason why workers at home should not respect that. It was wartime for both, not wartime for the soldier and peacetime for the civilian; the only difference was that the soldiers were laying down their lives for the cause. Women must be allowed to do men's jobs and there would have to be an expansion of the skilled workforce with the introduction of trainees or 'dilutees', and that was likely to cause problems with the skilled workers who jealously guarded the various areas work for skilled men. It is interesting to note what Lloyd George had to say to a meeting in Manchester and again the following day in Liverpool and to see what the response was.

[26]With special reference to what I expected from Lancashire, I added in my Manchester speech: — "Lancashire's private works, when they are fully engaged and after you have mobilized them, can turn out a quarter of a million of high-explosive shells a month. A gentleman near me tells me that you can turn out a lot more. Well, the more the merrier; but we want you to start from that and then work up in the direction of a million."

On the following day I spoke in similar terms at Liverpool. I repeated my reassurance to the workers about the temporary nature of the relaxations of ordinary rules and practices that they were being asked to accept. A resolution was carried, pledging those present to do all they could to increase the output of munitions. This resolution was seconded in a significant speech delivered by one of the workmen's representatives. It is worth quoting: ----- Mr. Clarke, a representative of the Amalgamated Society of Engineers seconded the resolution.

He said: "we have learned now that things are not going so well at the front as we thought they were. Certain newspapers have hidden the truth from us, and have presented too rosy a picture. It was only yesterday when they heard Mr. Lloyd George's speech that the workmen realised the terrible urgency of the matter. Now that we know, I am sure that there will be no difficulty."

A press comment on this speech stated: -----

The general feeling in representative trade union circles in London with regard to Mr. Lloyd George's speech is one of unanimous agreement. One prominent trade unionist said: "we are delighted with the definiteness of the speech, and only wish it had been given eight months ago. We have been annoyed at the campaign in favour of conscription, because we knew there were hundreds of thousands of men for whom no equipment could be immediately obtained."

At this time serious discussion was taking place about the about the amount of hours lost through alcohol abuse in some of the large industrial towns and in response to this the government set up a committee to report on the problem and make recommendations, they were charged with looking at what it would cost the Government to buy all the shares in the brewery companies and all of the public houses and off licences throughout the country. Serious thought was given to the complete closure of public houses in areas where munitions were produced and manufacturers were keen to go along with that setting forward a very strong case based on the history of absenteeism in their factories. Even the King was given to demonstrating that rich and poor alike would have to meet these strictures and offered to become teetotal for the duration of the war, he was also prepared to ban all alcoholic drink from all the Royal residences for the duration of the war as testimony that the well off would be treated no different than the working classes. This was confirmed later in some small way when Lord Rawlinson Commander of the Fourth Army was invited to breakfast with King

George V whilst on visit from the front, he hinted at the fact that the Royals were doing there bit and said that the King gave him a whiting for breakfast. Whiting then of course being the cheapest of fish.

In France the sale of absinthe had been banned and in Russia the sale of vodka also, and it was felt that it would be in the interests of the nation as a whole to look at the problem of alcohol consumption at home. There was a pub on every corner in those days, beer was cheap and the pubs were always full during opening hours. Even the women liked to drink in those days particularly in the evenings at the weekend where they would congregate in the 'Snug'. Often if they could not get to the pub then they would take a jug with a cloth over it to the end of the bar for consumption at home. It was the done thing in those days when the pub was the centre of social life in every town and village in the country; many of the pubs had bowling greens and were only a stones throw away, there were also the working men's and social clubs, community life was very strong and the social life that went with it was important to everyone. It was a done thing for a person to go down the pub and be greeted by all the lads in the vault, then to tell the barman to 'get them in' for those that were his drinking pals. In late 1915 a bill was passed to prevent just that, a 'No treating order' where it was a punishable offence to buy beer for someone else's consumption; each person had to buy his or her own ale. The bad part of it was the amount of time lost in industry through alcohol consumption which was far more than it is now, beer was cheap and to some manufacturers it was a headache, so they were pleased to give their vote to the abolition of drink in some areas, they also had the support of the Band of Hope Teetotal Mission as well.

The problem of drink had grown so bad that almost

every town had it's own teetotal mission that people were encouraged to attend. Lloyd George really got the bit between his teeth with the business of drunkenness but of course that sort of thing was anathema to him, although he was born in Manchester he spent all of his childhood in a small village, Llanystumdwy on the Lleyn Peninsula between Criccieth and Pwllheli, his upbringing in that environment probably set him against drinking, he would have little understanding of what part beer played in the lives of most people who lived in the bigger towns and he chose Bangor in North Wales to make his first speech about the evils of drink, and he peddled the 'Kings Pledge' using Bangor where the pubs were closed on Sundays as a safe platform to get the message across to the rest of the country. He informed them of the 'the great powers' invested in the government to deal with the problem and that they were going to use them, how they were going to use them was not yet known at that stage, and would be a matter for consultation.

He quoted Lord Kitchener and Sir John French, the Commander in Chief of the B.E.F., who told of terrible tales wrought by heavy drinking and their message to Lloyd George was to ban all alcohol for the duration of the war. Well he was on home ground at Bangor, North Wales where there was little in the way of industrial manufacture and would not be affected by alcohol abuse to the extent that say Tyneside, Liverpool, Manchester or Birmingham might, not to mention Glasgow. Nevertheless the response was loud and clear from the public and in the House of Commons where his plans were opposed; especially by the hard drinking Prime Minister Asquith. It restricted his proposed plans to the point where it could be considered a defeat; nevertheless stiff regulations were imposed in the large towns and ports on the opening hours of pubs where it was considered that drinking would have the greatest impact on the war effort. There were also heavy taxes imposed on beer and spirits as the war progressed and by the end of the war beer consumption nationally was less than half what it was in 1914, from that one assumes that drunkenness was alleviated to a great extent and the production of munitions not greatly impaired.

Efforts were being made to increase production but it was impossible to supply at the level that Sir John French was demanding, besides the War Office was quite blinkered and had little ability to see the overall situation, it had little flexibility either in changing to meet the needs of those at the front because of the constraints that it placed upon itself through an archaic system of arms procurement, they had no wish to be left with mountains of munitions if the war went the Allies way and turned out to be a short war[1], but this war was not like any other war. A letter from Lord Kitchener to Sir John French illustrates the level of thinking regarding the use of ammunition. Lord Kitchener wrote to the effect that it was impossible to attain production levels required for the number of shells needed, but having regard for that, operations should not be broken off for that reason alone and that once mounted an attack should proceed until the objectives had been achieved with or without the support of artillery.

It is clear that the British Imperial general Staff were slow to recognize the requirements of the B.E.F. in the current type of warfare and in particular the need for HE shells as opposed to Shrapnel, at the same time they were unsympathetic to the demands of Sir John French in asking for shells of any kind at the rate that he required them. He had been told in no uncertain terms by Lord Kitchener that even with maximum production, the Woolwich Arsenal would be unable to meet his demands. On the other hand Kitchener could not wave a wand and produce all the ammunition required and why could not Sir John understand that. The truth was that the job had to be done, Kitchener made that clear, but Sir John was not being made the butcher and either the Government gave him the means to do the job or it had to go. French was firmly of the opinion that the Asquith Government had almost brought the British Empire to its knees and decided then that he would do something about it. He turned to one of his staff officers and confided his thoughts to him, the officer reminded him of the consequences of any such action, that he would almost certainly be relieved of his post of G.O.C. British forces in France, this of course was a measure of his deep concern for his troops.

Shell Scandal!

Following the exposure of the ammunition shortage at the front, Lord Northcliffe blamed Lord Kitchener and published 'The Times' headline 'SHELL SCANDEL – Lord Kitcheners Tragic Blunder'. There were numerous accounts from serving officers of requests for shells being answered by all sorts of excuses, the Ordnance Corps depots behind the front line being empty of shells and battery Commanders being warned that there must be no shellfire without the Generals orders because of the dire shortages. In France they had a different approach altogether and had made contingency plans in peace time for the reasons that have already been mentioned, they had tackled the problem in peacetime and harnessed the nations manufacturing capacity and channelled it to the sector where those capabilities would be most productive, the problem for france was that a large part of the industrial capacity was in the occupied north. Another aspect that left the British with a problem after the first few months of the war was recruitment. France and Germany already had conscription in place but Britain historically had no need of that. Had the C.I.D. (Committee of Imperial Defence) been more informed as to what contingency plans France had in place then perhaps there would have been no 'shell scandal' and a better understanding of what France expected from the Entente. The needs of France and Germany, in terms of preparation may have been very similar but the reality for Britain was that the C.I.D. had other pressing needs to deal with at home.

In 1914 The British had a very small army and at no time had the occasion arisen where Britain needed to maintain an army to match the continental armies in size, Britain was merely a fringe player in Europe. As long as we could send a token army and provide Naval support, supplies and finance as we had done in the past we would always keep the channel open. At the outbreak of war there was a call for a nominal 100,000 volunteers, a level that the government obviously thought adequate as an initial requirement, and also a level of intake that could be coped with. But when the British public began to volunteer on the scale that they did, there was nothing to equip them with, no uniforms, beds, rifles, guns, the capacity to feed them, or any of the other mountains of paraphernalia that an army needs to make itself viable. What was needed more than anything was time, time in order to get a thousand and one systems into place, but things were moving along at the pace dictated by Germany and Austria where plans had long been laid at their convenience, not to the convenience of Britain.

The first Battle of Ypres, or known to the French as 'the Battle of Armentieres', in October 1914 almost saw the Germans almost break through and take the channel ports, the result of that would have been to cut off the means of communication with the British ports and Paris would have fallen. But the British line held and from that point the opposing armies were bogged down in the trenches and the western front, save for a well-planned tactical retreat by the German army to the Hindenberg line in 1917, nothing really changed over the next 4 years. Huge battles were fought for miniscule gains that were just as quickly lost quickly lost by the well-developed German system of counter attack. By the end of 1915 practically all the regular soldiers serving with the colours had been wiped out, the British army now consisted mainly of Territorial and New Army recruits.

DAILY ROUTINE IN THE ARMY

Reveille. 6.00am. Christians awake.

Parade. 6.30am. When he cometh.

Breakfast. 7.ooam. Meekly wait and murmur not.

Coy. Parade. 7.30am. We all cling together like the Ivy.

Arms drill. 8.45am. Fight the good fight.

Kit inspection 9.45am. All things bright and beautiful.

P.T 10.45am. Here we suffer grief and pain.

Defaulters 12.00am. The photo Wallah has arrived.
Dinner. 1.00pm. Come all Ye Faithful!

Lecture. 2.15pm. Tell me the old, old story.

Tea   4.00pm We do not know, we cannot tell.

First post 9.30pm. All safely gathered in.

Last post 10.00pm. He answers for us all.

Lights out. 10.15pm. Peace perfect peace.

***

18

Munitions Production

At home huge manufacturing and supply mechanisms had to be set in motion with the output of factories diverted to the needs of the military, in every area there was a desperate shortage and probably the most important was the need for shells, machine guns and rifles. During the pre war period when Lloyd George was the Chancellor of the Exchequer he had kept a tight hold on the purse strings and consequently ensured that the war Office only got what was felt necessary. The allocation of Machine guns was kept at a very low level and it was not until the war started and the shortages caused such tragic casualties that L.G. became committed to ensuring that this matter was addressed. Not until he became Prime Minister himself did he ensure that the army was supplied with sufficient needs in equipment and in so doing was quick to take the credit, when it came to supplying manpower L.G. was not so helpful.

As Prime Minister he was aware of the appalling casualties at the front and did not want to be seen as the one responsible for that, heavy artillery and machine guns were the things that would reduce the need for so much loss of life and if they did not have them history would point the finger at Lloyd George, he was canny enough to ensure that did not happen, but perhaps he also felt that with the right equipment the War could be brought to a speedy end. The reality in 1914 was however that through his policy of cutting back on defence funding in peacetime, he ensured that when the British Expedition Force went to France they had one Machine gun for every three or four of the German Army and that they had enough ammunition to feed the Royal Artillery with no more than four rounds per gun per day whilst the Germans were using 30 to 40 rounds per gun per day.

The Germans had long recognised the immense value of the machine gun and were extremely well equipped with them, something in the order of six or even eight per battalion, there were even reports of 16 per battalion, whereas the British Army had two for each Battalion with no provision made for reserve stock or for training use in the UK. To put that in some sort of perspective, a Company would consist of about 220 men and so there would be one Machine gun per 440 men, the Germans on the other hand would have at least one machine gun for every 150 men and probably considerably more. If the British Tommy was adept with the .303 rifle the Germans in turn demonstrated the devastating effects of the machine gun over and over again throughout the war.

However, from Oct. 1914 the war became 'trench warfare' and the machine gun was the weapon above all else in countering enemy attacks when used in conjunction with barbed wire entanglements. Heavy artillery of course did the most damage; a lengthy opening barrage that hopefully would cut the barbed wire entanglements and soften up the enemy did this. Then followed by of a creeping barrage in front of the advancing troops in order to pin the enemy down in their trenches. The problem was that as soon as the troops went over the top they were confronted by nothing but pounded mud and huge shell craters filled with water from the rains, that in itself was as much an obstacle in most cases as the enemy, it was a killer, men got into it one way or another and could not get out. The Germans then, far from having been softened up, were waiting with machine guns to mow them down as they approached the wire that in most cases had not been cut. The Germans went very deep with their trenches to a secondary level and were secure from the British bombardments so that as soon as the bombardment was lifted and the British troops went over the top to attack, the Germans were back in their positions with their machineguns waiting. The creeping barrage was developed in Rawlinsons fourth army and was to prove extremely effective, however there was a learning period when some tragic mistakes were made before the artillery mastered the technique.

As far as fighting equipment was concerned the humble spade must take its place and was a piece of equipment that played a massive roll in the war. Quite apart from artillery damage in pounding the earth to smithereens, the ground itself was also under continuous attack from the spade that was in use day and night for 4 years, and proving itself to be one of the most vital pieces of equipment of the whole war. The trenches were an absolute maze, they were given street names and troops moving up would enter the trenches a long way from the front line and march great zigzag distances to replace the troops awaiting relief, they were in the line, in support and in reserve all living in the trenches. Never can there have been so much trenching done as the hundreds of miles dug at the Western Front from the Belgian coast to Switzerland, every soldier worked on the trenches to keep them in order and particularly to keep themselves secure and dry. But it was those soldiers who had worked down the pit or navvying in various parts of the country who were moved into Pioneer companies and showed just how to make short work of trenching. In most cases the German trenches were deeper and of a more permanent build and offering more protection during bombardments. This allowed them to sit out the bombardments well below ground and them come out to man their Machine guns as the British advanced with the standard Lee Enfield .303 rifle.

My own introduction to the Lee Enfield .303 rifle was as a boy at home, my father came home on leave on being posted overseas, he had his full kit with him, big pack, small pack, ammo pouches over his greatcoat, he had his kitbag and rifle as well. He took everything back with him but left the rifle in the built in wardrobe in my parent's bedroom. I don't suppose that it was unusual to see a soldier with his rifle in those days, perhaps on a 48 before being posted abroad or to another location. My father knew of course that he ought not to have had it, and I cannot think what on earth he thought he might use it for. It was kept in a built in Wardrobe that went over the stairwell from Mum and Dads bedroom and of course we understood that no one had to know about it. After the war my Father would often bring it out and show my brother and I how to set the rangefinder, take it apart and clean it, use the oil bottle, 4 by 2 and pull-through located in the rifle butt, how to lie on the ground legs spread out and hold the rifle to take aim, everything but fire it so when I eventually went in the army it was familiar to me.

There must have been a large number of 303's in civvy St. after the war because one day there was an announcement that there was to be an amnesty; anyone handing in a gun before a prescribed date would be allowed to do so with no questions asked. Perhaps my father felt that he was unable to walk into the police station 3 years after the War ended, hand in his rifle and walk out without some record of that on file and his later being called to account. Maybe he did not trust them to keep some record of the fact that he had kept the rifle perhaps for later use. It could have been simply that being a postman and well known he did not want to be seen or word get round of him having kept an army issue rifle, I cannot say. However he went out quietly late one night and threw it in the Leeds and Liverpool canal, he climbed over the wall of the Ordnance Mill, long since burnt down, and went down to the canal on the opposite bank to the towpath by Appleby's flour mill (Daisyfield cornmill) and threw it in, I doubt that it is still there but it would be interesting if it were.

It was not the only time that he climbed over the gate at the old Coddington's factory yard either. In 1947 we had a very severe winter, snows six feet deep in our street and fuel was very hard to get. I recall spending Saturday mornings at the gasworks queuing for coke, the weather was bitterly cold with deep snow everywhere, long icicles hanging and thick rutted ice on the road and pavements were it had been cleared of snow, there were no cars to grind it into slush in those days and the temperatures stayed so low. My brother and I had a flat wagon from old pram wheels (in big demand at that time) and flat timber; it came in useful for carrying sacks of coke from the gasworks on Saturday mornings, the only day they were open.

We used to have to go early to get in the long queue at the 'pop hole' just inside the Gasworks gates for a ticket after which you could get in the long queue inside the yard itself, to wait in turn for your bag to be filled at a point out of sight further up the huge cobbled yard. They would call for you to get your sack (one Cwt. Per person so you needed two coal sacks since coke was lighter than coal) and it was a route march to the huge pile of coke at the other end of the yard. The coke was dumped from overhead trolleys that ran along on a gantry from the coke furnaces. You held open the sack and the man shovelled it in with a size 10 shovel, it was hard on the knuckles if the coke hit your hand going in and being so cold of course it smarted where a bit of bark came off.

We wore only short pants and wooden soled clogs with clog irons on the bottom, and long socks, I suppose the good thing was that the pants were lined in those days and came to your knees, nevertheless we seemed to do nothing but shiver. To combat that we used to make winter warmers and I suppose that year we had them all the time. They were made from a cocoa tin with a lot of holes punched in each end, inside was a bunch of cotton weft from the spindles that were rejected at the cotton mill and this was set alight, it was not quick to ignite so we would blow and blow and then put the cap on and run round like an aeroplane to get the air through it. Needless to say they got too hot to hold at times but it was surprising how long they lasted.

You had to provide your own sacks and string at the gasworks, if the sack was a sugar sack there was lots to tie up at the neck, but if it was a coal sack you had the devil's own job keeping the coke in as you pulled it along on the truck because it had to be upright. I remember my father on hearing how we struggled up the cobbled steep part of Bruce St. with its high curbs, giving us the benefit of his advice. "Next time you come up that hill push the truck, it is always much easier to push something uphill than to pull it", sure enough he never went to the gasworks himself. We went for the old lady next-door and other people close by in the street that my mother had volunteered us for, we would get threepence and have to hand it over to my mother, and look happy about it as if we would not have it any other way. So having done one trip we would turn round and do another before the gasworks closed at 12 Noon.

Well, the reason my father went over the gate at Coddingtons factory on this occasion was that there was a huge pile of coal used for the Bankfield Mill boilers next door. So late one night he got my older brother to go with him and stand guard in the shadows by the gate while he climbed over to pinch some coal in a sack, I was not allowed to join them but stood at the backyard door ready to whistle if anyone came across the spare land in between. Coal was rationed and what we did get from the coalman was mainly slack, grey very low-grade shale like coal that burned with little heat. But this was anthracite, hard, clean, shiny nuggets that burned very hot and was easy to bag. He would not have thought of doing it but there was no fuel for the fire to be had and the temptation was too great, once the coal ration was used up that was it, all that the coal merchant had was blocks of peat which I understand came from Ireland, the smell of it burning was delightful but it gave off very little heat, of course there was no such thing a central heating. Everything was still rationed in 1947, Manny Shinwell was the Minister of Fuel or 'Minister of no fuel' as my mother used to say, John Strachey was the Minister of food and at the shop my mother used to ask for her miniscule ration of 'Strachey bacon' which oddly, tasted better than anything you can buy now. Life then was very little different than 1916 and a world removed from life today.

Following the 'Call to arms' by Lord Kitchener on posters put up throughout the country, the recruitment process had a sort of snowball effect, a sense of 'we are all in it together' it was an adventure, and nobody was wanting to be left out, there was a certain amount of cajoling in the factories and pubs aimed at those who where not disposed to volunteering, but it was an opportunity to be in a man's world, well ordered and disciplined gave rise to a feeling of pride, a sense of doing ones duty to King and Country and of course that is exactly what Kitchener appealed to. Also there was the fact that the only opportunity to travel abroad for most men in those days was with the army or navy and the urge to join for men working very long hours was perhaps, hard to resist.

Many of these conscripts had trained in the Territorial's and enjoyed the comradeship and training at summer camps, they had families so full time service was not for them. Here was the chance to see a bit of short-term action, they said it would be over by Christmas and who could blame them for wanting to breaking out of a humdrum existence for a short while. It might not what today's generation might think of as a worthwhile break in this day and age, but life was vastly different then. In Lancashire they mainly worked in the cotton mills for very long hours and that lifestyle was replicated for others in various ways throughout the country. All too quickly those in the Territorial's, on being asked, responded at once, agreeing to serve in Imperial service, they found themselves undergoing intensive training before eventually going into the front line. When eventually they got into France they had a big shock, it was not what they expected. From the early days at Mons and Le Cateau there were heavy casualties and many must have pondered on what they had let themselves in for. The fact that they may have had other strong reasons for wanting to go besides patriotism does not detract from the courage and loyalty of those who went, or indeed to say that they would not have gone had they known what it would be like, of course they would have gone, but it probably was not how they saw it when they volunteered. They showed enormous courage and bravery, the wounded suffered without complaint in a war that was a disaster of epic proportions, Germans, French, British and Russians etc threw themselves at the command of the well cushioned General Staff, like lemmings over a cliff.

19

Battalions, Brigades and Divisions

My paternal grandfather and a my great uncle on my mothers side were both territorials with the 4th battalion the East Lancashire Regiment when War was declared; later my grandfather was transferred to the 8th battalion the East Lancashire Regiment, one of the new service battalions formed at Fulwood Barracks Preston. My maternal Grandfather enlisted with the 4th battalion Kings Own having been a territorial in peacetime and his brother volunteered for the 1/7th battalion T.A. the Lancashire Fusiliers, one of the New Army battalions raised at Salford. On my wife's side her great Uncle served with the 1/4th battalion the East Lancashire regiment having been with them in the Territorials, he was later transferred to the 1st Battalion KSLI (Kings Shropshire Light Infantry), just as many soldiers were moved to other battalions at the front in order to replace losses through killed and wounded.

Battalions of these famous Lancashire regiments formed Brigades mainly alongside other Lancashire battalions and they stayed together in a Division providing support for each other as they moved in and out of the front line, this was the basis of the Brigade system in the British Army. Many of these County battalions no longer exist; the battalions of the New Army of course were immediately disbanded at the end of the Great War. Many of the British regular army regiments no longer exist as a result of several amalgamations of the various divisions (Kings, Queens, Highland, Guards etc). An example of that is the amalgamation of the 1st and 2nd Life Guards in 1928 to form the present Life Guards. Likewise in 1969 The Royal Horse Guards and the 1st Dragoon Guards amalgamated to form the Blues and Royals who along with the Life Guards make up the present Household Cavalry.

Since WWII the changes have taken place at regular intervals so that now many cherished and famous regiments no longer exist. The East Lancashire and South Lancashire Regiments joined with the Loyals to form the Queen's Lancashire regiment based at Preston, and the Kings own and the Border Regt. amalgamated to form the Kings Own Border Regt. with their depot at Carlisle. More recently these two regiments have amalgamated once more along with the Kings Liverpool Regt. and the Queen's Lancashire Regt. to form what is now The Duke of Lancaster's Regiment, the current Duke of Lancaster is of course the Queen. The history of the regiments of the British army are the basis of the very strong loyalty amongst the troops that serve with them, I know my father was always keen to stress that to him it was the Kings Own Royal Regt., there were Kings Regiments and there were Kings Own Regiments, but there was only one Kings Own Royal Regt. It was a matter of pride that each Regt. was known for past achievements, for instance the 'Six VC's before breakfast' of the 1st Batt. Lancashire Fusiliers at Gallipoli, throughout the British army these older regiments engendered a feeling of enormous pride in those who served with them, and that was evident throughout the regiment, something that stayed permanently with anyone who served.

The exception in Lancashire County was the Lancashire Fusiliers; they amalgamated with the Northumberland Fusiliers, the Royal Fusiliers and the Warwickshire Regt. as the Royal Regiment of Fusiliers with their depot at the Tower of London, and sadly, even as I write, the 2nd battalion has been listed for disbandment. Others regular regiments of the British Army, with long and proud histories like the Manchester Regiment, the York and Lancaster Regiment and many more were disbanded long ago. They were proud and famous Regiments that fought with exceptional courage and self-lessness throughout the two world Wars and there was great sadness when they went out of existence. The present proposals will see the British Army reduced by a nominal 20% from 100,000 to 80,000, the smallest it has ever been, before the Suez crisis the Army strength was some 340,000 and from the turn of the last century that was probably as low as it got, since the crisis Suez the cutbacks have gradually reduced the size and by the end of the current cuts the British Army will be one quarter of its size in 1956. The question is not whether we need a army of 350,000, the question is, can we defend ourselves and our dependencies with 80,000 troops?

The movements and experiences of the Lancashire Battalions at the front, was typical of what happened to thousands of men all over the country who 'joined up' and in so doing changed the face of family life in Britain for a generation. In Kitcheners New Army men were encouraged to join up with their pals and they were assured that they would be trained and posted together, these were known as the 'Pals' Regiments. At the outset of war there were 4 battalions to a Brigade but as the War dragged on and casualties increased it was necessary to reduce that to 3 battalions per brigade. These brigades were made up more and more of new army battalions as the war progressed and these are some examples of four battalion brigades.

The 125th Brigade made up of the Lancashire Fusiliers 1/5th, 1/6th, 1/7th and 1/8th battalions.

The 126th brigade comprised 1/4th and 1/5th battalions East Lancashire Regiment along with the 9th (Old-ham) and 1/10th (Ashton-Under-Lyne) battalions of the Manchester Regiment.

The 127th Brigade comprised the 1/5th, 1/6th, 1/7th, and 1/8th Battalions of the Manchester Regiment.

A division was made up of three brigades and the three brigades mentioned here formed the 42nd or East Lancashire Division. Other Divisions were made up of Battalions from the Kings Own Royal Regiment (Lancaster), The Loyal North Lancashire Regiment and the South Lancashire Regiment and so on throughout the British army. Although these brigades and divisions would move from one Corps to another and one Army to another, in general they remained unchanged at Divisional level. An army Brigade was commanded by a Brigadier General (rank now defunct in the British army and designated simply 'Brigadier'); a Division was commanded by a Major General, a Corps by a Lt. General, and an army commanded by a General with the overall command in a theatre of War commanded by a Field Marshal, a rank that is now abolished.

The Regular Army, Territorial, and Service Battalions.

The British Army order of precedence is a complicated issue and although individual regiments of Foot in 1914 were still fiercely proud of their seniority as designated by the number of Foot, it is now largely a thing of the past. However prior to the Great War it was still an important matter amongst regiments when seniority counted so much, even though the County system had been in force since the late nineteenth century. The County system meant that regiments were affiliated to Counties and designated by the County name, e.g. The Warwickshire's, The Devonshire Regt, The Durham light Infantry etc. The pecking order was designated by

250

who took precedence over whom but even then it was a complicated business. The Lancashire regiments that I have already mentioned were, Kings Own 4th Foot, (senior regiment in the Kings Division) Lancashire Fusiliers 20th Foot or better known as the XXth and the East Lancashire regiment the 30th Foot.

The County Regiments of the British army consisted mainly of two regular battalions with the colours, 1st and 2nd, (one based in the UK and one overseas, usually India, South Africa, the Sudan, Jamaica etc.) and two territorial battalions that would be the 4th and 5th battalions. There would also be a reserve battalion that would normally be the 3rd battalion and made up of men who had served as regulars with the colours and were now on the reserve. It was usual for a soldier to sign on with the colours for 7 years and if he did not stay on in the army he would be discharged and go on the reserve for 5 years. This is exactly what my father did between the Wars. In the event of war the territorial battalions would be called up and take over the duties of the regular battalions in order to release them for Active Service, or what would now be termed Operational Duties. Originally the Territorial Battalions were not required to serve overseas, their role was home defence. During the South Africa War the Territorial Battalions volunteered specifically to go and fight and so at that time a precedent was created that allowed the Territorial's (on a voluntary basis) to become 1st line battalions in time of War.

On enlistment with the Territorial's a recruit had the choice of signing for overseas service or not and it would appear that at the outbreak of WWI few of the Territorials had taken up the option. They were battalions raised from within localised areas and consequently there was a very strong bond of loyalty to that particular battalion. For instance the 4th battalion TA East

Lancashire Regiment was based at Canterbury St. Barracks, Blackburn with company outposts at Darwen and Clitheroe whilst the 5th battalion TA was based at The Barracks, Burnley, with outposts at Accrington, Padiham, Bacup and Haslingden.

When the 1st line Territorial battalions were required to go into the line or to the front, there would be further battalions raised, for example the 4th battalion would become the 1/4th with the new battalion designated the 2/4th battalion and so on. This also applied to the 'Service' battalions that were raised through recruitment for Kitcheners 'New Army'. These would be designated 6th, 7th, and so on. An example of this was the 7th battalion of the Lancashire Fusiliers that was raised as a Salford TA battalion, the overspill from this battalion formed the nucleus of another battalion and so the 7th became the 1/7th and the new battalion was the 2/7th, both battalions were raised locally from Salford and the surrounding area within the traditional recruiting area of the Lancashire Fusiliers and were known as 'Pals' regiments.

Kitchener was keen to recruit on a local basis with a view to encouraging close comradeship and loyalties, even guaranteeing to keep Pals together wherever possible. It should perhaps be mentioned here that Lord Kitchener had little time for the Territorial Army and thought that they were pseudo or pretend soldiers who would not prove themselves if called on to give service to their country. On the other hand he had a vision of a New Army raised from volunteers who were prepared to be soldiers at the time of greatest need, they would answer the call and they would fight for each other. As it happened what had been an enormous rush to volunteer in 1914 quickly became a trickle and conscription had to be introduced.

Other examples of locally raised Service battalions

and known as 'The Pals', 'The Accrington' pals of the 11th (service) battalion the East Lancashire Regiment raised in Accrington in 1914 is an example, (two companies of that battalion were actually raised in Blackburn) others were the Stockbroker Battalion, The 10th (Service) Battalion of the Royal Fusiliers, Salford Pals 5 battalions, the Liverpool Pals 4 battalions, the Manchester Pals 8 battalions and many others from all over the Country.

It is perhaps interesting to note to what extent the British army has contracted since pre war days. Taking the Lancashire Fusiliers as an example, they are now amalgamated with the Northumberland Fusiliers, The Royal Warwickshire Regiment and the Royal Fusiliers and make up what is now the Royal Regiment of Fusiliers with their depot at the Tower of London. These four amalgamated regiments consist today of only two regular Battalions and this clearly illustrates the huge reduction in the number of battalions in the present day British Army compared to the peacetime establishment before the Great War. In this case there would have been 8 regular battalions, 8 territorial battalions and 4 reserve battalions in the four regiments, i.e. 20 battalions

One final point worth noting is that it was impossible for all the 'service' battalions of a given regiment to be recruited on a local basis, for instance the 'Cheshire Regiment' raised 35 battalions in the 'Great War', the Royal Welch Fusiliers 44 battalions and even they were eclipsed by several other Regiments. It therefore follows that many of the recruits to the various regiments had little or nothing in common with the regiments in which they found themselves, recruits were drafted to where they were needed and this started very early in the war. It is not inconceivable therefore that a soldier could leave his regiment at the front injured, be admitted to a base hospital only to return 3 months later to find that he barely knew anyone, such were the casualties and the wastage of human life. It was inevitable that as the war progressed and each battalion suffered the heavy losses that they did, a County Regiment would have changed the soldiers in it's ranks over and over until those members left probably had nothing to do with the regiment other than they had been drafted to one of it's battalions.

The first battle of Ypres saw the virtual annihilation of the regular soldiers of the battalions that went with the B.E.F., the replacements were elements of the New Army, new in every sense but they nevertheless gave an excellent account of themselves. The General staff looked at the use of manpower in a totally different way, when making their plans against the enemy one of the main considerations was how many men they were likely to lose, and therefore what replacements they would need in order to achieve their planned objectives, other ranks, NCO's, WO's and Subalterns really were gun fodder.

The General Officer Commanding and all his senior staff were of course billeted in mansions/stately houses commandeered as required and sited perhaps 25 miles behind the front line. They lived a life little different than that they would live at home as the upper class rich, the job just happened to involve the loss of life on a huge scale by which they were largely unaffected.

OUR HUMBLE REQUEST

Oh! Lord above we not all Wesley's or John
Bunyan's
But grant us our humble prayer and give us
steak and onions.

From cutlets and from curry stew, Lord kindly
us deliver,
And from the beasts we're forced to eat, please
cut out their liver.

Oh! Lord above we are not all saints, for some-
times we say 'Damn',
But hear us as we humbly pray for something
better than jam.

Please, a little milk and sugar to strengthen up
our tea,
Grant us these simple little wants and we'll
send thanks to thee.

**

Moving soldiers around to unfamiliar circumstances is
exactly the position in which my grandfather found
himself as his Battalion the 4th East Lancashire Regt,
now fully trained and designated the 1/4th, embarked
along with the 1/5th for Egypt but leaving him behind,
he was posted to the newly formed 8th (service) battal-
ion, that had been raised at Preston and was now sta-
tioned in the West Country, this was so that a nucleus
of trained soldiers, albeit territorial's would make up
the numbers of a battalion of raw recruits.

My great uncle, Benjamin Leaver of the same 4th
battalion, being an old regular soldier with the colours
and having served in the Boer War brought valuable
skills that were needed in the training of raw recruits.
He, along with others that had previous service, was
required to stay at the Bury camp that had been desig-
nated a Training Depot. He became a founder member
as it were of the 2/4th battalion with a robust recruiting
campaign in the Blackburn and Burnley areas.

20

The 1st Somme
July - November 1916

This was the year that the volunteers of Kitcheners new army saw the first major offensive made by the B.E.F. in a joint effort with the French. The balance was in fact uneven in that the British had 3 times more divisions involved than the French, the German attack on Verdun had taken away two thirds of the French forces and so the Somme was always considered to be a British affair.

Haig was now a Field Marshal, G.O.C. of the BEF and was being pressed by the French G.O.C. General Joffre to make a combined British /French attack on the Somme. Haig however, was not happy about the choice of front chosen by Joffre for the intended assault, it offered no worthwhile gains, would not significantly weaken the enemy and was extremely well defended. He felt that an all out attack in the Ypres area with the possibility of capturing the important supply transport network around Roulers and Kourtrai would be a far more profitable venture. Another worry of Haig's was that the raw recruits of the new army were not yet ready to carry such a massive assault as that envisaged by Joffre, and he considered the French army to be weak and demoralised and unlikely to see the battle through. However, the allied meeting that took place at Chantilly in December 1915 had outlined a strategy for a combined assault and the matter had been agreed, at a later meeting the plan was further outlined and the detail left to the supreme army commanders, General Foch himself played a large part in the detailed planning of that.

Kitchener too was pressing Haig and was of the opinion that the British would now have to shoulder the burden, that as far as he could see the French had had enough and were worn out, Foch also had only recently made that same observation to Henry Wilson (whilst GOC Liaison officer to the French High Command). The B.E.F. had grown considerably and by July 1st 1916, the day of the opening battle of the Somme consisted of some 1,400,000 men, but there was concern at the War office and G.O.C. in France that these young recruits should not be exposed to battle before being brought to a high standard of training.

Henry Wilson was now the commander of the Fourth Army Corps and although he had no further responsibility for liaison between the French and the British High Commands, he took the opportunity to visit those with whom he had developed strong relationships on the French side. On the 11th of June whilst visiting General Foch he got into conversation with Clemenceau, the Prime Minister who hinted at removal of Marshal Joffre the French C. in C. The candidates to replace Joffre were Petain, Foch and De Castelnau, Clemenceau indicated that he was in favour of Foch, and being his long time friend, so was Henry Wilson. It may be an indication of the esteem that Wilson was held in by Clemenceau that he spoke so intimately with Wilson, or perhaps he wanted Wilson to denegrate Joffre, something of course he would not do.

There appears to be no further indication that Clemenceau discussed the matter with anyone else but it does have a parallel that occurred a few months later. In June 1916 Kitchener had been on his way to Northern Russia in HMS Hampshire when the ship went down with all hands, there was speculation that she had been torpedoed by a German submarine, but the weight of opinion veered towards the ship having hit a mine.

There were other conspiracy theories but they seem not to be very convincing. On Kitcheners demise, Lloyd George moved from Minister of Munitions to Secretary of State For War to replace him, and one of the first things that Lloyd George did on taking up his new appointment was to visit the British troops in France; he also met with General Foch at the French GHQ. Henry Rawlinson Commander of the 4th Army,[27] records that Foch visited him and told him of Lloyd Georges visit, he said that Lloyd George had asked a lot of questions about why the B.E.F. did not fare so well as the French in so many aspects and openly inviting Foch to 'crab' on Sir Douglas Haig. Foch had then expressed the opinion that Lloyd George had inferred that Haig's position was not very secured. After the Conversation with Lloyd George and Rawlinson, Foch arranged to meet Douglas Haig and spent some considerable time with him in private going over what had what had transpired and of course Haig was thankful for the advice.

The whole of the planning for the battle of the Somme was thrown into turmoil when on February 21st the Germans attacked Verdun. The French 10th Army was operating between the British 1st and 3rd armies, Haig had been resisting pressure from Joffre to relieve the 10th and take over that front, now he readily agreed and the 10th Army was transferred for the defence of Verdun, as a result the balance of divisions involved in the coming battle of The Somme was drastically changed. General Rawlinson's Fourth Army was in excess of 500,000 men, of those some 100,000 were involved as the battle opened at 7.30am on July 1st, and a total of more than 150,000 men attacked the German positions. By the end of the first day the British alone had lost almost 60,000 officers and men, 19,500 dead, 35,000 wounded and some 2500 missing. To give an example, the Accrington Pals (11th Service Battalion

East Lancashire Regiment) lost 21 officers and 585 men out of a battalion of some 850, this was the New Army and they were comparatively raw recruits. Nothing in British War history has ever come near to such losses on one day.

Matey

Not coming back tonight Matey
And relief is coming through.
Were all going out tonight Matey,
Only we're leaving you.

Gawd! It's a bloody sin Matey'
Now that we've finished the fight.
We go when relief's come in Matey,
But you're staying here tonight.

Over the top is cold Matey,
You lie on the field alone.
Didn't I love you of old Matey
Dearer than the blood of my own.

You were my dearest chum Matey,
(Gawd! But you're face is white).
But now though, relief's have come,
Matey
I'm going alone tonight.

I'd sooner the bullet was mine Matey,
Going out on my own.
Leaving you here in the line Matey,
All by yourself, alone.

Chum O' mine and your dead, Matey,
And this is the way we part.

The bullet went through your head Matey,
But Gawd! It went through my heart.

***

The British regular Army no longer existed in real terms after the battles of 1915; the fighting was now done by battalions of the new Army and the Territorials, the New Army were literally thrown in at the deep end. To give some idea of the level of preparedness of these battalions was it is worth looking at a typical example. One of Kitchener's pet projects was the Pals Battalions where recruits were drawn from local areas. The Accrington Pals is one such battalion. The Mayor of Accrington at the time was Captain John Harwood whose enthusiasm encouraged hundreds of men to enlist into the 11th Service Battalion, The Accrington Pals. Recruiting started on the 14th of September 1914 and within ten days 36 officers and 1100 other ranks had enlisted. Two came from Company's from Accrington, two from Blackburn about 4 miles away, and smaller units (platoons) from Burnley and Chorley both within a few miles of Accrington. Initially the battalion was scattered with the men billeted in their own homes, still in civilian clothes and having to travel to training areas at Burnley and Accrington each day. Few of those recruited had any experience and towards the end of February 1915, having moved into billets at Caernarvon, the Commanding Officer, Adjutant and other senior officers were replaced by experienced officers of the Regular Army who transfered from other Regiments. The blue militia uniforms that they had been issued with were replaced by khaki and they settled to more intensive training. In May they moved to Staffordshire and again in July were billeted at Ripon in Yorkshire.

In this short time they had formed themselves into a competent fighting unit, now considered to be a body of men, well trained and able to work with a good team spirit. In November they moved to Salisbury ready for active service and in December they embarked ship for Egypt, there they spent the next 15 months in the Suez Canal area. On March 2nd 1916 they embarked aboard the Llandovery Castle and on the 8th of March disembarked at Marseilles. The following morning March 9th they boarded a rickety, drafty old train and travelled slowly north to Picardy and the Western Front where they arrived in time to prepare for the First Battle of the Somme. For so many it would be their final journey.

The General Reserve (which later became the Fifth Army) at the time, under the Command of General Hubert Gough, was billeted close to Rawlinson's Fourth Army and was placed at Rawlinson's disposal, by the 7th of July the General Reserve (soon to be designated the fifth army) had commenced an attack on Olliviers in co-operation with the Fourth Army and this initial stage saw the breakthrough of the German first line of defence, albeit at tremendous cost in casualties. This was to be repeated over and over through the months to November, attack after attack for little gain and so the war, instead of being a decisive victory became a wearing down war, it was a stalemate that the Germans felt that they would not survive, but nevertheless managed to hold out. The Germans had mounted the costly attack at Verdun in February but owing to the fact that the Russians and the British held firm to the allied agreements made at Chantilly the Germans were compelled to pull back from Verdun. The Russians had attacked the Austrians in what was known as the Brusilov offensive so called after the Russian army group commander, the attack was highly successful and saw them take half a million Austro Hungarian prisoners. The

British had attacked at the Somme leaving General Erich Von Falkenhayn, the German C. in C. on the horns of a dilemma and little option but to withdraw from Verdun. In August Generals Nivelle and Mangin triumphantly retook Fort Douaumont and the Verdun episode was finally brought to a close, the loss of life on both sides was enormous. Whenever there was a lull in the fighting, burial parties were sent out to dig mass graves for those that were killed and lay out on the field, this photograph will give some idea of the size of these operations as this 42nd division burial party sets out.

The newly developed tank introduced in September 1916

4th Battalion East Lanc's 1917. The platoon Sgt has a make-shift periscope to view the german lines, made from a mirror at the end of his bayonet.

Heavy field gun with Asbury type breech mechanism. Used in long opening barrages before the troops went over the top.

On the firestep, a soldier keeps a watchful eye for Raiding parties whilst four of his comrades take a well earned nap.

Joffre was again now pushing for an all out attack and in September the British attacked using the newly invented tank, this new device was initially designated an armoured machine gun and became a part of the Heavy Machine Gun Section. The tank was a new, untried means of warfare that proved not to be very reliable in the early stages and success was on a small but increasing scale. At the outset only some 70% of the available tanks were ready to join in the battle, they were dispersed to various parts of the front but many of them did not even engage the enemy. In the case of the attack on High Wood, of the four tanks involved 3 got bogged down and the fourth was destroyed by shellfire. Nevertheless they put the fear of God in the Germans and although again there was no outright victory this second part of the battle of the Somme came to a close in

November with the taking of Ancre, a village that along with Thiepval on the other side of the valley had been a main objective when the Battle opened on July 1st. This small victory gave the troops a new confidence after such a hard battle to take it. Again in November Gough's reserve divisions, newly renamed Fifth Army, took Beaumont Hamel to the North west of Thiepval and that gave a great boost to moral having been fought over for so long.

A meeting of the Allies brought an end to activities, the conditions that the troops survived under were appalling, the winter rains had turned the battlefields to slimy, muddy wastelands and the worst of the weather was yet to come. Although in November 1916 they had not beaten the Germans they felt superior, it was felt that they had them on the run and with a bit of luck could finish them in the coming year. Haig was confidant that the Germans were weakening and that a good push would see victory for the Entente. At the end of 1916 the Germans were also glad of the break in hostilities, the war of attrition was wearing them down, moral was very low following the loss of important positions from which they had dominated the front and a host of letters sent from home found on German prisoners told of the disillusionment at the worsening living conditions back home in Germany. The lack of successes at Verdun and on the Somme saw changes in the German High Command; Falkenhayn was stood down and sent off to Palestine, he was replaced by a successful duo from the Eastern front, Count Erich Von Ludendorf and Field Marshal Paul Von Hindenberg, confirming that all was not going well for the Germans on either the East or Western fronts.

A.D. 1916

The sky shows cold where the roof has been,
But the stars of night are none the dimmer,
Where the home once stood, the ruins are seen,
But the brazier gleams with a cheery glimmer.

And the old goes and the new life fills,
The scenes of many a peasant story,
And the bursting shells on the sentried hills,
Whisper of death but shout of glory.

Gutted and ripped, the stricken earth,
Where the bones of the restless dead are show-
ing,
But the great earth breathes of life and birth.
And the ruin shrinks from the blossom blowing.

The old life fails but the new life comes,
Over the ruins, scarred and hoary.
Though the thunder of guns and the roll of
drums;
But make for death, whilst they shout of glory.

***

By early December 1916 General Joffre had been ap-
pointed Field Marshal and shunted of to an advisory
post away from the direct machinations of war, in ef-
fect relieved of his Command. In his place came Gen-
eral Nivelle, fresh from his victory at Verdun, he was
the current hero and talked anyone and everyone into
believing that he had the wherewithal to wage war on
the Germans and see them off French soil. Although
there was some doubt on the part of the French politi-
cians at Nivelle's proposed strategy and that he was

'the man', he had little difficulty in convincing a receptive Lloyd George who was happy to listen to anyone with a plan, particularly a French plan rather than anything Field Marshal Haig and his staff might propose. France and Germany had paid a very high price at Verdun, the French casualties, dead wounded and missing, amounted to some 380,000 and the Germans some 340,000. The villages in the area around Verdun were completely obliterated, declared a closed zone and later planted out with trees. A place to house the bones of French and German soldiers removed from the battlefield was erected at Douaumont where the bones of some 130,000 soldiers are housed. It was death and injury on a scale that beggars belief.

Just as Falkenhayn had identified two strategic breakthrough points, Belfort and Verdun, where a breakthrough on a narrow front would see thousands of troops pour through and attack from behind, so the Battle of the Somme had been planned by the French as an allied venture, a desperate hope that there might be a breakthrough that would see the Germans driven out of France and across the Rhine. It had been rejected as a suitable plan by the British GHQ and also by the politicians at home for very good reasons as seen from the British point of view. But the Allied meetings at Chantilly in November 1915 and February 1916 saw a change in thinking and it was considered in the interests of Allied co-operation that the attack on the Somme should go ahead with full co-operation from The British Army. In the event, the three armed forces of Britain, Germany and France lost a total of 1,400,000 men between July 1st and November 15th, the War office stating that the German losses accounted for 630,000 of those. But in the end, although the battle of the Somme exposed the myth of German military superiority, there was no victor and Germany was still a powerful and entrenched force. The British had fought a series of five exhausting battles and gained a significant amount of ground, and it was demoralising after the sacrifice they had made to hear the Secretary of State Lloyd George denigrate the efforts of the British Forces at the Somme.

Lloyd George, after his visit to Flanders where he sought to extract comment from Foch about the British effort and in particular about Douglas Haig, made a statement saying, 'the (British) garrison artillery in France is entirely untrained, it cannot shoot and is quite unfitted to work the perfect weapons that I have provided' he also demanded a report from Sir Henry Rawlinson on the performance of the artillery in the recent battles. Rawlinson replied with a very positive report in which he wrote in part [28]"The Battle of the Somme has been a great and trying artillery struggle. Without the effective assistance of heavy howitzer and counter battery groups the successes which have attended the efforts of the Fourth Army could never have been attained". He also wrote in his diary with regard to the aspects of Lloyd Georges visit '--- now I hear he has been criticizing our heavy artillery, which is very hard on men who have been working like heroes. What is the reason for it? Is it the casualties? Is it our tactics, or just dislike of Haig? It has been said that Lloyd Georges mistrust of Haig stemmed from the losses sustained, the reality was that the French had taken greater losses throughout the war but still that did not diminish Lloyd George's faith in the French Military leadership that had, overall, proven to be less effective than the British.

1917

Nivelle's Grand Plan. Lloyd Georges scheming.

In the latter months of 1916 Joffre and Haig had begun to make plans for 1917, there was a feeling of optimism that the Allies on the Western front could finish the War in 1917 even though Joffre had commented that the French troops were worn out. The planned offensive was to be in February 1917 but all that planning was disrupted when Joffre was removed. Marshal Petain seemed to be the obvious choice to replace him and Painleve, the French Secretary for War, supported him. However General Nivelle was now the popular French hero after his success at Verdun and he, supported by the French Foreign Secretary Briand, had different ideas. Petain was confident that he would replace Joffre with Nivelle as his deputy but things became a little distorted when it became known that had Petain been elevated to the post of French GOC, Douglas Haig would have been expected to liaise with Petain through Nivelle putting Haig in an inferior and therefore intolerable position, he would be seen as a subordinate rather than an ally. The plan was wholly unacceptable and the upshot was that General Nivelle, with the support of Briand and Lloyd George, ensconced himself in the position of Commander in Chief to which there seemed to be no opposition. He was confident that he had the answer to the German threat, his system had worked at Verdun and he sold it to everyone so effectively that he got all the help he needed to get on with it. His plan was an elaboration of Joffre's original plan, to break through on a front between Reims and Soissons, the 2nd Battle of the Aisne.

The influence and the decisions about the direction

of the war were coming mainly from Britain and Lloyd George had great confidence in General Nivelle, his mother was English, his father French and he himself spoke fluent English. Lloyd George found that he could speak to Nivelle without an interpreter and not only was Nivelle enthusiastic and optimistic, he was also good at getting across his point of view. Lloyd George was on his side and put his weight behind the Nivelle Grand Plan. The British would undertake their side of the plan and co-operate fully with a view to bringing the enemy to the negotiating table.

Initially the plan had a cool reception from the British GHQ, they had more pressing needs, indeed initially Nivelle's French subordinates were themselves vehemently opposed to the plan that he had hatched. The French Government, influenced by Marshal Petain, who favoured small local attacks rather than the grand strategy, was also sceptical questioning the wisdom of the plan and threatening to abort the whole idea. Britain's immediate concern was with the amount of shipping lost to German submarine attacks that had brought the country to near starvation, and the need to put the German submarine facility at Zeebrugge out of action, as with Sir John French, Haig's wish since taking overall Command had been that the British should operate in the North from the Ypres area to the coast and the plan to incorporate an assault on the German U boat facilities could be enabled by a breakout from the Ypres salient, this would be something Lloyd George would surely agree too. But the French were not having that; they were determined to keep French forces between the BEF and the coast. It may have sounded ludicrous to the British at the time had they known, but the French were concerned that when the war came to a close that the British might decide to hold onto the territory that they occupied with their armed forces on the

French/ Belgian border along with the Channel Ports, such was the lack of trust that existed between the allies. The French were not so interested in saving the channel ports as they were in saving Paris, and to that end the British were there to be used.

In March 1917 a meeting was held in Calais attended by Lloyd George, Douglas Haig, Sir Eric Geddes, Sir William Roberston, General Nivelle, Briand and others to discuss matters related to the forthcoming offensive and matters of rail transportation. The meeting began at 3.30pm and after an hour of discussion about the finer details of transportation to which Lloyd George obviously did not contribute, he suggested that the matter of transportation be discussed at a separate meeting with the interested parties and with that the group broke for tea. The meeting resumed at about 5.30pm and Nivelle outlined his plans for the coming offensive, his 'Grand Plan', and on conclusion asked if there were any questions. At that point Lloyd George, interpreted through Briand said that he wanted Nivelle to tell the whole story, what about your relations with Haig, obviously he wanted to know about the disagreements that had occurred between them and in doing so put Haig on a spot. Haig says that he was surprised at this intimate probing by Lloyd George, but nothing came of it since any differences that they had concerned tactical matters and were not considered part of the overall plan.

The meeting broke again for dinner when LG asked the French delegation to come back after dinner with their suggestions for a command structure. In the light of events that followed it is abundantly clear that Lloyd George had discussed all this with the French beforehand and that the meeting was a sham. After dinner Haig went to see Sir William Robertson who was in a rage about the French proposals that had been passed to him as he was having dinner, ostensibly these French proposals for an Allied command structure had been given to LG not an hour after the meeting had broken for dinner. During the period they were at Calais Lloyd George on two occasions had deliberately avoided personal contact with Douglas Haig, before the meeting Haig had suggested that he and LG should meet privately, this LG managed to avoid on the pretext of meeting with Briand. The second opportunity would have been at or after dinner but LG did not attend saying he was ill, he did not therefore meet with the CIGS or the G.O.C. BEF privately, preferring instead to speak clandestinely with the French contingent.

Robertson pointed out immediately the dangerous position into which Lloyd George was putting the British Forces, they would be brought fully under French command, there was to be no General Officer Commanding the BEF and no General HQ staff. Instead there would be simply a British staff officer based at French GHQ Compeigne and all orders to the British forces would be from Nivelles Chief of Staff via the British Staff liaison officer; that liaison officer was to be Sir Henry Wilson.

It was felt at the time that Lloyd George had prior knowledge of the French proposals, the implications of which were profound, the British armies in France would be under the Command of General Nivelle who in turn was answerable to the French Government, it followed therefore that all British forces would be totally under French control. Haig and Robertson found it unbelievable that Lloyd George could be so naïve, not to mention underhanded, as to contemplate such a move. This was not simply a case of the French suggesting that the British army be under it's command, although Joffre felt that appropriate, this was a British Prime Minister prepared to sell his Military High

Command down the river to satisfy what appears to have been a total lack of trust in the British High Command by the French. There can be no other explanation other than Lloyd George connived with the French to bring about this plan whilst deliberately excluding Robertson and Haig from any discussions. It seemed inconceivable then, and even moreso now, that the French delegation could have left that meeting and within one hour formulated detailed proposals to move the British army under French Command. Lloyd George obviously knew about and contributed to such a plan and agreed its contents before the meeting was held. Field Marshals Robertson and Haig boiled over and they put a flea in Lloyd Georges ear, the love affair with the French and the denigration of the British forces had gone too far, although there is no evidence that Lloyd George ever recognized, or owned to just how contemptuous his behind the scenes dealings with the French had been.

Lloyd George having been convinced of Nivelle's Grand Plan, and having previously openly expressed his contempt for the British High Command, was more than happy to subborn Sir Douglas Haig and place the British army under the command of the French. Nivelle convinced Lloyd George that the French plan would put a swift end to the war, he also thought that by sanctioning it the unacceptable level of casualties would come to an end and the war would be over. However the consequences of such a foolish agreement were, firstly the losses would increase, the British were interested in maintaining the security of the Channel ports, but France was more interested in saving Paris and to that end, since the French were worn out, (Joffre's word for it was exhausted) the British troops would be doing all the fighting having first been moved into the French lines, (this actually happened following the

German March offensive, 1918). When this was made clear to Lloyd George he hastily called a further meeting in London with the Chief of Imperial General Staff, Field Marshal Sir William Robertson, with General Nivelle present, at that meeting the agreed French proposal was set aside as not acceptable to the British Government and a new set of conditions applied. Haig retained full command of the BEF and so was able to negotiate with Nivelle and the British Government to get his own plan off the ground for an attack at the Northern end of the British front at Ypres once the Nivelle Grand plan was out of the way.

Haig was appalled at Lloyd Georges scheming and had lost all trust in his will to support the British High Command in their efforts, the ability of Lloyd George and Sir Douglas Haig to work together towards an end of the war was poor at the best of times, now it was virtually non existent. [29]General Gough makes reference to a visit that he made to GHQ where he spoke with Field Marshal Haig and noted that he showed signs of being worried. He said to me 'of course if they (the Government) don't approve of me, they had better appoint someone else'-- and then glancing at me rather suspiciously it seemed, he added—'is it going to be you?' He then went on to say that there was no question as to who was the better Prime Minister to serve under, Asquith or Lloyd George. He found that Asquith was loyally supportive and receptive of his suggestions and would do his best to see these implemented whereas Lloyd George far from helping would place every obstacle in his way, ---'in fact he hampers the conduct of the war'. Lloyd George had only been appointed Prime Minister in early Dec 1916 but Haig had long had him summed up as regards his attitude to the British High Command, the relationship between Lloyd George and Douglas Haig was akin to that of a dog and a lamppost.

Field Marshal Sir Henry Wilson also comments in his diaries on a conversation with Lord Milner who was a member of the War Cabinet.[30] --- 'he says that Lord Milner told him that Lloyd George wanted to get rid of Douglas Haig. Wilson replied that he would have nothing to do with that sort of business and that if the War Cabinet did not did not approve of Haig then they ought to remove him, but not as a result of any discussion that Lloyd George may have had with General Nivelle'. On being appointed Secretary of State for War after Kitcheners demise, Lloyd George had visited Haig in France and on his return to England had made several disparaging comments about him, he was saddened by the enormous casualties and openly stated that he considered the Battle of the Somme a disaster. It was perhaps not surprising that he sought to change the order of things when he became Prime Minister and had been looking for ammunition from French sources that he could use against Haig. Somehow Lloyd George seemed to have lost sight of the fact that the Somme offensive was a French initiative, that it was opposed by Douglas Haig and that it was Lloyd George who committed him to the French proposals by agreeing to them at the Chantilly conference.

At the end of 1916 the British settled down in their new winter quarters in depressing circumstances of rain, hail and snow, the weather was appalling but they were still harassing the enemy taking several thousand German prisoners in January and February 1917. The enemy counter attacks had subsided although they staunchly defended the villages that they occupied from well-concealed machine gun nests, the reason for that gradually became clear. The army air corps flights over the German positions had reported extensive new defences being built well behind their existing lines, these were no small undertaking but a massive defence system long a line from close to Arras for some 75 miles to Soissons known as the 'Hindenberg line', it linked to the Drocourt-Queant line that extended north to the west of Armentieres. It was to the Hindenberg Line that the Germans withdrew leaving the allies to occupy the devastated ground that they had vacated. Roads, railways, bridges etc all laid to ruin and within that desolate area the Germans left well concealed machine gun outposts that posed real danger to the troops as they moved onto the new ground. The new German defences were obviously constructed to resist any sort of attack and were intended to be far more permanent than anything that had previously existed. It consisted of deep entrenchments on a first, second and third line with considerable distances between each line, these defences were considered by the Germans to be impregnable by the enemy.

The winter and early spring conditions continued to be almost unbearable and as the push forward continued it became clear that the Germans were in retreat, the new ground that they occupied that was previously untouched behind the German lines was now in ruins, roads, bridges, villages and churches etc. In order to secure the needs of transport and communication the British troops were kept busy with road and bridge construction along with trenching in order to hold their newly won positions, it was the worst winter of the war and the main enemy during that period was mud. During the month of March the flying Corps was busy over the German lines and feeding back information about the massive adjustment that the Germans had made in moving back 10 miles or so to the Hindenberg line. They were taking heavy losses as a result of newer and better aircraft that had been brought into service by the Germans.

During his meeting with Lloyd George, Nivelle had

expressed a wish that Sir Henry Wilson join his staff at Compeigne as the British Staff Officer to the French High Command. In the event the French proposals were of course thrown out but a watered down version was adopted and this left the opportunity for Nivelle to again seek to have Sir Henry by his side. In a discussion with Wilson, Nivelle confided that it would be impossible for Haig and himself to work together effectively without Wilson as a go between; Wilson was by all accounts indispensable (we can no longer ask him but his diaries leave us in no doubt). Although he had railed against taking the post to Haig, Milner & Robertson, Wilson promised Nivelle that he would speak with Haig about the matter. When they met at GHQ Haig told Wilson that he had received orders on occasions from General Nivelle regarding action he was to take regarding the coming offensive that left Haig with the feeling that he was in a master and dog situation, he felt that Nivelle had ignored the fact that the French proposal that the British Army be placed under French command had not been adopted and treated Haig as a subordinate. Henry Wilson accepted the post and subsequently was able to calm matters by pointing out to General Nivelle that Field Marshal Haig would be more likely to respond positively if he were treated as an equal, which from then he most certainly was. Haig on the other hand, even though he was looking to action in the North, was keen to support the French in line with his original orders from Lord Kitchener, and within what he considered his capabilities, with Wilson liaising he felt things would improve and for the short time that Nivelle was C. in C. they respected each others positions and worked well together.

There has been a lot of harsh comment about Haig and his command of the British Forces, particularly with regard to The Somme, Arras, Cambrai and Passchendaele. It is as well to remember that Haig was not the architect of the first two battles and was not at all keen to being involved in either one of them, but as C. in C. of the Expeditionary Force he was charged with supporting the French in the best possible way. Of course the decision to carry out these offensives was taken by the politicians of both countries and already we have seen that Lloyd George was quite prepared to put the British Forces in France under the command of a French General, what a disaster that would have been. Haig was not there to conduct some grand strategy aimed at defeating the Germans; that was never a possibility, but on Kitchener's original orders he was there to support France. This was a war of attrition, there was no possibility that either side could sweep the enemy away, that became clear only by launching attack after attack against the wire and machine guns, with the resulting cost in human life to both sides. It also resulted in loss of faith in the Allied military leaders who were grasping at initiatives that might see a breakthrough; in the demoralisation of troops and the mass mutinies in the French army. Haig may not have been a genius; it seems that we were a little short on military genius, but we had good talkers like Henry Wilson and Brigadier General Charteris who kept everyone buoyant. But the French and Germans had also lost faith in their top commanders and got rid of them so Haig was in good company, he was still there, his staff said not a bad word about him and that might indicate that they found him a good leader. He was not without his faults of course, and to read some of the comments about him one would wonder how he ever attained the rank that he did. Perhaps Haig's strengths lay not in being a genius on the battlefield but in being a good soldier, able to maintain 'good order and military discipline' for the rest he did what he was told without question and if that involved loss of life on an epic scale then that just had to be. In this world there are 'doer's' and 'thinkers', Haig was a doer, Wilson was a thinker.

21

The 4ᵗʰ & 8ᵗʰ Battalions the East Lancashire Regiment

My paternal grandfather was born in Blackburn in 1882, he married when he was quite young, his wife Maria was born at Houghton Bottoms between Blackburn and Leyland in Lancashire and later moved to live in Blackburn. He was a territorial and was called up for service in WWI with the 4ᵗʰ battalion the East Lancashire Regiment and later was transferred to the 8ᵗʰ Service battalion. He was killed on a bitterly cold and snow-swept morning on the third day of the Battle of Arras, posted 'missing presumed dead'. His story is that of thousands of men who went and never came back; this briefly follows his time in the 8th East Lancashire Regiment that fought at Arras, an account that could be that of any one of the thousands that were conscripted to battalions throughout the country, and how events developed for them from the moment of call up.

THE RIFLE

"What do you do with your rifle son"?
"I clean it every day, and rub it with an oily rag,
To keep the rust away,
I slope, present, and port the thing,
When sweating on parade.
I strop my razor on the thing,
The bayonet stand is made,
For me to hang my mirror on.

I often use it too,
As a handle for the Dixie, sir,
To lug around the stew".
"But did you ever fire it son?
"Just once, but never more.
I fired it at a German trench'
And then my work was o'er.
The Sergeant down the barrel glanced,
And then he said to me,
Your rifles dirty, penalty, seven days C.B.

***

With the declaration of war in August 1914 began mobilisation, the various companies of the 4th battalion The East Lancashire regiment started to report to the Battalion HQ and for several days were billeted there, this was the 4th battalion depot at Canterbury St. Barracks in the centre of Blackburn. On the 19th of August they marched over Haslingden Moor the 16 miles to Bury, the 5th battalion ELR Burnley and district, had marched from Burnley down the Rossendale Valley to Bury where both battalions remained billeted, re-kitting and training for almost three weeks. On the 9th of September the 4th Battalion followed the 5th by train to Southampton where they embarked on the 'SS Deseado', a first class cruise liner of the Royal Mail Line converted to troopship. The following day they sailed for Egypt as part of a convoy with a Royal Naval escort. There was tremendous disappointment amongst the men of the Brigade that they were not going to France and Flanders to join in the action, but there were those of the 4th battalion who were even more disappointed at not even leaving Bury.

Friday night in the billet

Gie' me a tin o' blackin' Gie mi' some oil for mi' lamp'
Gie' me a sheet o' emery, gei me a tuppeny stamp,
Ere' gie' mi' one of your chinstraps, reach me your polishing rags,
Blimey ain't this an existence, 'ere gimme' a packet of fags.

***

When the 4th Battalion The East Lancashire Regiment (now known as the 1/4th for the duration of the War) left Chesham Fold Camp en-route to Egypt, there were a number of men left behind, some of these were perhaps veterans of the South African War, soldiers able to contribute to the training of the rush of raw recruits who were enlisting in the training and 'service' battalions, others were maybe not fit for overseas service or too old for front line duties. My great uncle Benjamin

Leaver became one of the core group around which the 2/4th battalion was formed and stayed at Bury training recruits until the dire necessity for troop replacements at the 3rd battle of Ypres (Passchendaele) in 1917 saw him moved into the front line. He had been wounded in the Boer War, and as an old soldier he was killed by a sniper bullet at Zonnebeke, Passchendaele on The 11th of October 1917.

John, my grandfather was transferred from 4th Battalion to Pokesdown in Wiltshire and was part of the nucleus forming the new 8th (service) Battalion East Lancashire Regiment. The 8th spent time in Colchester and on the Salisbury Plain undergoing intensive training and honing their skills in readiness to take their place at the front, whereas the new 2/4th at Bury became a training Battalion sending up replacements to the front line Battalions

The 'Battle of Arras' was a tactical diversion aimed at taking German divisions away from the Champagne area to enable the new French Commander in Chief, General Nivelle to mount his ostensibly, brilliant offensive. Nivelle's plans seemed to offer a means of making progress and he was given the full support of the French and British Governments. His intention was to make a breach in the enemy lines through which would pour allied forces to attack the Germans from behind (the breach being made by French Forces). To enable Nivelle to relieve sufficient of his French Divisions in carrying out this 'Grand Plan' he needed the British to extend their front further South to take in the French line between the River Somme and the River Oise, this would require a further commitment of some 6-8 Divisions, Douglas Haig baulked at this. He said that in order to relieve the French and take on the extended line he would need to have several Divisions diverted from Salonika to the Western Front. He maintained that five of his fifty-five divisions were not available for one reason or another; sickness, injury etc therefore his resources were already stretched. His anxiety was of little concern to the new Prime Minister, David Lloyd George, indeed he might well have relished the idea that he could oppose Haig's viewpoint since he had made plain the fact that he had no confidence in him. However quite apart from his manpower concerns, Haig, like several of Nivelles HQ staff, had no confidence in Nivelle's plan.

22

The Battle of Arras

The battle was scheduled to commence on the 8th of April but was put back to zero hour 5.30 am April 9th 1917. For the previous five days there had been a continuous artillery barrage in what was the heaviest bombardment the British had ever made, it involved the use of some 3400 guns and on the 9th after a few initial hold-ups the attack was a stunning success, on the first and second days of the battle all objectives were taken except for the little hill town of Monchy Le Preux where the Royal Fusiliers found very heavy resistance. The town was on a high promontory and was well defended by the Germans; from Monchy they could see the plain in front of them as far as Arras and therefore able to observe every move that the British made, they were not likely to give up such a valuable piece of high ground easily. In order to counteract this German advantage in mounting the attack from Arras and to conceal the activities of the British troops as they massed ready for the attack, it had been necessary to use the huge caves on the east side of Arras and even to extend them.

The following account briefly covers a section of the attacking front that was allotted to the 112th brigade, the 8th East Lancashire Regt., 6th Bedfordshire, 10th Loyal North Lancashire Regiment and the 11th Royal Warwickshire and in particular the 8th East Lancashire Regt my grandfathers battalion, the build up to the Battle of Arras for that battalion and the route they had taken to get there.

The 8th battalion sailed from Dover and arrived at

Boulogne the next morning, their ship having been escorted by a destroyer. They disembarked and marched from the quayside with the band playing to the barracks nearby followed by "half the female population of the town". Next morning the battalion formed up and carried out what was described as a "triumphal march" through the town Before taking time off to send postcards and exchange money etc. Late the following night, August 2nd, the battalion started by train northwards towards Calais rejoining the battalion advance party who were already on the train having landed earlier and further south at the port of Le Havre, their destination, the outskirts of Ardres, was finally arrived at after a circuitous march from a village station.

Over the next few days the battalion marched via Nordasques to St Omer where they joined the rest of the 112th Brigade, they then marched on to Hazebrouck where on The 8th of August the G.O.C. Second Army, Lt. General Sir Herbert Plumer, inspected the battalion. It speaks highly of the General that he took the time to meet and inspect this new brigade almost within the week of arrival.

The Brigade to which the 8th East Lanc's belonged constituted 4 Battalions, the others being, The 8th Bedfordshire's, 11th Warwickshire's and the 10th Loyal North Lancashire Regiment, they were one of the three brigades making up the 37th Division, (110th, 111th and 112th) in the 2nd Corps of the Second Army. The Brigade would stay together through all the battles that they fought in but shifting regularly from Corps to Corps and across the various Armies designated First to Fifth.

Toward the end of August the 37th division moved south, by train to Doullens and then marched to Mailly-Maillet just north of Albert and close to the German front line. Here the battalions were split up and allocated to regiments in the front line in order to gain experience in the front line trenches. The 8th ELR started to receive the first instruction in trench Warfare when the four companies A, B, C & D were attached to the regiments of the 12th Brigade, (4th Div.) which were, The Lancashire Fusiliers, The Kings Own Royal Regt. (Lancaster), The South Lancashire Regiment and the Essex Regiment. These were regular battalions that were at the battle of Le Cateau. They had the experience of night patrols to locate German wire cutting parties, snipers and bombing parties etc. The four companies of my Grandfathers battalion the 8th ELR, were now in the front line and finding it exhilarating, each company was keen to learn and prove themselves in the front line, by the time they were relieved by the Seaforth Highlanders they had suffered casualties and were beginning to know first hand what the war was about. On being relieved they moved back to Englbelmer for a three-day rest period.

On the 5th of September the Battalion marched from Bertrancourt to billets at St Amand, where they were accommodated in barns, on the 15th of September the 8th ELR relieved the 10th Royal Fusiliers and for the first time held a section of the front line. This is where they stayed for several months, two weeks in the trenches and two weeks in the billets. A description of the church at Foncquevillers, the little village in ruins through which they had to pass to the front line, and taken from the 'History of the East Lancashire Regiment' says simply. "The church although still standing had gaping holes everywhere and was roofless". I paused at that point to wonder just how many churches in towns and villages in Northern France and Belgium had suffered that same fate, it is obvious that there was a sadness amongst the soldiers on the front line at the terrible damage done to the lovely old buildings in the

towns and villages and yet they counted for nothing
when weighed against the enormous loss of life by HE,
shrapnel and machine gunfire.

A SOLDIERS PRAYER

Givenchy village lies a wreck, Givenchy
church is bare,
No more the village maidens come to say their
vespers there.
The alter rails are wrenched apart, with rubble
littered o'er,
The sacred, broken sanctuary lamp lies broken
on the floor.
And mute upon the crucifix he looks upon it all,
The Great white Christ the shrapnel scourged
upon the eastern wall.
He sees the churchyard delved by shells, the
tombstone flung about,
Dead men's skulls, and white, white bones the
shells have shovelled out.

The trenches running line by line, through
meadow fields of green,
The bayonets on the parapet, the wasting flesh
between.
Around Givenchy's ruined church the levels
poppy red,
is set-aside for silent hosts, the legions of the
dead.

And when at night on sentry go, with danger
keeping tryst,
I see upon the crucifix the blood stained form of
Christ.

Defiled and maimed, the merciful, on vigil all
the time,
Pitying his children's wrath, their passions and
their crime.

Mute, mute he hangs upon his cross, the symbol
of his pain,
And as men scourged him long ago, they
scourged him once again.
There in the lonely, war lit night, to Christ the
Lord I call,
Forgive the ones who work thee harm, O Lord
forgive us all.

***

The trenches were in good condition in this part of the
line with ample dugouts and wire beds, after about a
week, night patrols started to go out and one humorous
account shows how one patrol almost managed to wipe
itself out and was a sharp lesson to those involved. It
seems that in the pitch black the patrol broke up and
lost touch with each other, the guards in the trenches
could hear bombs going off and could only wonder at
what was happening. When the various members of the
squad got back they reported that they had all met 'en-
emy' patrols and had bombed them, until they realised
they were bombing each other. Luckily on this occasion
there were no casualties. However almost on every tour
in the line some were killed and others wounded, often
there would be heavy casualties especially if an attack
was mounted and counter attack by the other side, but
shelling itself took the greatest toll.
 Below. photo of 4th Battalion East Lanc's Regt.
Front line troops in a saphead at Givenchy. 'Grub up' time
whilst one keeps an eye on the German lines. Note the peri-
scope is wrapped to stop sun glinting and aiding snipers

A Royal Horse Artillery 18 pounder field gun.

The periods at St. Amand out of the line was usually spent fulfilling fatigues and providing support for their opposite number in the line, the 10th Royal Fusiliers. One welcome development was the installation of hot baths at the divisional HQ 4 miles away, this allowed them to have a hot soak and change their underclothes every three weeks. The mind boggles at the enormous discomfort suffered by the men in the trenches and that was the easy part of their existence, during periods of heavy shelling or other enemy activity it was often not possible for relief's to get through or for food to be brought up to the lines. And yet they might be knee deep in mud and exhausted from mounting attacks or repulsing enemy attacks. Taking your boots off at any time in the line was a punishable offence.

As time went on the weather worsened into November and coupled with the Heavy German shelling the trenches became impassable. So much so that it was necessary to attempt relief over the top until the German machine-gun fire put a stop to it. Each spell in the line was more miserable than the last; the trenches sometimes waste deep in water and the German shelling all the time increasing. At this time ammunition for the British guns was in very short supply and may have been perhaps only 5 rounds per gun per day. The casualties also increased and the whole routine took on a monotonous grind. It was during this period that the Battalion won it's first VC. This account is taken from the Regimental History of the East Lancashire Regiment.

At 'stand to' one morning Pte. Young saw Sgt. Allen lying wounded in front of our wire and immediately went to his rescue. Climbing the parapet, he received a bullet that shattered his lower jaw, undeterred and heedless of the enemy fire, he pushed on and reached

Sgt. Allen by which time Pte.Green had come to assist him, together they brought him in. Later, terribly wounded, as he was, Pte. Young walked up to the village dressing station. For this gallant act he received the Victoria Cross, while Pte. Green was given the D.C.M. (Distinguished Conduct Medal)

The routine was broken only by heavier bombardments and limited attacks by the Germans, two officers were killed by sniper fire, Lt. Winser hit in the head and Capt. Hammond in the thigh, both died a few days later, so pressed was the medical support that a wound of any sort could prove fatal through loss of blood despite the best efforts of the medical orderlies. The enemy activity increased and the casualties with it, in July 1916 the 1st Battle of the Somme began with massive bombardments of the enemy positions and the use of gas, something that the Germans had first used, the reaction was, quote 'like putting a stick in a wasps nest'. The men where building up to the excitement of going over the top and were busy polishing their bayonets as they watched the devastation wreaked by the heavy guns.

And so life went on until on the 4th of April 1917 the 8th battalion the East Lancashire Regiment left for Arras, from Rebreuviette they marched via Liencourt, Avesnes le Comte, Hauteville, and Wanquentin and on to Warlus. They arrived on the morning of the 8th of April where the whole of the 112th brigade met and bivouacked in a field. At 3.30am the next morning in pouring rain the Regiment was stood to and set off to march the six kilometres to d'Amiens in the western suburbs of Arras. This was the start of Battle of Arras.

MARCHING

I fancy it's not 'arf me chance,
To go on plodding neath my pack.
Parading like a snail through France,
My 'ouse upon me blooming back.

My wants are few but what I need,
Aint not so much of bully stew,
Nor biscuits that's a mongrels feed'
But Matey, just twix me and you.

When winks the early evening star,
And shadows o'er the trenches come.
I wish the Sergeants brought a jar,
And issues double tots of rum.

***

The battle was due to begin that day but it was put back until the 9th, in any case the 8th East Lanc's were in reserve and not needed until the final assault on Moncy le preux. When the 3rd, 12th and 15th divisions had taken their objectives by passing the Black, Blue and Brown lines, the 37th division, of which the 8th East Lanc's were part, would then pass through their lines for the final assault. A front had been allocated to the 8th East Lanc's and the 6th Bedfordshire's along the Northeast side of the of the Arras/Cambrai road, They were to be supported by the 10th Loyal North Lancashire Regt. and the 11th Royal Warwickshire Regt.

The 8th Kings Own had breakfast, it stopped raining and the sun came out, welcome after the bitter cold

1916/17 winter. By 9.00am the battalion entering the town to occupy the old British trenches on the Arras/Cambrai road. At about 1.30pm the Battalion moved up to the German trenches that had been cleared by the troops that went in on the first wave, their job was now to capture the final objective that was the Brown line.

It was after 5.00pm when they moved up again for the final push, but things were not going right and there was a difficult obstacle to be cleared in the Tilloy les Mofflaines area. A joint effort by two companies of the Essex Regiment and 'A' company of the 8th East Lanc's was unsuccessful in clearing the German trenches. 'A' company under Captain Edmondson had entered the German trenches at two points with bombing groups and Lewis gunners as well a riflemen, however the Essex companies were unable to co-operate and 'A' company had to retreat. It was now dark, heavy snow was falling, and it was bitterly cold. Early next morning the 37th Div. was moved back to the old German trenches until the brown line objective had been achieved ready for them to launch the final attack on the front at Monchy le Preux and on the line between the Arras/Cambrai road and the River Scarpe.

At 1.30pm on the 10th of April, after a short delay, they were off, having been lined up ready to go they made excellent progress with few casualties, but the attack was 24 hours late and that had given the enemy time to prepare, moving in heavy artillery and reinforcements allowed by the quick defeat of Nivelle's offensive, which of course was the main offensive. Regardless of this the 37th Div. was informed that there would be no artillery to cover them until it could be moved up which would be no sooner than 2 hours later.

At this point the Germans were clearly seen digging in between Moncy-le-Preux and the Cambrai Arras road, there was also increasingly heavy artillery fire from heavy field guns and 4.2 howitzers. The 111th brigade were meeting stiff opposition in front of Moncy-le-Preux and the East Lanc's company under Captain Wright had lost touch with the 10th Royal Fusiliers who were on the right of the 111th Brigade front (left of the 112th Brigade). In the event Captain Wright had been killed and the East Lanc's and the Bedfordshire's were under heavy machine gun and rifle fire but managed to drive forward in rushes taking Les Fosses farm adjacent to the Arras-Cambrai road in a joint attack around 5.30pm.

Soon after this the advance was halted by heavy German short-range fire and an artillery officer came forward to say that the guns were ready to cover them if they knew where they were (they were asking for the range). But heavy snow started to fall and the only means of communication was by runner. Taking advantage of a heavy snowstorm the attack pressed forward for several hundred yards and started digging in just short of the La Bergere - Monchy-le-Preux road at around 6pm, soon after signallers arrived to lay a line to Brigade H.Q.

They pressed forward as soon as possible but could not make much ground against the enemy, heavy snow and the bitter cold. Rations were brought up and there was a 'Tommy cooker' for every two men that ensured everyone got a hot drink. As they settled for the night in that freezing cold it is recorded, as mentioned in a previous chapter, that a flock of wild geese passed overhead honking as they went, that must have been a poignant moment during that break in the fighting, if anything would mark out that night from all the rest then surely it was those geese and it is not hard to imagine the thoughts the men must have had of peace and home.

Orders for the whole of the 37th Div. to attack at 5.15am on the 11th were not received until 4.30am on that day by the 112th brigade, a message was received saying that a covering barrage would be laid down at 5.00am and lifted at 5.30am, (which was of course received far too late) and that the advance was to continue. This of course left very little time to get the orders out to the companies who were deployed in advance of the La-Bergere – Moncy le Preux road. There is however no detailed information recorded in the war diaries as to the exact positions of the companies at this juncture and therefore it would be impossible to know at this stage any precise detail of what happened. The orders for the 112th brigade were that the 11th Warwickshire Regt. and the 10th Loyal North Lancashire regiment were to pass through the lines of the 8th East Lancashire Regiment And the Bedfordshire Regt. with the objective of capturing Guemappe on the right and to join up with the 111th brigade on the left.

When the Loyal North Lancashire Regt. Passed through the other Battalions they came under very heavy fire from the front and the left flank which created great confusion, at this point the two leading companies of the 8th East Lanc's, led by Capt. Edmondson, dashed forward, Edmundson was immediately killed. The other two companies also moved forward and became mixed with the Loyal North Lancashire's, the 11th Warwick's and elements of the cavalry all of course were dug in ahead of the La-Bergere – Monchy-le-Preux road.

There was now only one officer left with the four companies and Lieutenant Taylor, although slightly wounded, went up from battalion headquarters. Little could be done by way of reorganisation as a result of counter attacks by the enemy, all of which were repulsed but by the time that the battalion was relieved on the night of the 11th/12th that had been achieved. The battalion pulled back to Tilloy-les-Mouflaines on relief and they once more had hot food, the following day they went back to Wanquentin and then Ambrines where they stayed until the 22nd cleaning up training and resting.

The battalion had marched into Arras on the morning of the 8th and by the 11th they were out of the front line for a short while, in that time my grandfather was one of those left behind, like Capt. Edmondson, never to be seen again. He was killed on the 11th in that desperate push forward in support of the Loyals and so he was in the final confused push beyond the La-Bergere – Moncy-le-Preux road when he was obliterated, maybe blown to shreds by a shell or lost in the mud of a shell hole like so many others in that tragic War, Just a wife and six more children without a father. My father was nine years 5 months old at the time and he had not known his father for the last two years anyway, so it is not really surprising that he never mentioned him.

I have often wished that I could have known that little bit more about the movements of the 8th Battalion East Lanc's in this one action, and through that the general movements of my grandfather, the company he was with that morning and just what happened at each stage during the 9th, 10th, and 11th of April 1917 to the point where he was killed. It would be impossible to know anything other than the broad details under normal circumstances and photographs are the thing that really capture a moment in time, there was however a significant occurrence that created a snapshot of what he was doing at a precise moment, it was not a visual one but one that nonetheless created that sort of immediate contact, as a result of it I do have some feeling that I share his experience for one fleeting moment. The incident, mentioned earlier, occurred as the battalion broke off their engagement with the Germans at about 5.30pm on the evening of the 10th. The ration parties managed to get hot tea brought up to the men through the lines, as they rested the men looked up to see a flock of geese honking as they winged their way through the crisp, clear evening air. That one fleeting moment is to me like a photograph, a moment captured in time, although I really know nothing of the detail of what happened to my grandfather during the war, I do know just for one brief moment exactly what he was doing, like a snapshot I can link that action to a time, he was looking up at those geese and that gives me a really good feeling. It is something that all the men saw and through it no doubt recognised the irony of their situation, the freedom of those geese on the wing, unknown to my grandfather however, death was but a few hours sleep away.

The troops of the British New Army had a very successful first day and the Canadians had an even greater victory by taking Vimy Ridge. The view from the ridge as seen by General Spears was quote, 'the plain of Douai lay below, a glimpse of another world, behind me a sea of churned up mud---beyond on the German side peaceful countryside with villages that from a distance appeared to be untouched by war. The Canadians were justly euphoric at the extent of their success with German artillery emplacements abandoned on the lower slopes of the Ridge. The Third and Fifth Armies continued to push forward but it became obvious that the lack of mobility on the 10th brought the 3rd Army to a halt and with that the opportunity that Haig had sought by turning the German flank had been lost.

The raw recruits of the New army had learned a great deal and in a way become battle hardened, unfortunately at Arras the mode of battle in those early stages had changed briefly from dogged trench warfare and wearing down tactics to a highly mobile war. Officers who had little or no experience of mobile warfare again in a learning situation, led these relatively new recruits; they lacked the necessary equipment and were moving across ground that had been churned up by five days of bombardment. The result was that the gains made on the 9th were not followed up before the Germans were able to bring up reserves. To borrow Churchill's watchword it was now a matter of 'buggering on' as the war once again took on that slow grind, the incessant wearing down of the enemy with small attacks along the front and at no small cost in casualties.

The situation was no better For Gough's Fifth Army as it attacked east from Bullecourt toward the Arras Cambrai road against heavily fortified German line. Had the Third Army managed to push past Moncy le Preux they would have quickly met up with the Fifth Army and the possibility of turning the German flank, but that did not happen. On the 11th the Australian Division attacked supported by tanks, none of which made it to the enemy wire Before being knocked out by artillery, although the Australians routed the enemy they were unable to hold on to the ground they had gained against a heavy German counter attack and they were pushed all the way back. On the 12th the Germans mounted a massive attack during which the Australians took heavy casualties, strung out thinly as they were over a wide section. On the following day, the 16th, after several delays and apologies the French attacked with fifty Divisions and 3000 guns. The weather was appalling; snow and sleet coupled with mud and the steep sides of the Aisne were the initial problems but almost as soon as it began word was coming back that the wire had not been cut, the West African troops that the French were using extensively were frozen stiff and unable to carry their weapons other than under their arms, they were unable to fix bayonets because of frozen hands and as the approached the still intact wire they were mown down by the enemy.

In General Gough's own words it was 'a miserable failure, (there is no other word)'. It was also clear that having fully defeated the Nivelle Grand Plan the Germans were rapidly transferring divisions to face the British Third Army under General Byng with the intention that they would yield no further ground in front of Arras.

One of the big problems with General Nivelle's plan was that everyone knew about it long before the event, it had been openly discussed in Paris and even Douglas Haig had called a interview to discuss the proposed plans. Haig said that he had revealed full details of the Nivelle plan but did not realise that the three Frenchmen present were journalists; the result was that the Germans knew all about it and were able to prepare for the attack. It was also reported that the Germans actually had a typed copy of the plan days before the battle. The effect of the defeat on the French Armies was profound; they had gone into battle with their tales up determined to rid France of the German menace, but a senior French General commented that if this battle was lost the French would not fight again, perhaps there was talk of mutiny amongst the troops, previously at Verdun there had been mutinies that were kept quiet and the British knew little of.

Sir William Robertson the C.I.G.S had written to Haig and said 'Poor Nivelle, he is going in with a rope round his neck', the politicians were very doubtful about the plan and he had been getting reports of serious misgivings from his Divisional Commanders. Joffre had said it, the French troops are exhausted and he was probably sacked as a result, there was no room for pessimism. Now that the French attacks had been repulsed by the Germans there were signs of mutiny that spread very quickly through the French Armies. Again the British were kept in the dark as to the extent but the French government became alarmed at this threat to the allies. Nivelle was immediately removed; his grandiose plan had not worked and had left France in terror of where it might end. It was later reported that some 200,000 French troops had mutinied. It was the High Command of this French army that Lloyd George was so happy to hand over full command of the British Army in France to, it would be hard to imagine that Lloyd Georges judgement would ever be worth a jot to anyone in the British High Command in future.

I was helped by, and I am greatly indebted to, the curator of the East Lancashire Regiment Museum at Townley Hall, Burnley in searching for material regarding the East Lancashire Regt and the movements of my grandfather in the early 1980's, nothing was too much trouble for him and I have to say to my discredit that I now cannot remember his name. The information was there for my father to know in his lifetime but all he ever knew was that his father was killed at Arras, not where or exactly when nor the miserable, bitter cold, snow covered dawn where he died, and I do not think he even knew that his Fathers name is engraved on the Memorial at Faubourg D'Amiens along with about 30,000 others killed in that one salient.

At the end of 1916 the British High Command considered that the outcome of the Somme offensive, the Germans retreat to the Hindenberg Line and the peace proposals put forward by Germany were indications that the Allies were making progress, they saw that the morale of the British troops was high and thoughts turned to the Flanders offensive. The behind the scenes conniving by Lloyd George and the French saw any such plans sidelined at least until the autumn of 1917.

Now the way was clear to dust off those plans and hope that at last Haig's long sought after battle plan could become a reality. In order for any such plan to be undertaken there needed to be a firm assurance that the German divisions currently tied up on the Russian front would not become available for transfer to the Western Front.

The British Army was making whatever progress there was, assisted by the French in that they kept the German divisions busy from the Oise to the Swiss border, but the French were fit only for defensive operations at that time and the British, although able to take on the enemy in Flanders with the more than fair chance of winning, could not realistically face that situation if the Russian front divisions were released. Any planned offensive also depended on War Cabinet approval and although supportive of the plan put forward by Haig they were equally concerned at the French ability to play a full part. The War Cabinet wanted assurances that the French would agree to a full commitment of French forces consistently and throughout the offensive.

Haig met with Petain at Amiens in May 1917 having already made available details of the planned operation. At that meeting Haig made it clear that before the British War Cabinet could consider approving the planned Ypres offensive they would have to have an assurance of a solid French commitment to a combined offensive. Haig went on to ask Petain if he was in a position to give those assurances, i.e. was he in command of the French forces and if he was did he intend to fulfil the promise made at the earlier Paris Conference. At this time but unbeknown to the British, the mutiny in the French Army was still at an early stage and later was to get far worse. Petain was trying to bring the matter under control by allotting more time for leave and R & R whilst reducing the length of time that men spent in the line but this information was not made available to Douglas Haig at that time. There had been a number of executions of the mutinous ringleaders and it was said that several hundred troops were herded into a section of no mans land and bombed by their own artillery. The British had heard rumours but were fed only the information that the French wanted them to know, nevertheless within GHQ there was little faith in the ability or will of the French Army to take the fight to the enemy.

Haig was quite insistent that Petain should answer his queries and readily accepted Petain at his word when he said that he would give his total support to Haig and keep the German divisions busy to the extent that they would be unable to transfer units to oppose the British front. Henry Wilson was present at the Amiens meeting and was not impressed with the fact that Haig had so readily accepted Petain's word. At this time Wilson was still the British Staff liaison officer to the French, but Nivelle had been got rid of and Petain having replaced Nivelle did not want Wilson on his staff, he did not trust him and felt that he should go, the rest of the French GHQ also saw him as a Nivelle supporter and shut him out. Wilson contacted Haig and stated his case, that he wanted out but felt that there was no place for him and that Haig did not want him back. Haig immediately put him at ease by saying that although he would rather have him as an important link between the allies, he would welcome his return to GHQ forthwith. Wilson's first move was to put pressure on Petain and have him set down in writing exactly how he was going to meet the commitments he had made to the combined British/French offensive, the outcome was what Wilson had suspected all along, that Petain had no intention of supporting Haig to anything other than what he felt the French army could sustain, in effect he would decide how far he could go and would go no further irrespective of the level of commitment to the offensive, therefore his reply in writing fell far short of what he had promised and had actually misled Haig into thinking, i.e. that he could wholly rely on the French C. in C. for support when in fact that was far from the case. Petain was only interested in defending his front and bringing the French Army back under control.

Petain had already told Wilson that he did not agree with Haig's plan, that it was too ambitious and too wide a front, he favoured attacks in depth on a narrow front with artillery and aircraft but not infantry. Wilson himself, although not in agreement with Petain, was also of the opinion that Haig's plan was misguided. Foch had made some scathing remarks to Wilson when they met in Paris in May, about who had suggested that Haig go on 'a ducks march through the inundations to Ostend and Zeebrugge' saying that the whole thing was futile and dangerous. Haig ignored what he considered to be negative comments, he played down the seriousness of the French lack of zeal, not really knowing that the underlying problem was mutiny, there was also the fact that he could not rely on French support. He also ignored the very important arguments put forward regarding the state of the ground, The Times correspondent, Colonel Repington had met with C.I.G.S and spoken at length about the dire consequences of attempting a breakout of the Ypres salient.

The area was low lying and largely below sea level, Flemish farmers who had developed a network of canals and drainage ditches that kept the fields from becoming waterlogged for most of the year had worked it for hundreds of years. However, in normal times the whole area was for the most part a wetland, but these were not normal times. At the outbreak of war the Belgians had flooded the area in order to slow the German advance and so now the water table was permanently high and flooding was frequent, there was also a desperate shortage of fresh water since the surface water had permeated and contaminated the artesian wells. It was impossible to dig trenches since they simply filled with water, the best they could do was to dig shallow dugouts and supplement these with parapets but there was no getting away from the deep, sticky mud and the trenches that were often knee deep in water. General Gough said 'No battle in history was ever fought under such conditions as that of Passchendaele'.

Repington along with others pointed out that mounting an offensive in this sort of terrain would be difficult enough, but how much worse was it going to be if there was to be a massive and sustained artillery barrage for days before an attack followed by a creeping barrage in front of the troops as they advanced After all the terrain had been under constant artillery battering for the previous three years and was already a barren landscape. Not only was the land waterlogged through lack of drainage the water was stagnant and the men being relieved at the front were coming back caked with mud and stinking, It was not hard to imagine the terrible conditions that the troops would be operating under but Haig chose to ignore this. None of these negative comments from various sources condemning Haig's plans were made known to the British Government, therefore there appeared to be no reason why it should not go ahead, particularly if there was a possibility that the ports of Ostend and Zeebrugge could be captured. The most eminent and influential military thinkers of the 20th Century, J.F.C. Fuller was to later comment that to have the B.E.F confront the German army alone and in such conditions 'was an act of sheer pigheadedness on the part of Field Marshal Haig'. However the opportunity for Douglas Haig to score a massive victory before the Americans came on the scene was irresistible, it was what he had long believed in and on becoming C. in C. had planned for. He wanted victory for the B.E.F. and to show that the Germans could be defeated, he carried on with his plan long after it should have been abandoned and that was what prompted the comment from J.F.C. Fuller.

The state of mutinous uprising in the French Army became progressively more acute and as a result the initial scheduled attacks by the French in June were abandoned. Petain sent one of his aides to the British GHQ with the intention of explaining away the need to postpone the attack that would sound plausible, without fully revealing the state of affairs regarding the level of indiscipline amongst the French troops and how that impacted on the readiness of the French Army to undertake the initial attack on the 2nd of June as planned. The June attack was abandoned but the planned July attack was not affected and would go ahead. The French explanation for all this was simply that the June attack was to be put back to the July date, a convenient way of putting off the June attack if ever there was one. The extent of the mutiny in the French Army was never really known to the British even though Petain had regularly visited Haig to express the dire situation he was in and to request that Sir Douglas keep the pressure on the Germans so as to relieve his demoralised troops, France was in a desperate state. It was long after the war before anyone really knew the real extent of the French mutinies. Had the Germans known even a whisper of the level of demoralisation in the French Army the whole course of the war could have turned out quite different.

I OFT GO OUT AT NIGHT

I oft go out at night time,
When all the sky's aflare.
And the little light's of battle,
Are dancing in the air.

I use my pick and shovel,
To dig a little hole.
And there I sit till morning,
A listening Patrol.

A silly little sickle,
Of moon is hung above.
Within the pond beside me,
The frogs are making love.

I see the German saphead,
A cow is lying there.
It's belly like a barrel,
Its legs are in the air.

The big guns rip and thunder,
The bullets whiz o'er head.
But o'er the sea in England,
Good people lie abed.

And over there in England,
May every honest soul.
Sleep sound while we keep watching,
On listening patrol.

***

The Battle of Arras continued until the middle of May when finally the Village of Bullecourt was taken, on the Aisne the French were experiencing heavy fighting against German counter attacks and it was clear that the B.E.F. was now faced with the fact that the French Army, having taken the brunt of the fighting since 1914 was a demoralised army ill equipped to offer support to Haig's Northern initiative, this was reinforced by the fact that Petain was making no commitment beyond the July initiative, he showed no commitment to the allied cause at this stage with regard to attacking moves, he was content to defend the front line and to wait for the American troops to arrive.

23

The Battle of Messines

The British attack at Messines Ridge was planned for the 7th of July 1917, although in itself a complete operation, to Haig it was the start of the third battle of Ypres and had long been planned for. Since the end of 1915 the main areas of action for the B.E.F. had been the Somme in 1916 and Arras in the Spring of 1917, the latter had gone on far longer than Haig would have wanted but it was unavoidable since the need to relieve pressure on the French was paramount. The Second Army under General Plumer in the Ypres salient had been kept busy for the last 2 years in the continuous wearing down war but had seen little real action, now it was time to take centre stage. Plumer was an avuncular figure and it is said that his troops often referred to as him affectionately as 'Daddy' because of his concern for them, he was considered an honest soldier, kind and generous and who cared deeply for the men under his command. It is said he gathered his men and gave them a brief encouraging jolly up before the battle, and so from that point of view perhaps the troops knew Plumer better than most army commanders would be known and consequently thought of him more affectionately.

At that time Haig did not think highly of Plumer, he felt that his concerns were more with the soldiers under his command than with the war itself, that he did not have the fire in him to lead the proposed Ypres offensive and on that basis he wanted to get rid of him, however Haig decided that he was unable to justify sacking Plumer, after all he was a very decent sort and had not failed in anyway whilst in command, he decided to leave things as they were but keep an eye on him, he would be in command of the Messines offensive. Plumer was a comic looking figure and perhaps that did not help, he was said to be the model for Colonel Blimp, the caricature of an army officer and easily written off at first sight because of his looks as a jolly, bumbling sort. However, during those two years in command he consolidated the position of the B.E.F. in the Ypres salient and although surrounded on three sides by German troops looking down on them from high ground successfully prevented the Germans from mounting any meaningful attacks. Now Plumer's star was in the ascendance, he was to prove that although he might be a comic figure in looks, he was actually a first class commander and as the war progressed he gave Haig cause to rethink his opinion of him after his brilliant victory at Messines.

Once the business of assisting General Nivelle with his 'Grand Plan' was out of the way, the possibility of driving through Passchendaele and on to Roulers, an important railhead and marshalling yards, would enable the allies to demolish the hub of important German communications and logistics and control the coast at Zeebrugge. This latter was of prime importance to the British Govt. in putting an end to the intensive German submarine activity and the massive loss in allied shipping tonnage. It had been suggested that the German submarine bases were in fact elsewhere and not at Zeebrugge, nevertheless, even if that were the case, Haig found this line of thought useful to his own plans for an attack east of Ypres.

Haig's reason for this was that he feared that the Germans would themselves attack along a front taking in the Ypres salient, driving south along the British left flank to the important town of Hazebrouck and cutting the allies off from their lines of supply, forcing them to accept enemy terms for peace. The Germans had made a massive attack on the 20th of October 1914, which was termed the 1st battle of Ypres, and at that time there was a great fear that they would break through and overrun the whole coastline down to Le Havre. Haig was all too well aware if that were to happen it would be the end for the allies, equally for the British to gain a victory in the opposite direction towards Roulers and the German Army headquarters at Courtrai, would deal a crippling blow to the enemy. Haig's plans would have to come later, which they did, in one of the most controversial battles of the War, the third battle of Ypres, commonly referred to as Passchendaele.

In mid May 1917, to the disappointment of Henry Rawlinson and his 4th Army, Haig appointed Hubert Gough at the head of the Fifth Army to lead the Ypres breakout with an attack on Pilckem Ridge, even though he had previously told Rawlinson that it was to be his task. Haig had been influenced by the way that Gough had gone about winning Bullecourt in the latter stages of Arras and was, like himself a cavalryman. Perhaps he saw in him the very person to sweep through and take the Gheluvelt plateau from the grasp of the German Commander Prince Rupprecht, followed by masses of charging cavalry. This would be the first and all important of his objectives, to secure the vital German hub at Roulers, this would allow Rawlinson to move on the Northern Coast, with the object of taking the main ports of Ostend and Zeebrugge, if and when Gough was successful in the Ypres offensive. Gough's brief was to capture the Passchendaele Ridge along with The Roulers and Thourout railway communications area beyond, having achieved that he was to move on northward and take the Houlthurst Forest area. Plumers Second Army would follow up and move into the area cleared by the Fifth Army to the east and north of Observatory Ridge, and Rawlinsons 4th Army would be clear to move on Ostend. The latter operation to be undertaken by Rawlinson was of course a late addition to Haigs initial Northern breakthrough plans, but it enabled him to obtain the authority that he needed in order to proceed with his original plan which was more limited in scope.

The secretary of state Lloyd George had expressed an opinion to C.I.G.S, Sir William Robertson, in June 1917 prior to becoming Prime Minister, that in view of the serious effect that German submarine attacks were having on transatlantic food supplies to Britain, it would be highly desirable if an attack could be mounted on the Belgian Channel ports with a view to capturing or disabling the submarine facilities. This was taken by the British High Command to be a main objective and was readily incorporated in the already well advanced plans for the Ypres offensive, it would of course not have been possible to attempt to take the Belgian ports without first pushing the Germans back successfully in the Roulers, Thourout area and the very difficult objective of Houlthurst Forest. The Battle of Messines was to go ahead, that was fully authorised, however no authority as yet had been given by the Government to proceed with any other planned offensive. The War Cabinet and the Government, although having an idea that Douglas Haig planned a major offensive, did not have comprehensive details of it at all in June 1917, these plans had been drawn up without consulting the War Cabinet or the Government in any detail.

At this point in the war the British forces in France were at their peak, some sixty plus divisions of well-trained troops of the New Army who, in the main, were now battle hardened. They now faced a major offensive but did not have the support of the French, added to which the Russian revolution had started in March

1917 therefore little was happening on the Eastern Front that might relieve pressure on the Western Front, Britain was facing the brunt of it now.

The Messines Ridge extended north in a semi circle westwards from near Ploegsteert Wood (known to the British as Plugstreet) in the south and extended some 11 miles to Observatory Ridge in the north, the whole of which was occupied by German forces. The object of the attack on the ridge was mainly to gain the high ground from which the German lookouts observed every move of the British below. It was essential that the heights were secured in order to secure the flank of the advance toward Passchendaele. The full length of the Messines Ridge was riddled with mine shafts, more than 20 in all some of them starting hundreds of yards behind the British front line. These shafts had been started in late 1915 and were dug by coalminers who had enlisted in the Royal Engineers and Pioneer Corps. They eventually extended well under the German lines, in some cases for half a mile or more. In order to create such long tunnels it was necessary to go very deep through the unstable sandy top soil into solid clay, this would allow the miners to work in silence so that the Germans had difficulty in hearing what was going on, not only that, at depths of more than one hundred feet the ammunition could be stored safely and not be detonated by enemy artillery fire directed on the ridge.

Mining conditions at Messines were extremely arduous in what was a massive operation, literally thousands of men were employed in the mines working shifts, those at the face lay on their backs wielding pick axes in hot, wet, confined spaces, digging at times through sand and then hard clay while others operated bellows to bring fresh air into the long tunnels from outside. Stored in these shafts were hundreds of tons of explosives that needed to be housed in sealed containers to protect it from the wet conditions, they were placed ready to blow up the ridge when the moment arrived although no one knew if the explosives would detonate after such long periods in storage. A great deal of preparation over the previous 12 months had gone into the planning of the Messines, Wytschaete attack, not least was the arrangement for getting supplies and troops to the Second Army front. This task was made easier by the work of Sir Eric Geddes, who had recently been brought in by Haig as the civilian director of transport and communication, his forte was railroads having had experience with railroad building in the American west and the Indian sub continent before joining the North Eastern Railways at home. His job attracted the nominal rank of Major General and as head of transportation he organised track laying on the whole of the Allied front along with rolling stock and engineers etc, so lines were laid to and along the Messines front to get the mountains of ammunition, guns, supplies, rations and troops to where they were needed with the minimum of effort.

In the build up to the battle guns were commandeered from battalions of other Army divisions to supplement those of the Second Army, and some 2300 guns were deployed of which no less than thirty percent were heavy calibre artillery. Already in late May a continuous barrage had been laid down on the forward slopes of the Messines Ridge that pounded the German trenches and artillery positions to such an extent that the enemy had lost more than half of the normal allocation of Howitzers and field guns. German air reconnaissance had indicated huge movements of troops and supplies to the Messines front indicating to Prince Rupprecht, the German Commander, that the continued action by the British on the Arras front was a cover for the main attack that would be on the Messines-

Wytschaete front. Too late, on the 3rd of June, he mounted a huge gas attack at Ploegteert Wood in which some 500 Australian troops were badly injured, knowing that the British attack was due to start any day he mounted an even larger gas attack on the 4$^{th.}$. Leon Wolf wrote, [31] "These last minute measures embarrassed the British but failed to hamper them to any large extent, except in the case of General Monash's 3rd Australians, 500 of whom were gassed en route. For once the 48 year old Bavarian Prince, Field Marshal of the Northern Armies on the Western Front, --------- had been too late with too little, outwitted underground, out manned and outgunned on the ground, and overpowered in the skies above. The Battle of Messines was lost by the Germans before it began, interrogation of prisoners later established how this long incessant shelling of the German positions had prevented relief coming in for those troops on the forward slopes of the ridge, that they had no supplies and were desperately short of food when the ridge was taken".

The 7th of June was the date for the commencement of the action and there was a great deal of anxiety within the British staff at whether or not the whole thing would be a success or not. The main concern was the fact that some of the explosives had been in the mineshafts for more than a year and may no longer be in good condition. Half an hour before the attack began the British guns fell silent and the German signal flares for artillery fire to commence was seen in the dawn sky, the firing lasted only a short time and was aimed at New Zealand troops that had crept into no mans land during the night in readiness for the off.

At 0310 hours on the morning on 7th June 1917, nineteen of the mines were blown at precisely the same time in a spectacular explosion that was heard as far away as London. Numerous attempts have been made by writers to describe the moment of the explosions and to give the reader some idea of the surreal scenario in which the troops went over the top to attack, A German soldier is credited with this description, --- nineteen gigantic roses with carmine petals rose up slowly and majestically out of the ground and then split into pieces with a mighty roar---. Suffice it for me to say that the whole top of the ridge lifted high into the sky followed by huge orange flames leaping hundreds of feet in the air and lighting the early morning sky. At the same time 80,000 troops went over the top to attack and an incredible bombardment by some 2300 guns spaced at an average interval of some 10 yards provided a creeping barrage. German prisoners later said that it was the most terrifying experience they had known, they ran, nerves shattered toward the safety of the British lines and were taken prisoner. The HQ staff of the Second Army all went to the top of Cassel Hill to witness the explosion and opening of the battle, General Plumer however is said to have knelt by his bed in prayer and on the hearing the first reports tears came in his eyes. Haig was right; he was a very human General. Without doubt the battle was a huge success; estimates vary between 7000 and 10,000 prisoners taken and in the order of 180-200 guns captured, the significance of this latter is equivalent to capturing the enemy colours, guns are in fact the colours of artillery regiments. On the 2nd day the German counter attacks were again held and by the end of that day the British had gained further ground. Later publications point to the contrary, that the acclaimed victory was not a victory at all.

Following the Battle of Messines the Lloyd George set up a committee to consider war policy across a wide spectrum of land, sea and air on all the allied fronts, he was of course reliant on senior military personel to advise him of future possible developments on the battle front, and to present plans in order to meet future needs. He had some ideas of his own about the moves he would like to see adopted, for instance he strongly supported the idea of bolstering the Italian effort and thought that by transferring British divisions to that front there may be a possibility of a breakthrough at Trieste by knocking out the Austrians, that way there would be fewer British casualties. However he found no support for this idea and there was even outright contempt for it from Robertson who told Douglas Haig that those 12 divisions that LG wanted would never be transferred whilst he was C.I.G.S. Being rather doubtful about France's possible intentions, LG also thought that a move on Syria would put Britain in a good bargaining position should France decide to enter unilateral peace negotiations with Germany, something that incredibly, according to General Foch, was a distinct possibility.

The Prime Minister was not convinced that Robertson or Haig had the ability to produce workable plans, he was bitterly opposed to Haig's plans for an Ypres offensive and in particular had decided that he wanted to get rid of Robertson. He put forward the idea that a duo of Field Marshal Sir John French and Lt. General Sir Henry Wilson should replace Robertson as C.I.G.S, but Wilson was not for this. Henry Wilson had been the British Staff Liaison Officer to the French GQH at the time of the Nivelle/Arras offensive, but now that Nivelle had been ousted and Petain had taken command he felt out on a limb. Petain did not want Wilson on his staff and having been virtually compelled to resign the post that he had grown to feel so uncomfortable in he was now back in London where he was called on to attend various meetings in an advisory capacity. It seems that he was highly thought of by the politicians (the frocks) but he was not so well thought of in the General Staff. He was a thinker, able to smooth out the bumps in relations between the

British and the French GHQ's, however at no time was he ever offered a command in action other than the temporary command of IVth Corps under General Rawlinson, during a quiet period that even allowed him to do the rounds visiting Paris etc. That perhaps indicates where his strengths lay; or perhaps the reason was distrust, stemming from his part in the Curragh incident that prevented his being offered a command? There was also the fact that he was perhaps seen as a little too close to the French. Whatever the reason he he did not baulk at passing comment on what ought to happen to commanders at the front, i.e. Haig and Gough, who had fought in the thick of it and had not spent their time scooting back and forth between England and France in endless discussions

Nonetheless he had his ear to the ground and during his farewell visit to France, Henry Wilson had noted a deep level of despondency among the French General staff and politicians in Paris, and also the commanders all along the French Line; he felt that they needed to be watched. He records in his diary that during this farewell visit, when he planned to reveal that he was to resign as Staff Liaison officer to the French GQH, he met with his old friend General De Castelnau who laid the blame for the current state of affairs on Lloyd George's readiness to accept the Nivelle Grand plan when so many staff on the British and French High Commands were against it. He also spelled out who he thought was responsible for the present state of affairs in France, he felt that the British Messines offensive was better than anything he could plan on his front but that it was not enough. Wilson also dined with General Foch and his wife at their apartment in Paris and later made comments on how General Foch was very concerned to get across the need for the British to take over more of the line down to the Oise and even Soissons in order to relieve the demoralised French.[32] "He (Foch) said that if we do not do this, the present Government would treat with the Boches for a peace, because the Army and France are tired out".

Mean while Lloyd George was countering the pressure from Robertson and Haig for more troops by his concern for the number of losses. This concern about losses was from the man who committed the B.E.F. to the French planned Somme offensive and the Nivelle Grand plan. In both cases he denigrated the British High Command for the staggering loss of life that ensued. Did he really think that troops could be thrown at such strongly defended German positions without loss of life, the very same cause of the current demoralised state of the French Army following Verdun where the troops were taking up the cry 'we will defend the trenches but we will not attack', the Poelus had refused to attack German machine guns any longer. There was also the fact that the situation was about to become much more difficult with the release of enormous numbers of troops from the Eastern Front

Having lost faith in the Allies ability to win the war Lloyd George was now hoping the American declaration of War would change the order of things. President Wilson had pressed Congress for an American declaration of War against Germany on the grounds that Germany had blockaded the west coast of the United States with submarine patrols and had tried to coerce Mexico into a pact against the USA. In April 1917 America declared war and joined the Allies but it was going to be a long time before they saw any action. Clearly there was a desperate need to come up with some viable strategic planning that might offer the Allies a way to end this war of attrition. The Kaiser was a dictator and there was no argument when he decided what he wanted done, by contrast the French were worn out, they had little fight left in them and had adopted a defence strategy based on Marshal Petain's softly, softly, approach to understanding and meeting the needs of the Poelus. The Russians had started a revolution and were sueing for peace with the Germans and were unlikely to be of any help whatsoever in bringing a swift end to the war. The Italians had suffered a massive defeat at the hands of the Austrians at Caporetti, Lloyd George had connived in an alliance with Nivelle that turned out to be a disaster for the Entente, added to which he had no time for, and gave no support to, his own courageous troops who now faced the brunt of the German offensive on the Western Front and would do so, as was now clear, until November 1918. The Germans had a distinct advantage in that Kaiser was able to make undisputed decisions, they were in a position to move quickly and react to any situation. By contrast the British army was shackled by the democratic procedure laid down by parliament and consequently too many different points of view to be taken into account before a decision could be reached. Haig had from the time of his appointment as GOC favoured a move North for the BEF and an offensive in Flanders. He had agreed to the Nivelle plan because he was obliged to follow the orders given to him by Kitchener, and when the French offensive was seen to be a failure, Haig allowed his divisions to remain in order to keep the Germans occupied and to relieve pressure on the French. At this point Haig decided that he would press ahead with his Flanders offensive and to some extent had managed to obtain the support of Lloyd George, but LG laid down conditions that the operation must be fully supported by the French and when it became clear that Petain had no intention to do other than hold off German attacks on his front LG dithered and authority for Haig to go ahead was waning.

24

Third Ypres – Passchendaele - Cambrai

Several meetings were held in June at whom Lloyd George made a strong case for moving men and guns to the Italian front. Haig and Robertson pointed out the risks in such a venture and also the advantages of the Haig plan if it was successful, but this was the sticking point, too many were against the plan and what they were trying to decide was whether or not several thousands of men would go on the attack in a few weeks time, and if they would ever come back. Haig made the position very clear when he said that peace talks were out of the question, they could attack in Italy or Flanders, they could wait for the Americans or just keep up the small attacks all along the front. But whatever they did the situation was not going to change and the important decision that had to be made, whatever that was, still was no nearer. In the end, Bonar Law made the suggestion that the matter should be left to the Military experts; they were the ones who presumably knew best. With that there was final agreement on this but it was not until Haig demanded to know whether or not he had the full support of the War Cabinet that on the 25th of July 1917 that he was finally given assurances that the War Cabinet would give its full support in the push to break out of the Ypres salient. They were still not clear what Haig's first objective was but made the proviso that should the casualties be too high that the offensive would be called off in favour of the mooted Italian offensive. Haig was now free to go ahead with the objective of securing the Passchendaele Ridge and hopefully to push the Germans back beyond the all-important town of Roulers.

Haig's plan was that the operation should be in stages, a bite and hold strategy that would allow reinforcement of the ground taken before moving on. His first objective was to secure the high ground on the right of the attacking force; this would secure the way with no fear of attack from German artillery or observation of movements. He had however entrusted Hubert Gough and his fifth army with control of the Ypres breakout and Gough had other ideas, he argued that it would be better to incorporate the opening moves into a total strategy whereby the offensive would be a continuous rapid push forward. In the end both Haig and Plumer agreed, Plumer saying that this breakthrough was what he had prepared for since 1915. In the event the high ground was not secured and in the end it proved fatal, Haig made a fatal mistake in allowing Gough to convince him into accepting a bad plan of attack.

Although final approval to attack was not received until July 25th, Haig had been authorized to make preparations, and the bombardment by the 5th and 2nd Armies opened up on July 16th firing some four and a half million shells, it is not difficult to imagine what state the ground was in when the barrage was lifted. The attack commenced on the 31st of July at around 3.00 hrs and good progress was made, Pilckem Ridge being taken before the weather changed and the rain came down. The ground was now mud as the Steenbeck overflowed and by the end of the day the front had advanced about a mile and a half with casualties of almost 30,000 men. The rain continued and the ground became more difficult, the Germans were using their heavy artillery to break up the ground before the attacking British Forces. General Gough recommended abandonment of the operation in the hope of a change in the weather and improvement in conditions, he felt that to carry on would be hopeless and the losses would be unacceptable. He pointed out that his troops were able to move only slowly, that guns were sinking into the mud whenever an attempt was made to move them, and that firing the guns only drove the spades and wheels deep into the soft earth, there was also great difficulty in moving ammunition and supply rations up to the front. Haig however was quite determined that a breakthrough could and should be achieved, this was the move he had planned for so long and he was determined to the extent that he appeared to be blind to the consequences, he ordered Gough to carry on. Pretty well all the tanks that had been brought up for the offensive were out of action, either out through enemy action or mechanical failure; many were simply bogged down in the mud and were sitting ducks. Late in September there seemed to be some small successes in this endless struggle that gave heart to the army Commanders and GHQ and the encouragement to go on.

A renewed attack was ordered for the 9th of October and for several days prior to this there was constant heavy rain again turning the ground into a quagmire. General Gough again was doubtful that the attack should go ahead but Haig was adamant, he was of the opinion that the Germans were exhausted and there was a real possibility they could finally be defeated, The attack went ahead on the 9th and was a complete failure just as Gough had foreseen, this was the day that my great Uncle, Benjamin Leaver, met his demise to a snipers bullet, I cannot but think that he and hundreds of other lost there lives on that day, just as others had done since July 25th, at the behest of a commander who was desperate to gain some sort of victory and to bring an end to the war whatever the cost in human lives. Haig ordered a renewed attack on the 12th of October he perhaps thought that there was a chance of ending the war before Christmas. The ground in front of the attacking line had been pounded to soft mud by the enemy and Gough contacted Plumer at his 2nd Army HQ to suggest that the attack be postponed, Plumer, having consulted his senior staff, thought differently and the attack went ahead. Haig was now determined that an all out push would see a breakthrough and the enemy driven out of Passchendaele.

The two Armies supported by the Canadian Corps made several such efforts but it was not until almost four weeks later on November 4th that they finally took the village of Passchendaele and brought to a close the long series of futile attempts to clear the Germans out of Flanders. On the 8th of Oct. Haig's Chief Intelligence Officer wrote in his diary, "--- with a great success tomorrow and good weather for a few more weeks, we may still clear the coast and win the war before Christmas". 10th Oct. Haig sent for me, ---- "he was still trying to find some ground for hope that we might still win through here this year, but there is none".

There had been rain each day since 4th Oct, and on the afternoon of the 10th it became torrential; the meteorological officers said that no improvement could be expected, yet Haig decided to press on, and his Army Commanders, although dubious, did not care to protest. The long struggle had been as much against the horrendous conditions as it had against the enemy, added to that the increased use of mustard gas by the Germans ensured that little progress was made. It is obvious that Haig set out with his original plan with the firm idea that not only was it achievable but that it would bring a quick end to the war, perhaps even by Christmas. But as the days and weeks went by he saw less and less evidence that this epic struggle would produce any real change in the virtual stalemate situation that existed.

Australian 4th division troops at Chateau Wood in the Ypres salient, October 1917

Wounded waiting for transport.

Haigs problem was either to persist in making that supreme effort again and again even at the horrendous loss of life that ensued, or call it of and rethink the whole plan by which they could rout the Germans. The latter was anathema to Haig and it seems that Passchendaele became the point of achievement that he had to conquer come what may, and for the time being it brought an end to the long weary saga. The final result was an advancement of only 5 miles and the loss of some 400,000 men. The Military Historian [33]J.F.C. Fuller, had accused Haig of 'an inexcusable piece of pigheadedness' and it was a fact that Haig's first concern was, in his own words to 'keep the breakfast table full', that is to say to keep the troops coming in to replace the losses. At this stage of the war that was his main headache and the reason why the powers that be at home had to scrape the bottom of the barrel. The name Passchendaele has stuck as the designation for the whole of the third Ypers offensive, perhaps it was given to the offensive by those who were there because it was the point that they finally reached and looked back on the 6 months of dire struggle, it perhaps epitomised the awful long and weary engagements, taking horrendous losses with nothing to show for it until, that disastrous period ended when the Canadians took Passchendaele. It was given the name, 3rd Battle of Ypres but it is more commonly known simply as Passchendaele, the whole 4/5 months was a campaign and the name itself became a byword for the lowest point of the war.

At home things were not at all rosy, there was a great deal of industrial unrest, there was the growing Irish problem and with the renewed German submarine offensive against Atlantic shipping greatly increased food shortages. The Kaiser claimed that Britain could not survive the loss of shipping on the scale envisaged for more than six months but he was proved wrong when the convoy escorts started to sink German submarines to such an extent that the Kaiser withdrew them, it would not help to win the war but at least Britain would not be starved into submission. The conscription age range had been widened and was now 18 to 51, the list of reserved occupations had also been revised and this widened the catchments considerably, besides this the non-combatant troops already in posts such as cooks, service Corps, Pay Corps, engineers etc. were now moved into the front line. Lloyd George wanted to know why so many troops had to be kept behind in England, was it not possible to move another 300,000 over to France? The matter was not so simple since amongst the number of men stationed in the UK was a large proportion of sick and wounded, there were also commonwealth troops that C.I.G.S had no direct control over. The fact remained that whilst the British manpower shortages in France and Belgium remained chronically low, the Germans were moving in as many as 10 divisions a month from the Russian front. The measures taken in widening the net to take in more conscripts and move non combatants to the front was what Haig now depended on to boost his manpower, the older, less fit, less mobile men. Lloyd George was concerned only with defending our positions and waiting for the Americans to pour in troops just as Petain was.

The Start of the 3rd Ypres in July 1917 saw the tank battalions unable to operate under the existing conditions, as far as Colonel Fuller, (J.F.C. Fuller) the commander of the tank Brigade, was concerned the 3rd Ypres was something they could not engage in because of the terrain and its condition. On that basis he began to develop a new strategy in which the tank battalions could operate in conditions more suited to tank warfare,

Haig however declared that it was not possible to fight on two fronts at the same time and therefore the tank operations had to be postponed in favour of, according to Fuller, a costly and futile Flanders campaign. Fuller discussed his plan with General Byng the Commanding Officer of the 3rd Army who was receptive to the idea but in a modified form. Fuller had devised a plan of attack involving some 380 Battle tanks and another 60 tanks in various support roles closely followed up by infantry. The plan was that the force would strike a heavy surprise blow at the enemy and then retreat having smashed their lines and capturing enemy guns and prisoners.

Byng wanted to turn the battle plan into a full-scale attack with the intention of breaking through and holding Cambrai and Bourlon Wood with a much greater force. He presented this idea to Haig who was in agreement and a date was set for the 20th of November, that day was the first real tank battle in history. In the initial stages the attack was a huge success pushing on a wide front as deep across enemy lines as they had during the whole of the 3rd Ypres campaign. Some 30% of the tanks were knocked out but it had little effect at that stage. There were many bad decisions taken which allowed the Germans to hold on until several divisions were moved up in support and they were able to counter attack. For the British there were no reserves and so they were pushed back until eventually Haig gave the order to retreat from the area.

The initial victory was well accepted in London and there was great rejoicing with the feeling perhaps that this was the beginning of the end. On the other hand the German G.O.C Von Ludendorf records in his memoirs that the British breakthrough of the Hindenberg positions in 1918 hailed the start of the defeat of the German army, in both cases it has long been well recognised just how premature they were. The reversal again saw Haig heavily criticised and he was by now at low ebb, Byng however was quick to blame his subordinates and poorly trained troops. The reality was that the men, having fought gallantly were exhausted and there was no support forthcoming, by contrast the Germans were fortunate to have divisions newly arrived from the Russian front and were able to move six more divisions into the area plus another 6 more divisions in readiness to mount a massive surprise counter attack. The British were caught on the hop by this surprise German counter attack just as much as the Germans were caught unprepared for the British tank offensive, which proved that it was difficult to introduce any new tactics that might change the face of the war and the idea that Fuller, the Commander of the tank brigade, proposed i.e. heavy surprise raids here and there along the front taking large numbers of enemy guns and prisoners may well have backfired.

Cambrai was notable for the fact that the attack was not preceded by a prolonged artillery bombardment; the creeping barrage technique was also replaced by the use of tanks in that the infantry moved forward taking cover behind the tanks. Specially equipped tanks also carried out the cutting of the wire far more effectively; something that over the whole of the war period had proved to be so hit and miss by artillery fire. It did also eliminate the huge losses from enemy machine gun fire and positively pointed to the use of tanks in battle as the way forward. The Mark IV tank was much superior to those in use at the Somme in 1916 but experience would show even greater development in the future. The German army recognised its value and developed the tank to a much superior standard than the British, French or Americans in the years between the wars, the Tiger tank used in WWII was, for its time, a devastating weapon. During my time with the colours, I was a

Field and AFV gun fitter in Armoured Workshops working mainly on Centurion tanks and in the1980's spent a day at the Bovington tank museum in Dorset, there I saw for the first time a WWII Tiger tank with its 88mm gun, and how incredibly ahead of it's time it was.

25

1918
Germany prepares for Victory offensive

The situation in France was now at a critical point, Field Marshal Haig was not supported by Lloyd George who felt that whatever strategy there was for bringing the war to an end had proved to be totally ineffective. He did not hide the fact that he had little time for The Chief of the General Staff, Sir William Robertson and the same applied to Douglas Haig along with the General staff at GHQ. Haig wrote to Robertson and said that if L.G. felt that he was not up to the task then he should sack him, if he wanted him to remain in command then the sniping had to stop. Haig was being pressurised by the War Cabinet to get rid of his DMI (Director of military operations) Brigadier General John Charteris, this on the basis he had consistently failed to provide accurate intelligence information to Douglas Haig resulting in failed offensives, he had apparently also made himself very unpopular with the HQ staff in the Army Corps. Although Haig thought highly of Charteris and was reluctant to accept his resignation, in the end he had little choice but to let him go. General Sir Launcelot Kiggell, Haigs Chief of staff, was another target considered lacking, Haig was loyal to his staff and it seemed would sooner he resign than see them treated as scapegoats but it so happened that Kiggell began to suffer with health problems and he too was replaced.

This was a rather unfortunate time for wholesale change at GHQ but there were also other changes going on that would take until March to put into place. During

January and February significant changes were made to the structure of the Brigades and Divisions in the BEF, the changes arose for the reason that so many of the battalions of the New Army were under strength and it was proving impossible to recruit sufficient men in order to bring the battalions up to strength. Divisions in the British forces were reduced from four to three brigades and brigades from four battalions to three, the existing battalions were then brought up to strength from the ones identified for disbandment, this latter in itself proved to be a massive headache. None of the GHQ staff or the Corps Commanders were pleased at the tremendous disruption these changes caused at a time when British Military Intelligence were quite accurately spelling out what the Germans were now planning following their huge increase in manpower from the Russian front. Traditionally the military had calculated an army's strength by divisions, it would not be good for moral to be seen smaller, better to reduce the number of brigades in a division than to have divisions up to strength but fewer of them, its called the Puffer fish mentality.

During January and February Haig met on several occasions with Petain and also his Army Commanders to assess and make plans to contain the German offensive that they expected sometime in mid March. They were also heavily occupied repairing and bolstering the inadequate defences that had been neglected during 1917 when the emphasis had been totally on attack. The main problem for the Army commanders was the chronic shortage of staff to carry out the work; the losses in the 3rd Ypres and the heavy losses at Cambrai had left the battalions sorely depleted. The Germans had in fact carefully planned several operations code named Michael timed to begin as the their attack progressed, this was known to the Germans as *Kaiserschlact,* 'Kaisers War'. Ludendorff assessed that if he attacked the French and defeated them he would still be faced by a defiant British Army that would be supported by the Americans. The only way to ensure victory was to defeat the British by driving them North onto the coast before the Americans could build up their forces in France, it was expected that the French would then capitulate and in fact plans for this were already foremost in Petains mind.

Following the Canadian taking of Passchendaele there was a feeling that the allies were on the winning side, even though the British were exhausted and the troops well down on the numbers required for the coming battles. The British front had been extended (to release French divisions to go into reserve) and General Gough of the 5th Army, who was now allocated 1/3 of the whole British front, had grave concerns about his ability to hold the whole 42 miles with the divisions at his disposal against the hugely superior German forces opposing him. Not only did he need fighting men, he also needed labour battalions to repair and provide the defences so badly lacking on the Somme after the Germans had applied their scorched earth tactics on withdrawing to the Hindenberg line. He wrote to Haig on the 1st of February to outline the shortages in manpower and to seek assurances that reserves would be available if there was real danger of a German breakthrough.

News had inadvertently reached British intelligence about German newspaper articles that had been relayed via Switzerland, from this it was established that the new 18th German Army Commander was a seasoned veteran from the Russian front with several successful battles to his credit; he was General Von Hutier. Other information had filtered through via aerial observation that the Germans were extremely active building new bridges across the St Quentin-Cambrai canal; new airfields were springing up, new roads, railways and hospitals. Haig had made clear in his reply to Gough that there could be no generous transfer of divisions to Gough's command, he did not have the men to do that without weakening his position in the North and possibly exposing the Northern channel ports to German occupation, Haig's demands for more men had fallen on deaf ears in Whithall. Following this Gough was in full agreement with Haig about what his task was to be, he was to hold but not break and retreat gradually in the way an elastic band would stretch, this would draw the Germans on, hopefully, in doing so they would also exhaust the enemy troops. The plan of course was not a retreat but intended to extend the German lines of communication to a point where they were exhausted and weakened, at that point Allied reserves held back specially for this situation would counter attack in great force. That was the plan.

Charteris, Haig's DMI (Director of military Intelligence) pointed out that the British now had a longer front to hold, little prospect of reinforcements and an enemy that had more manpower on the western front than at any time since the war began. He also pointed out that the British had a reduced army, in fact there were 300,000 more men in January 1918 than there were in January 1917, but with a much longer line to hold, the the manpower situation was reduced to what it was a year ago, not a very happy state of affairs. Now that the Russians had signed the Brest- Litovsk agreement and ceased hostilities the Governments of the Entente were in turmoil. The German and Austrian Armies on the Russian front were now moving back and it allowed Germany to move another 62 divisions to the Western Front. The staff at GHQ had for some considerable time been assessing where the German attack would come from, they not only guessed the date pretty well correctly, they had also pinpointed the place where they would attack, the latter was not too difficult to work out since they knew the enemy was all to well aware that the Fifth Army was now covering such a long front with few divisions.

Haig's concerns about Petain.

With the absence of agreement at the Supreme War Council regarding the length of line that the French and British should each be responsible for the situation became acute, the Council was threatened with the resignation of the French Prime Minister Clemenceau if Haig did not agree to his requests. Haig made arrangements to meet personally with Petain and together they agreed that the British would take over more of the line and extend it to 125 miles which was Haig's initial offer before Clemenceau's threat, it was also some ten miles Shorter than Clemenceau had demanded, the War Council at Versailles however, decided to accept this arrangement. Haig's main concerns were the shortage of men and the possibility of a split being opened up between the French and British under German attack, with this in mind he spoke on several occasions with Petain about mutual support if that should occur and Petain agreed that it was imperative that contact between the British and French Forces should not be breached, that he would offer what help he could. At a subsequent meeting Haig became alarmed when Petain said that if the French gave way under a German advance he would move his troops South toward Beauvais, Haig at once realised that the French intended to expose the British flank, when asked if that was his intention Petain revealed that he had orders from his Government that in the event of a German breakthrough he was to marshal all his resources around Paris to save the Capital. If such a gap opened the British would of course have been driven north, rounded up at the Channel ports and defeated, that is what Ludendorff intended, or at least hoped for. It followed therefore that if there was to be any hope of defeating the Germans it was essential that the French and British lines should be intact, if the Germans managed to create a gap then the war would be over and Germany victorious. In his memoirs Ludendorff made the point that he believed that France would put national interests before those of the Entente and this greatly influenced his plan of attack.

CIGS, William Robertson, was ever suspicious of Lloyd George's previous attempts to undermine the General Staff and to influence the progress of the war by the several devious moves he had made. In February the Supreme War Council at Versailles introduced a War Executive Committee chaired by General Foch with the job of controlling a General Reserve for use in any emergency on the Western front. Robertson took exception to the fact that L.G. had appointed Sir Henry Wilson as the British representative on the Executive Council without his knowledge and was of the opinion that under such an arrangement his authority as Chief of the General Staff would be undermined. He believed that executive decisions regarding the British armed Forces in France fell in his domain and Robertson pointed this out in a confrontation with Lloyd George stating that either he (Robertson) or his deputy should attend meetings of the Joint War Executive if decisions were likely to made affecting the BEF. He also made it clear that he objected to British reserves not being under the direct control of the GOC British Forces in France. In a letter to General Plumer in early February 1918 Robertson wrote 'it is impossible to have chiefs of staff dealing with operations in all respects except reserves and to have people with no other responsibilities dealing with reserves and nothing else'. Foch was of course Robertson's counterpart as the Chief of the General Staff in France and whether or not he would have relinquished that post to become chairman of the War Executive Committee was unclear.

As a result of that meeting Lloyd George offered Robertson the post of representative at Versailles but with reduced responsibilities as Chief of the General Staff, several other options were also discussed but Robertson was not interested in any of them, even if they were viable, he therefore offered to resign, Lloyd George had got what he wanted, Robertson felt that if he did not have the support of the Prime Minister he had no alternative but to go. When Rawlinson was the British member of the Executive War Council at Versailles he wrote in his diary on the 23 February 'I shall need all my tact to get the question of the reserve settled, it ought never to have been raised, I cannot help thinking there is some political motive behind it. If it is L.G's method of getting rid of Wullie, (Robertson) it is a cumbrous and dangerous way of doing it. I must have another talk with D.H.'

The King was most upset and advocated that Robertson must not go, Douglas Haig told the King that there was no reason why he should not go and L.G. said that if he did not go the Govt would resign. Robertson was moved to the post of G.O.C. Eastern Command at home and Henry Wilson appointed in his place as CIGS. Lloyd George then instructed Douglas Haig to appoint a representative to the Versailles post, Haig chose the Commander of the Fourth Army, Sir Henry Rawlinson on the condition that he could have Plumer back from Italy.

The idea of a Reserve under the command of The War Executive would have meant that Foch, as Chairman, would have the authority to select the reserve forces by thinning out all along the front irrespective of the wishes of the various Army commanders. This caused a great deal of unrest, Haig was very much opposed to it and when Foch asked Haig to release nine divisions to go into reserve Haig flatly refused saying he would resign first. At a subsequent meeting of the Supreme War Council in London following Haig's refusal, it was decided that the idea of a General Reserve was not going to work and should be abandoned, Haig had shown as always that he was not prepared to make any promises that he could not keep, he also knew that should the Germans break through it would not be Foch who took the blame, but Haig no matter what the situation was viz a viz reserves. Foch was now Chairman of the Executive War Council that had no function, the French Prime Minister Clemenceau had agreed to the abandonment of the project, but Foch had registered his disapproval at Clemeneau's decision and that led to some bad feeling between them. The French politicians and General Staff were suffering a *crisis de nerfs,* and under the circumstances Lloyd George was anxious enough that he sent Milner, the Secretary of State for War, off to Versailles post haste to get some idea of what was happening with regard to planning for the impending German onslaught and the consequences of that for the British forces.

The die was now cast, from the first days of the Russian revolution it had been clear that war on the Eastern Front would cease and that the German Army would concentrate entirely on the western front, politicians and military leaders had been consumed by this coming alarming aspect of the war, the expected massive assault with which Germany would, hopefully, end the war victoriously. The French had plans to save Paris in the event of a breakthrough by the Germans, the

British sought assurance that France would answer the call if the Germans threatened to split the French and the British, Lloyd George was concerned about the losses, Petain struggled to raise morale amongst the French troops, it now seemed that everyone was keenly aware of the need to pull together as a coordinated whole against a hugely strengthened enemy rather than the fragmented Entente force that existed.

26

Second and Third Somme

At any time since the War began, the fall of France would have seen the German occupation of the whole of France and Belgium, the Channel ports invested and the complete isolation of the British Isles. In 1918 the Germans aimed their attack mainly at the British lines the strategy being that if the British were beaten then the French would collapse, Ludendorff had decided to aim his attack at the weakest point where the two armies met, The French left and the Fifth Army right. It was well understood by both Haig and Petain that the Germans rallying cry was *England der feind,* 'England the enemy', and that the expected heavy blow would be directed at the British front.

Byng's Third Army covered 26 miles of front with 10 divisions in the line and 7 in support opposed by 25 German divisions. The Fifth Army under Hubert Gough covered a front of 42 miles with 11 divisions in line and 4 in support opposed by 43 German divisions. The difficult situation that the Fifth Army faced was well known by Haig who had tried his utmost in vain to get reinforcements sent out from England, Lloyd George was fully aware of the situation but initially had given no support whatever to the BEF, now limited replenishments were coming out, mainly fresh faced youngsters with no concept of what they were to face, L.G.'s contribution in the first two days of the big German push was to step up the pressure on America to send troops as soon as possible, The BEF had of course been sold short before and the situation now was no different. The Fifth and Third armies were in a depleted state and in no condition to go to war against not only vastly superior numbers but also seasoned storm troopers from the Russian Front.

On the 21st of March the battlefield was covered in a thick fog, the German attack began at 4.30 am with a tremendous barrage of over 6000 guns and a large proportion of the rounds were gas. The main blow was initially against the Fifth Army and then to the extreme right of the Third Army, these two armies were split by the Somme, a major error in not having both banks of the river under one command. So successful was the German attack that the British had little opportunity to adhere to the tactics agreed with GHQ, i.e. to give way gradually, holding as long as possible without putting the men in jeopardy before withdrawing, instead the whole violent thrust created an ongoing situation of utter chaos for the overwhelmed British troops. As Plumer later said 'these new recruits do not know their business'. During the first two days 21st – 23rd March the Fifth army lost about 350 field and 150 heavy guns, the heavy fog worked in favour of the advancing Germans in that it allowed them unseen to surround some of the Fifth Army units, it was also helpful in that it allowed those units if the Fifth Army to retreat in broad daylight, something they would have had great difficulty in doing in clear weather. Some reports say that many of the British troops abandoned their post and fled and that whole units surrendered and were taken prisoner, it is a fact that some 22,000 were taken prisoner and the losses were horrendous. Other reports speak of men remaining at their posts until they ran out of ammunition and were either wiped out, taken prisoner or joined the stragglers slowly moving to the rear. The roads were blocked with troops retreating and civilians with the few belongings they could carry, following the German move to the Hindenberg Line some

18 months previously, farmers and land workers had been gradually moving back to work the land, now they were driven out again and the British forces, weary and exhausted, many injured with no real means of meeting their needs could do nothing but get out themselves. At midday on the 23rd March GHQ issued an order to the Third Army to prepare a line from the Somme, through Albert to Gommecourt that left little doubt that a retreat was imminent, in the late afternoon GHQ issued another order,

'Fifth Army must hold the Somme at all costs. There must be no withdrawal from this line. It is of the greatest importance that the Fifth Army should affect a junction with the French on their right without delay. Third and Fifth armies should keep in closest touch in order to secure their junction and must mutually assist each other in maintaining Peronne as a pivot'[34].

The situation was at that time extremely serious and Gough had instructions [35]both written and spoken, that since the crisis in manpower was a grave threat to Haig's widened front, too many risks in battle were not to be taken with the Fifth Army; that its divisions were to be nursed as carefully as possible if a determined assault upon them were made by superior numbers; and that it might well be desirable to fall back to the rearguard defences of Peronne and the Somme while linking up with the Third Army on the north and preparing for counter-blows. Obviously the weak point (Fifth Army) was a matter of grave concern to Haig but he was unable to bring the army up to strength. The orders issued to Hubert Gough contradicted each other, but in the event he could do nothing but react in the best way possible to a hopeless situation.

On the 23rd on the Gommecourt Front My Grandfathers younger brother William Clough was taken prisoner, he is mentioned earlier with the poem that was sold round the streets to collect for his wife. I can find no record of where he was held by the German medics, whether eyes were removed in a field hospital or a war hospital in Germany.

March 1918 warrants a book alone dedicated to the battle of St Quentin in order to describe in detail what happened, in fact there are two books that I can think of that do just that, William Moore's, 'See How They Run', and William Shaw Sparrow's, 'The Fifth Army in 1918'. At the time, blame for what happened was placed squarely on the shoulders of Hubert Gough, as time went by others were apportioned blame for their part in the humiliating defeat, people started to analyse what happened and came round to exonerating Gough in the main. Haig was also blamed, as was Lloyd George for with holding replenishment troops when they were in fact available in the UK, the local commanders down to company level and the troops themselves did not escape severe critism either. The fact is that Ludendorff had taken his time to ensure that all the necessary ingredients were in place for three months before he attacked, his troops were fresh; he had massive resources and he set out in his own words 'to chop a hole' through the Entente weak point. It was a case of, a weak British front left by the British Government and refused support by a French Commander to face a powerful enemy, and when the inevitable happened the British Government was not having humiliation heaped on it and therefore needed a scapegoat.

Unfortunately Ludendorff fell foul of Clauzwitz's theory and by the 25th March his troops had over extended their line of communications, the men were tired and hungry and this allowed the allies to hang on and prevent the occupation of Amiens. It was at this point that the pressure from the Germans slackened and the blows started to fall elsewhere. The Fifth Army was battered but the Germans had not broken through.

Foch later described the situation, [36]"the German soldiers were inspired by enthusiasm and by complete confidence. The British Armies had to face the most formidable assault of the whole war.

The war correspondent Hamilton Fyfe later wrote, "The Germans had so many divisions they could take them out of the line as soon as the were tired and let them recover. Our men had no intervals. They were on their feet day and night. When they were not fighting they were falling back or hastily improving old defensive positions----". Fyfe, being a war correspondent on the spot at the time wanted to to report the facts as he saw them, censorship prevented him from doing that and it was not until after the war that he wrote of what he saw.

On the German Front Ludendorff briefed correspondents and said. "The British fought tenaciously and concealed their machine guns with great skill---"

Following the losses in the battles of 1917 at Arras, Cambrai and the 3rd Ypres, when the manpower of the British Army in France was dangerously low, Haig had been pressing for more recruits to be sent out from England but Lloyd George was not responding on the basis of the heavy losses that had already occurred in the war, he was holding back replenishment troops in order to compel Haig to fight a defensive war until the Americans came. It had been necessary therefore to comb through the existing ranks to find men to send to the front and that meant that cooks, pioneers, engineers, admin staff and any non combatant staff that could be spared were dragooned into the front line, this also included men up to the age of 50. At home there was screening of the various army units for men who could be spared, there was also a review of all those men who were working in civilian jobs holding reserved status certificates in the quest to find eligible recruits, men who were classified as B grade medically were also drafted in. Following the German Spring offensive the War Cabinet, realised the shortsightedness of having held back replenishment troops to a large extent, was now implementing measures to put that right.

Lloyd George addressed The House with regard to the raising of the age of conscription in the British Military Service act of 1916 and also applying it to Ireland, that had previously been exempt. There was a heated exchange with regard to the latter with comments from Irish MP's such as, you will never get any conscripts from Ireland, ---you come and get them, ---you will have another war on your hands. On the 16th of April the act of 1916 was extended to Ireland and as a result anti conscription groups were set up across the country supported by the Bishops. Every Roman Catholic was asked to sign a petition at the church door on the 21st of April 1918, to the effect that they would deny the British Govt. the right to enforce compulsory conscription in Ireland, and a solemn pledge to support one and other and to resist conscription by the most effective means at their disposal. As a result conscription was not enforced..

At home, war correspondent Colonel Repington wrote in the Morning Post "I notice that Government Press is doing it's best to unload the responsibilities of it's masters onto the soldiers, and especially to blame our Command in France and our FIFTH ARMY for the success of the German attack on the 21st of March and subsequent days. The War Office permit these insinuations and innuendoes to be published, broadcast without reply, and therefore I am entitled to defend my old campaigning comrades and to establish the facts----"

It referred to the unpardonable speech made by Lloyd George in the House of Commons regarding available troops at the front, the deputy Chief of the General Staff Major General Frederick Maurice took umbrage at LG's blatent misrepresentation of official figures and fired a memo off to his chief Sir Henry Wilson, who was now CIGS. Wilson ignored the memo, and with that General Maurice contacted Col. Repington with a copy of the correct figures that he then reported on in the press. On becoming aware of Maurice's actions, Lloyd George sent for Sir Henry Wilson, who had already started a witchhunt to find the leak. The outcome was that Maurice was compelled to resign his post.

Douglas Haig's concerns about the French level of thinking with regard to the coming German offensive had obviously been well founded. He had already pressed Petain into admitting that in the event of a gap opening between the British and French he would turn south to Paris; this was expected of him by Clemenceau and the French Government, Petain had in fact relayed these instructions to General Fayolle, Commander of the French First and Third Army groups. The potential consequence of that was that the British Forces would be outflanked on the right, driven back on the Channel Ports and surrounded on all sides, this was the problem that Haig had to consider and what measures were required to ensure that the British/French line held. Petain of course was concerned with the interests of his country but that did not warrant turning his armies south and leaving the British isolated in the event of a break-through, if the Germans had managed to breach the line then the war would have been lost and France occupied irrespective of what happened to the British Army.

Foch wants a General Reserve, under his control.

Foch had already decided that he had to have a sizeable general reserve of French troops under his control and had, with the enthusiastic support of Lloyd George, almost achieved that. Had it not been for the actions of Douglas Haig in refusing to move divisions into reserve under Foch's control, it was highly likely that Foch would have found himself below the rank of Haig and Petain, but in ful control of their reserve forces. Fortunately Clemenceau was in agreement with the argument put forward by Douglas Haig and the matter was dropped. Clemenceau was not prepared to go against Haig, the British were doing all the work, never the less he was fully supportive of Foch, who at that stage was desperate to gain control over a major aspect of the conflict. Foch tried to appeal but this was rejected, but as we shall see, he does not give up and in the end succeeds in getting himself in an even more commanding position.

On the 26th of March a high level meeting was convened at the Hotel De Ville at Doullens, it was attended by the top political and military brass but excluding Gough, a point that will be looked at in more detail later. A major effort was now needed and some very careful planning to face the assault that was threatening to sweep the allies away, it was time for Lloyd George to stop pressing for a possible solution on the Italian or Salonika fronts, the Western Front was now where the war would be won or lost and the Americans were taking overlong to build up their forces in France. It must however be remembered that the British Fifth and Third Armies along with the French under Fayolle, had been in full retreat for the last 5 days under the massive German attack whilst this meeting was in progress, the good news was that the Germans were wilting, their troops were exhausted and they were having difficulty getting supplies over such long lines and the allied lines were holding.

Finally there was agreement that Foch should be elevated to Supremo or Generalissimo (although there are those who would object to the latter designation on the basis that he did not have complete control over the Allied Armies) with immediate effect. Needs must and here was a man who was anxious to get on with the job whether or not the Americans could take a full part at the present time, Foch had lots of vigour and aggression in him toward the Germans. He was also a senior General who had not held a command since the end of the 1st Somme in 1916, although he was ever anxious to get involved in the fighting at the front. Foch had a plan, just as Nivelle had a plan in 1917, and he wanted to create an opportunity to use it. He had contrived with support of Lloyd George to get himself in a position where he could create and control a general reserve, but that was rejected, now apparently, he was in charge of Allied strategy. Heaven knows that there was a desperate need at this stage to establish common aims and coordinate the movements of the Allied forces. This was never more evident considering the state of the battered Fifth and Third Armies plus the French under Fayolle. Petain had declared the Fifth Army a defeated army and had turned away, in effect casting them adrift when he could have supplied reserve divisions to give support, his comments at the Doullens meeting were caustic with regard to the Fifth Army and totally unwarranted from an officer charged with revitalizing a defeated and mutinous French Army.

Foch's appointment was made in a moment of panic fearing that the British and French would be separated, each looking to its own interests, and in Petain's case this had been made patently clear, this possibilty of a separation had been Haig's concern all along. Petain had assured Haig he would provide relief at the Somme but was shocked by what he heard of the Fifth Army. Ostensibly keeping to his commitment to Haig he said he was sending 15 Divisions, but then the next day, the 24th he changed his mind when he informed Haig that he considered the attack on the Fifth Army was a feint and he expected an imminent attack in the Champagne region. With that Haig turned to his Commanders of the First and Second Armies, Horne and Plumer asking them to thin their fronts in Flanders, they did as he asked and Haig got 6 Divisions to move south, he also got 5 divisions from Petain. With Foch in post, Haig had now shed the responsibilities that were the cause of much of his apprehension, he could sit back and let Foch take the strain, as for Hubert Gough, already transferred under the Command of General Fayolle and then relieved of his post. Seeing Gough hung out to dry must have seemed a great pity, courageous, honourable, grossly unsupported, but what could Haig do?

The Fact that Petain did not keep to his promise of support for the British at the Somme only served to highlight the weak position that Foch found himself. He did not have the authority to tell the Army Commanders to deploy troops wherever they were most needed; only Haig and Petain had the authority to deploy reserves in their armies. From that point of view he realised that he was going to have difficulty raising a reserve at all that would be controlled by him under his new Command, a matter now needing only written confirmation by the allied leaders. Foch's plan, unlike Nivelle's idea of punching holes and racing through, was to collect a massive reserve that would be available for a sweeping counter attack, assuming the Germans could be drawn on sufficiently to over extend their lines and therefore weaken their position. There were two problems with this; one was the fact that he could not be sure where the next attack would occur and so where to mass his reserves in readiness, he opted for an area south west of Amien, a point considered by Douglas Haig to be too far away from what he thought would be the next German offensive i.e. the Ypres salient. The second problem was the fact that the severely under-manned British Army would have to take the brunt of the fighting with little prospect of support whilst accumulated a reserve behind he lines.

General Foch's war experiences started as a French Corps Commander where he suffered a heavy defeat at Morhange in 1914, after the 1st Somme he fell into disfavour when he, along with other French commanders, was held responsible for the huge loss of life. During the battle of the Somme he reached the age of retirement but was kept on the active list, when Nivelle was elevated to Commander in Chief in early 1917 he found work for him at Senlis where he was charged with the task of producing a plan of action in the event of Germany violating Swiss neutrality, this he completed in early January 1917. Shortly after that he transferred to Army HQ at Mirecourt until the 30th of March where he assumed temporary command of the 7th and 8th Armies whilst the incumbent C. in C. General Castelnau was on a visit to Russia, this was the French *sectuer du calmes* or 'quiet front'. He later worked on the drawing up of plans in order to meet the expected German assault on the Western Front following the release of German and Austrian Armies from the Russian front, otherwise he was employed in an advisory capacity to General Nivelle.

Although Lloyd George was not present at the 'Doullens meeting' the appointment was what he had wanted, a Commander in Chief that would have command over the British Forces rather than Douglas Haig, it was for him a highly acceptable move, for others it was less welcome. Clemenceau said bitingly to Foch 'you have now got the command you wanted' to which Foch replied something about commanding a cause already lost, but alas! it was his patriotic duty! That probably sizes up the man's ego; however reluctant Foch would have us believe that he was, Clemenceau was not fooled; Foch had put himself up for the job. The situation was a compromise, the best of a bad lot, but Foch saw it as his calling. Haig on the other hand had already moved the Fifth Army under the command of General Fayolle, and at the Doullens meeting when the matter was being discussed, Foch had railed against Petains timidity, and with that Haig took the opportunity to say to Foch, 'if you would give me advice I would happily follow it', it seemed that Haig was happy to shift the overall responsibility onto to the French, he considered the Fifth Army to now be a French problem since Gough's Fifth army was under Fayolles command, perhaps now the Fifth would get French support when it was needed. Haig had also moved General Congreve's VII Corps from Gough's left across the Somme to join with Byng's Third Army.

Foch, full of vigour, set off immediately to put his plans into action. He made it his first task to meet the various army commanders and, made Gough's HQ his first port of call, one can imagine what was going through Foch's mind, 'I'll sort this one out', (General Gough had received a message asking him to be at his HQ in the afternoon) There Foch made some extremely serious insinuations that called into question the resolve of General Gough, a commander who had shown great courage and resolution in the face of insurmountable odds with little or no support from the French who repeatedly said they were sending in reserve divisions but did not, they purposely kept them back, neither had

Haig been able to provide him with the two extra divisions that he had pressed for on the basis that they were needed in the event of an enemy attack in the Ypres area.

During the visit by Foch, Gough was treated like a naughty schoolboy; questions were fired at him such as, why are you here in your HQ and not at the front with your men? He was given no chance to reply to any of the questions put to him. Throughout the war all matters conducted between the French and the British were carried out in French, English was never spoken and although Gough had a good command of French he was not sufficiently fluent in the language that he was able to counteract the rude and excited manner in which he was addressed by Foch, this of course put him at a great disadvantage. The reality of the situation was that a British army commander of equal rank ought never to have been addressed in such an overbearing manner particularly since the addressing officer was a posturing foreign national. Sir George Aston[37] comments on an interview that took place with Foch after his retirement in which he described his method of dealing with Allied Commanders. He said that he would discuss a plan with them and let them mull it over so that they felt that they had arrived at the decision themselves, he then would leave them a little note prepared by Weygand (his Aide) and says that this aimed at creating a feeling of mutual cooperation rather than being talked down to by a superior officer. He said that this 'come over and see me and we will chat about it' may have been a lengthy process but 'we got there in the end'. All one can say is that perhaps this was his view looking back, but no doubt Hubert Gough would see it in a somewhat different light.

It seemed obvious to Gough that things had been said at the Doullens meeting that had caused Foch to be in such an animated state on arrival at Dury with his little shadow, General Weygand. The reality was that Gough was reasonably satisfied and confident with the current situation of the Fifth Army since it had completely frustrated Ludendorff's plans and saved Amiens, albeit at great cost. It was never going to be easy and this was made clear by Gough when the date of the attack was known, time and again he pointed out that the number of men he had under his command to cover the extended front that he had been allocated, were totally inadequate, he was grossly over extended. The men under his command had fought themselves to a standstill and Foch appeared to be completely ignorant of what the Fifth Army had achieved under virtually hopeless circumstances. The fact that General Gough was now under the command of the French General Fayolle on his right meant that he was not invited to the Doullens meeting on the 26th, although the other British army commanders were there. It could be said that he was deliberately shut out and that is probably nearer the truth of the matter.

Henry Wilson wrote in his diary[38]

"--- left with Milner and went to Dury. Gough just established his headquarters there, but as our meeting had been changed to Doullens (from Dury) we pushed on through Amiens". Here was an opportunity for the Chief of the Imperial General Staff to visit a British Army Commander at the front, who for five days had fought, with a severely weakened army, one of the most intensive battles of the war. A commander who could have given Wilson and Milner (the Secretary of State for War) an up to minute report of the current situation at the front, and they 'just pushed on', that is the sort of support General Gough could now expect from a superior who had never commanded a unit in battle who that same day entered in his diary,[39] "---- then I dis-

353

cussed the removal of Gough and told Haig he could have Rawly (Rawlinson), and Rawly's old fourth Army staff from Versailles to replace Gough, Haig agreed to this."

Had Gough been invited to attend the Doullens meeting he could have presented a report that might have enabled those present to see things in a different light, but unfortunately those who did attend simply spoke of the ground lost under Gough's command. At that meeting Petain was openly speaking of the cowardice of the Fifth Army, that the Fifth was a broken army, finished, and in Paris such stories were reported in the press, they also circulated in London. The fact that the French with double the numbers in men, were themselves scurrying back faster and further than the Fifth army was of little consequence, nor to was the fact that on that very morning a command from the Third Army Commander, General Byng, having been misinterpreted an order from GHQ caused the wholesale retreat of Congreves VIIth Corps to across the Somme leaving Gough's right totally exposed to German enfilade fire.[40]

Foch stormed out of Gough's HQ at Dury ordering General Gough to hold the ground that they stood on, under no circumstances must there be any further retreat, *Jamais reculer!* In Gough's own words he says, "--the impression that Foch made on me was naturally not a favourable one. Excitable and evidently apt to jump to conclusions, he did not inspire me with respect or confidence". Gough was totally surprised and filled with indignation but in the interests of military discipline he carried out his orders. There has now been time enough to analyse and evaluate the conduct of the Fifth Army and without doubt those crucial days under Gough's command were the bedrock on which in 1918, the Armistice and final victory were founded. Later we shall see that the Germans were denied Amiens, they were then denied Hazebrouck by Plumers 2nd Army, the enemy broke through the French and raced to the Marne but by then Foch had what the British did not have, reserves, with which he struck a crippling blow.

On March the 27th after spending the day visiting brigade and divisional units Gough arrived back at Dury around 5pm to find that he had a visitor from GHQ. Haigs Military Secretary General Ruggles-Brise, he asked to see Gough alone and as it were delivered the Coup de Grace. Gough says '—he told me as nicely as he could that the Chief thought that I and my staff must be very tired, so he had decided to put Rawlinson in and the Staff of the Fourth Army to take command. On the 28th of March Rawlinson took command and on the 2nd of April the Fifth Army ceased to exist, the units being incorporated into the Fourth Army. General Gough, having suffered the ignominy of being relieved of his command during battle was invited to dine with Haig at GHQ on the 31st of March, it was Good Friday and there he was informed that he would be taking command of a trench digging party from Amiens to the coast, Haig did not entirely trust the French and in the event that they allowed the Germans to split the French and British Forces, Haig wanted to have a defensive line already prepared. Fortunately Gough was spared the degradation of taking command of a pioneer digging army when a few days later he was discharged home on half pay.

John Terraine put it succinctly when he said'[41] 'Gough and his army had not fought in vain; it was a cruel fate that brought dismissal after so gallant a fight against such hopeless odds'. And Plumer, who had returned to command the second Army from his brief command in Italy on the 13th of March, made the following comment[42]. 'For such a disaster a scapegoat was required. Rightly or wrongly, and against Haig's protests, the War Cabinet ordered that Gough should be the sacrifice'.

By the 26th March the Germans had not succeeded in taking any major objective and now their attack was weakening, they were attacking all along the Somme/Arras front but a call to Foch for reserves were ignored, what Foch's appointment signified was the importance placed on Petain's plan to turn south to Paris if the French army found itself in great danger. Unfortunately it also cast the British Fifth and Third Army Commanders in a grossly incompetent light and ended the illustrious career of a very fine soldier. What were the public at home to make of it, that the British were proving to be so incompetent that they needed a French, largely unsuccessful General, to take charge? Did he have some magic powers that would enable the undermanned British Forces to push the Germans over the Rhine? Foch's debut as Supremo started with three successive defeats in two weeks, are Generals to be removed because they do not always win, if that is the case why was Foch not removed, (in fact even at so early a stage, amongst the French General Staff there were calls for him to be replaced by Petain).

Foch's simple plan was to build a General Reserve of French troops under his executive command, until that was achieved the job in hand for the French and the British was to hold on the their positions defending whatever the cost. In the main, the British were the ones doing the fighting, Where was General Foch to get these reserves from? The answer was simple, to take troops from the quiet areas of the French front into reserve and replace them with worn out British troops; this was referred to as *Roulement*. The war weary British Fifth and Third Army soldiers would not move to an area behind the British lines for rest and recuperation in the normal way but go straight into the line on the French front. It was well known that the Germans planned their big attack to be against the British front on the Somme and that manpower numbers were dangerously low, it follows therefore that Foch was quite prepared to leave the British depleted front to take the brunt of it. Perhaps his hope was that the British would buckle under the strain and a creating a situation that would allow a counter stroke with his mass of reserves thereby securing a French victory.

The German military strategist *Clauzewitz* said that an army should be aware of gaining a massive victory and yet be unable to gain from it, if its troops and lines of communication were exhausted and no reserves available to follow through, the probable outcome of what might have been a victory would turn to total defeat, this of course would depend on your opponent having the ability to produce a counterstroke anyway. This counterstroke was the basis of Foch's plan, but in achieving it the British Army would face a terrible task. The opponent in this game of chess, Count Erich Von Ludendorff was working at plans that would prevent the build up of a General Reserve, just as Foch hoped that the Germans would over extend themselves and be unable to hold on to their gains, so Ludendorff was hoping to compel the Allies to use up all their reserves thus leaving the Somme and Arras exposed. The Germans had two main objectives; one was to split the Anglo/French Front, the other to 'chop a hole' through Flanders to Hazebrouck and the coast. From that Petain, the French C.in C, deduced that there would likely be a third plan, and that plan would be an offensive in the Aisne/Champagne area to draw off divisions from other areas of the front. This could have been the reasoning behind his withholding divisions needed to support the Fifth and Third armies. Whatever his reason for coming to that conclusion he did not tell Haig why he expected such an attack, events will show however, that although his timing was a bit out, he was right. However the attack on that front was only mounted as a result of the German failure to breach the British lines, and having said that it was not grounds for standing aside and seeing the British Fifth Army destroyed.

Foch's experience in the war could not compare with that of Douglas Haig whose seamless involvement at the front from mid 1915 onwards had seen him in command of all the major battles on the British front, and before that, campaigns in India and South Africa. The fact is that there was no way that the French would ever serve under British command and of course Haig knew that, he never sought to command the Entente Forces, on the contrary he offered his loyal support to Foch and fully supported his appointment. Haig did this because his sole aim was an end to the war, and that could not be achieved whilst Petain put national interest before a united front. Shaw Sparrow [43] makes the following crucial observations, "that this so called unity of command under Foch did not include the Americans", (one year after declaring war the Americans were still not engaged) the British were retreating and at that moment Lloyd George was begging President Wilson to send his troops as fast as he could. What were people to think of that, British troops needed a competent French General to lead them plus the support of the American troops? Especially when there were 1.5 million recruits in England. Was it expected by Lloyd George that Foch was a miracle worker, infact Foch had suffered three defeats during the war, one of them at the Chemin Des Dames that threatened the outcome of the crucial Battle of the Marne in 1915; these defeats were serious enough to see him relieved of his command and replaced by Marshal Petain. Shaw Sparrow goes on to say, "When these matters are weighed and measured, I am certain that it would have been much fairer to Foch, and much fairer, of course, to our national pedigree and just pride, if the act of appointing a French Generalissimo had been deferred till the retreat had ended, and till Mr. Lloyd George had explained frankly that Gough, through no fault of his own, began the battle perilously short of men; had received reinforcements with a slowness that could not be avoided; and yet had baffled the immense efforts of Von Hutier and Von Marwitz, winning time for both the arrival of piecemeal relief and for the incoming of US troops". Of course Foch would not have agreed with this and it was perhaps in Haigs interests since he would never be in a position of overall control that he should support someone who was, not only that, there was the added bonus that 'the ball would be in someone else's court'. In any event the whole situation must have been galling and belittling to Douglas Haig, a conscientious man who was dedicated to his task and ever optimistic. His position was a tenuous one because of the relationship with Lloyd George, an inveterate Francophile who had no time for the British General Staff in France. Added to this Haig, to his credit, in the higher interests of achieving victory, had supported to the full the appointment of Foch, a somewhat proud General who initially treated Marshal Haig as a subordinate.

America had not joined the Allies but declared itself to be in some associate status, besides that General Pershing the US Commander in Chief was reluctant to have his troops under other than American command, "the American people would not accept such an arrangement". However when Foch became the Supremo, Pershing offered to make his troops available under Foch's command, his only proviso was that the US troops be kept together as divisions, units that were in fact larger than a French or British Division. The previous suggestion of a reserve under the control of Foch would have seen him, as a General, of inferior rank to both Haig and Petain, sharing command in a way that could have only been detrimental to Haig's efforts to move things on. Foch was now 66 and had probably given up hope that his time of greatness would ever come, but here was the call, and he rose to it superbly displaying all the superior arrogance of Le Proverbial Coq Sportif, even though he did not have a designated title. Haig asked Foch pointedly if he would send in reserves to support the British in the event of break-through by German forces, General Foch eventually replied that on no account must the French and British front be separated, if the attack were to develop the French Army would send five infantry divisions and four cavalry divisions. Alternatively if the attack falls on the French, Haig would provide six infantry divisions and six artillery divisions, the proviso here as pointed out by Foch was that the latter would not apply if the British were under heavy attack themselves.

All this of course had already been planned between Douglas Haig and Marshal Petain, but according to the latter the defence of Paris came first which left in doubt whether there was a plan at all. Now it was accepted as the plan of action by the Supreme Commander above all other plans which of course, for Marshal Haig, set-tled the issue of whether support would be forthcoming at the greatest point of danger. As will be seen later, initially all this did not make it any easier for Haig to work with Foch, at times Haig despaired at the lack of cooperation and at Foch's single mindedness with re-gard to creating a general reserve at the expense of the BEF. The defence of Amiens was said to be foremost in Foch's mind but to a large extent that had been taken care of, the German offensive on that front had been stopped before he was appointed Supremo. Ludendorff's remark that the French would not try too hard to help the beleaguered B.E.F was reiterated by Von Hutier's[44] Chief of Staff Gen. Maj. Von Sauberzweig when he said, "---it need not be anticipated that the French will run themselves off their legs to the help of their Entente comrades". There was no rush to bolster the Divisions of the Fifth and third Armies in the March offensive, but, as will be seen, matters were dealt with differently when the enemy attacked on the French front at the Chemin Des Dames in July.

At this stage in the war there were strong British feelings with regard to the March 1918 offensive, and there existed a heartless attitude on the part of the French public towards the British effort. At GHQ however, it was felt that Petain had let down the Fifth and Third Armies in the period before Foch was appointed and when they faced the fiercest onslaught of the war. Nevertheless, having been what Foch considered to be uncooperative, Haig was now to become exactly the opposite and agreement was reached on mutual support by movement of divisions in the event of a dangerous situation occurring based on the plans worked out earlier between Haig and Petain, it only remained to be seen whether or not Foch would also find reasons not to fulfil these obligations.

Haig wrote to Foch on the April 6th saying that his plans were not adequate to deal with the overall military problem as it existed, and in particular that of the BEF who were taking all the strain, he demanded that French troops should take over some of the line and take a fair share in the battle. In view of the fact that the enemy were attacking heavily in an attempt to take Hazebrouck and Calais he badly needed reserve divisions to be moved up ready to support the BEF if and when required. Foch refused to offer any help or to take over any of the line and on the 7th Haig sent a message to CIGS, Sir Henry Wilson saying that he needed him to come in person to France. Wilson saw Foch and again Foch refused to move with regard to using his divisions in of support Haig, they had all three been over concerned about a possible German blow aimed at Arras/La Bassee but were taken by surprise when the attack did come. On the 9th the Germans attacked in great force against the British front from the Le Bassee Canal to Armentieres and again on the British line of the Lys to Estaires, another violent attack. Armentieres was abandoned and by the 11th the battle waged along the whole front with the British forced back to Neuve Eglise. On the 12th Haig, in his Order of the day, addressed his men with his 'backs to the wall' speech saying,

---- "words fail me to express the admiration which I feel for the splendid resistance offered by all ranks in our army, many of us are now tired. To those I would say that victory belongs to the side that holds out the longest, --------- there is no course open to us but to fight it out. Every position must be held to the last man. There must be no retirement. With our backs to the wall, and believing in the justice of our cause, each one of us must fight on to the end".

Many of these troops had already suffered the trauma of *Kaiserschlact* in the period from the 21st of March having been drawn off from the First and Second Armies and transferred to the Somme, now they were again facing a much superior force and a reported 110 German divisions were used along the whole front. Foch's sole concern appeared to be the saving of France, and if the BEF was destroyed in the process, so be it, surely this was not what the British came to France for, to be sidelined and destroyed for the sake of self interest. Sir John French had pinpointed the spirit of the BEF's reason for being in France when he spoke of Napoleon on his arrival at Cherbourg,

----"would he not have rejoiced at this friendly invasion of France by Englands good yeomen, who were now offering their lives to save France from the possible destruction as a power of first class".

Ludendorff was desperate to punch a hole somewhere that he could dash through and this was to be the knockout punch, the Germans could smell victory, life back in Germany was getting very difficult, shortages of everything and especially food was giving rise to serious unrest amongst the population. Having pushed the British forces back on the Somme for 15 miles they got a glimpse of what life was like for those living on the other side of the wire, and it came as a shock to realise that the submarine blockade had not made any significant difference with regard to supplies in what had been a relatively quiet part of the front, obviously in the west they were not suffering in the way that the German people were. At the front there were reports from German officers of their men cutting up dead horses, such was the lack of supplies.

And yet, absurdly, it seemed that to Foch and Clemenceau Britain was not pulling her weight. When Clemenceau spoke of sending two Colonels to Britain to examine our manpower the matter was reported at once to Henry Wilson by Maj. Gen. Spears; liaison Officer between Wilson and the French. Wilson was incensed and pointed out a few facts and indicating who was taking the strain, that our 60 divisions had a loss of 300,000[45], and that the French 60/70 divisions had a loss of 100,000, one third of British losses. Ouch! And we only came to help.

On the 10th April Wilson[46] made an entry in his diary, 'Foch is looking for a title for himself. Apparently he wanted a designation giving him more authority! Foch was aiming at Generalissimo status, he outlined the limitations imposed on his appointment by the 'Doullens Agreement' in a meeting with the 'Tiger', as Clemenceau was informally known. Foch advocated that the role of coordinator of the allied effort was simply inadequate and that more powers regarding the wider conflict needed to be conferred upon him, the Americans were now entering the war and he wanted full control of all allied forces from the North Sea to the Adriatic, he had a plan! Clemenceau of course gave him his full support and called a meeting in the Town Hall at Beauvais on April 3rd at which the following resolution was adopted.

"General Foch is charged by the British French and American Governments with the coordination of the action of the Allies on the Western Front. To this end all powers necessary to secure effective realisation are conferred on him. The British, French and American governments for this purpose entrust to General Foch the strategic directions of military operations. The commanders in chief of the British French and American armies have full control of the tactical employment of their forces. Each commander in chief will have the right of appeal to his Government if, in his opinion, the safety of his army is compromised by any order received from General Foch".

One cannot but think that the effect on French public morale at the appointment of a French Generalissimo with wide ranging powers over all Allied forces would go unnoticed by Clemenceau, the French Prime Minister. However the wide-ranging powers that Foch sought were not forthcoming, the theatre of operation as far as he was concerned would be confined to France. Clemenceau had put forward the designation of Commander in Chief Allied Forces but it was rejected, the appointment made at the 'Doullens Agreement' had referred only to France. The Belgians were not included anyway since under the Belgian constitution they remained under the Command of King Albert. Lloyd George attended the Beauvais conference having landed at Boulogne and travelled by car through the area where British troops recently engaged in battle were moving, in his memoirs Foch records[47], 'it seems evident that the order and morale of these (*British*) units did not furnish him with a pleasant picture of the situation; for apart from arriving very late, he seemed to bring with him a most gloomy impression'. It seems a particularly superfluous comment to make, almost as if his imagination had run away with him whilst writing up his diary. The British/Commonwealth troops in the area of Amiens were under no great pressure in early April and certainly Rawlinson gave no indication that his men were of low morale at that time.

Foch goes on to say---"he was not long however, in shaking this off and recovering his characteristic animation and energy", and while the session was in progress he, Lloyd George, made this statement regarding myself; ---"the English people have confidence in you. Your nomination as Commander in Chief of the Allied Armies has nowhere been so well received as in my country". One can imagine Douglas Haig cringing at the submissiveness of the man and wondering why he could not be so staunchly supportive of our own competent General Staff, but perhaps mercifully it was whispered, and Haig knew nothing of it.

It seemed that Foch was hoping to put himself in a similar position to that of Erich Von Ludendorff, but that was not remotely possible, when the latter gave an order there was no debate, it was not questioned. The Entente on the other hand consisted of two democratically elected governments and all the decision-making problems that one associates with that. The opposition, i.e. Germany, albeit a monarchy, was a dictatorship in

365

which the decision making process was not open to question nor was there an electorate to consider with regard to losses at the front. Not having been allowed to broaden the terms of his appointment, Foch was still in a position to achieve what he originally set out to do; that was to control a strong reserve; if Foch's plans succeeded it would be an all French reserve with the British holding the line.

On April 14th an important meeting was held at which Haig again pressed home the fact that since the 21st of March the British Army had borne the brunt of the fighting and in the process had exhausted his reserves, he had not asked for French troops in the battle line nor even in the actual battle zone, all he did ask was that the small reserve under General Maistre Commander of the D.A.N, (Detachment Armee du Nord) situated between the Somme and Arras should be moved further North and ready to be called on. Foch held to his previous position and declared that he would not relieve whilst the battle was in progress, and Wilson summed it up by saying, if you will not relieve in battle there would be little point relieving after the battle. Haig found Foch difficult to work with; he was opposed to his short term thinking but of course Foch was not interested in any ideas that Douglas Haig, might have, Foch had his own agenda and he was not sharing it with Haig or anyone else, this of course gave rise to acrimonious feelings.

As a result of Foch's single minded quest to form a reserve and his reluctance to take Haig into his confidence with regard to future planning, accusations were made saying that the French were looking after their own interests at the expense of the hard pressed British, this led later to meetings where Clemenceau and Foch were confronted point blank by Henry Wilson, Milner (Secretary of state for War) and Haig about Foch's cavalier attitude to the British. Two divisions of French Infantry and three cavalry divisions had moved into Flanders under the command of General Plumer, but he was not allowed to use these divisions without Foch's approval. The situation on the Second army front was very serious and Henry Wilson wrote in his diary, [48] ---- "Plumer had a long talk with me before Foch came in, he is quite clear that if the Boches attack heavily he cannot hold the line of hills (Messines, Wytschaete, Kemmel Hill) much longer, he cannot trust his troops, they are untrained, and although as brave as possible, simply do not know their business".

Replenishment troops had begun to arrive from the UK but the numbers were totally inadequate and the divisional strength in the Second Army was severely depleted, some 10 divisions only remaining. A little later Foch arrived; he and Henry Wilson went on to have a strained exchange of opinions. Wilson had spent a great deal of his time in France and since the early days of the Entente Cordial he and Foch had been close friends, however since Foch had been allotted the role of Supremo their relationship had soured somewhat and when Foch made unwelcome comments on the subject of manpower shortage, Henry Wilson's reply was that the French should lower conscription age from nineteen years of age to eighteen as in the British Army, and that might help. He also commented on the movement of British troops into the French line from Reims to the swiss border. Wilson was quite adamant that it would be totally unsatisfactory for British troops to be transported to Lorraine or Alsace since the distance from the British front would be too great, Foch arranged for the Corps that did move into French Lines to be sent to the Chemin des Dames in the Champagne region, but as it turned out, after the exhausted themselves in battle with the Fifth and Third armies they would not be there to rest.

Foch went on to Second Army HQ to see Herbert Plumer and to give him his orders, i.e. '*Jemais reculer*' and then for an hour proceeded to lecture the highly experienced and respected Plumer on how he should handle his men, and the tactics he should use to defend Kemmel Hill etc. Foch never really left the post of Professor at the Ecole Superior de Guerre and obviously was quite happy to let everyone have the benefit of that whenever the chance arose. It is difficult to know what Haig's feelings were on this, after all he was the Commander in Chief of British Forces in France and here was a French General, whose job was purely of a strategic nature and based at French GHQ, involving himself in tactical decision making on the British front line. By the 17th April, at the Battle of the Lys, Plumer had withdrawn completely from the Passchendaele Ridge and the Ypres salient and set up a defending perimeter around Ypres. The next day the Germans again mounted a heavy assault against the hills that ran From Messines to Mount Kemmel, skilled enfilade machine gun fire from key British positions destroyed the German attack. They made another attempt the next day but with the same result and this was followed by a seven-day lull.

From the 17th - 20th the Germans attacked heavily but were repulsed, the British were now being partly relieved by the two reserve divisions that Foch had agreed to attach to the D.A.N. Since the start of the Lys offensive the British had brilliantly defended Kemmel Hill but had now been relieved by the French. On the 25th the Germans attacked again and took just one hour to sweep the French off Kemmel Hill and take 6500 prisoners. That was, of course a serious embarrassment for General Foch, particularly since he had declared to General Du Cane, the British Liaison officer to Foch, only ten days before at the height of the battle "the Battle of Hazebrouk is finished". One wonders if his believing that prompted him to allow his French reserves to go into the line.

On the 29th the Germans again made an all out attack to break through to the Coast and again it failed miserably. The German Commander General Von Kuhl commented.

"--- that they had failed to compel the evacuation of the Ypres position, the Channel ports had not been reached--- the second great offensive had not brought about the hoped for decision".

Haig made a comment regarding the strained relations between General Plumer and the French. [49]'The French have been very trying and poor old Plumer has had a most anxious time! The Belgians had proved far easier to work with, and this was brought out in a letter from the Earl of Athlone-----and that neither King Albert nor his people desired having to have the French alongside them. The Belgians he told the King (George V) would do anything for General Plumer.

When the end of hostilities came on the Eastern Front in November 1917, Ludendoff found himself in a very powerful position, he could take his time regrouping, to improve lines of support, supply and communications in readiness for the big break through. Not only was their position advantageous from the point of view of manpower, the front was not shared by any other ally, for instance Austria, and therefore there was no conflict of interest. By comparison the Allied situation had changed to the point where Foch was now Supremo, not officially in overall control but actually fulfilling that role in that he was bypassing Douglas Haig and talking to British Army Commanders as to what they should do, this of course created a situation of unrest amongst the General Staff. Petain had nursed the

French Army through an extended period since the disastrous Nivelle campaign and the mutinies following Verdun, after this long period when, for the Poelus, offensive action had been out of the question and they were prepared only to defend *La patrie,* there was hope that once again they could be a strong, viable force.

At home Henry Wilson and Lloyd George were talking of plans looking forward to 1919 and even 1920. Foch was also beavering away at plans in which he favoured an all out attempt to defeat the Germans in April 1919, there was a distinct feeling that it would take time for the British Army to recover and any offensive would be out of the question until the coming year. It seemed that everyone was forward planning for when the U.S Forces came in greater numbers. Thankfully Douglas Haig saw things differently He wanted the war ended before 1918 was out, and his thoughts revolved mainly around how that could be achieved. Of course he had thought that 1917 might produce the same sort of results and that had ended in a disastrous year. Haig was in a precarious position in that he was made to feel that he was The General Officer Commanding British Forces in France only on sufferance, writing to Lord Derby he had said he that in his opinion 'we are all expendable' and that if the War Cabinet felt that he should go then so be it, just tell me and I will resign. He also added 'but I doubt you will find a suitable replacement just now'. Lloyd George asked Wilson, did he think that he should accept Haig's resignation; Wilson thought that they should wait, echoing Haigs comment by saying there was no obvious replacement for him at that time. One could well understand it if Haig felt disillusioned by his present, tenuous situation since he also commanded a severely weakened army, he faced a re-energized, powerful enemy and had to contend with the difficulties in working with Foch, who he considered 'obstinate and selfish' and from whom he could expect heavy demands but little help. However, at no time did Haig allow his feelings towards Foch to interfere with their working relationship, and evidence of his conscientious and optimistic nature showed as he applied himself fully to plans for countermoves that would cancel the recent German gains as the Battle of the Lys ended.

27

Chemin des Dames and Second Marne

From mid May until July figures show that British losses over the period were in the region of 300,000, some 90,000 of those were missing presumed dead or had been taken prisoner. Of the 100 French Divisions only 32 had been involved in the action from 21st March and the losses were in the region of 92,000. The German army had lost in the region of 500,000 men, nevertheless, with divisions still transferring from the Russian Front Ludendorff could count on reserves of around 90 divisions giving him a superiority of some 25 divisions over the Allies. The Americans were arriving belatedly and toward the end of May there would be some 120,000 untrained US troops in France. Foch was keen to relieve French divisions for his General Reserve and at his meetings at British GHQ in April he had aired his plans for what he termed *Roulement*, his idea was that the weary, exhausted British divisions that were now being relieved, should not be moved behind their own lines for essential rest and recuperation, but to a quiet area of the French front line. This was Foch's means of building up his reserves by robbing Peter to pay Paul, and it created a bad feeling between Wilson and Foch. Amongst the first British troops to be transferred to the 'secteurs calmes du front Francais', the calm sectors, were some of the divisions that had seen the hardest fighting with the Fifth and Third armies, they were the 8th, 50th, 21st, 19th and 25th. They were allocated a position on the right of the legendary Chemin Des Dames, a long ridge to the south of and roughly parallel with the River Aisne. This is where the British would spend their precious R&R, alas unknown to the French and in great secrecy Ludendorff was massing troops and equipment some few miles north at the town of Laon, it seems incredible that the French never became aware of this, the build up to some 30 divisions and an estimated 5000 guns should normally have been spotted by spies or civilians, even aircraft, but so good was the German camouflage of guns and supplies that nothing was fed back to French intelligence.

Although the move to the French 'quiet Front' was intended to be restful period, the officers and NCO's of the British divisions were kept busy at lectures about the French system of operating, and they in turn took the time to pass this on the O.R's as a matter of course. The French obviously thought it was important that the British (Les Khakis) be brought up to scratch in the French way of doing things in order to increase the level of cooperation in the event of an enemy assault. Some of the French who had been in these trenches for some time and were accustomed to German activity in the area, had recently noted an increase in the number of single artillery shots, to them it was an an indicaton that the enemy had brought new guns into the area that were being tested and calibrated in readiness for use. The British divisional Commanders, unlike the French Commander they were now under, had already seen heavy fighting over an extended period at the Somme and had first hand experience of being in the front line. They had advised that the British divisions should be dug in on the reverse slopes of the Chemin des Dames but the French claimed that the mass of 30 German divisions poised to attack, large as it was, in fact was a massive diversion and so ignored the advice. Once over the Chemin Des Dames the enemy plan was to create a defensive position on the River Vesle, that was the extent of the German planning at that stage, although, with luck, lack of opposition from the French might well provide the opportunity for a race to the Marne.

The British were out and about at night cutting a way through the German wire and looking for what they could find, they captured a German subaltern and on being questioned he denied that there were attack preparations in progress but his interrogators had a bad feeling about the information he was giving them. A soldier captured by the French talked more freely and indicated the time that the enemy attack was to take place, and in an attempt to get some sort of confirmation on that the German subaltern was handed over to the French Secret Police, the Deuxieme Bureau. They gave him a choice, either tell the truth or be taken out and shot forthwith, he opted to tell what he knew and corroborated the information given by the soldier. Again signals were sent out to the British divisions that the enemy would attack at 0100 hours, surely this was not the intention, battle weary British troops now defending a quiet part of the French Front as they sang, 'Here we are, here we are, Oh! Here we are again!

THE RETURN

There's a tramp of feet in the morning, an oath from the N.C.O
As up the road to the trenches, the brown Battalions go.

Guns and rifles and wagons, transport and horses and men.
Up with the flush of the dawning, and back with the night again.

Back again from the battle, from the mates we have left behind.

Our officers are gloomy, the N.C.O's are kind.

Then a Jews harp breaks the silence, purring an
old refrain,
Singing the song of the soldier, "Here we are
again"

Here we are, here we are, Oh! Here we are
again.
Some have gone west, best of the best, lying out
in the rain.

Stiff as stones in the open, out of the doing for
good,
They'll never come back to advance or attack,
But by God! Don't we wish that they could?
***

The German gains on the Somme, at Arras and Lys as
they pushed the British hard back had produced no im-
portant gains, they had failed to break through the Brit-
ish front in some of the most intensive attacks of the
war and Ludendorff now looked for some way to bluff
the Allies. He drew up plans to send a huge force to
cross the Aisne, drive over the Chemin des Dames and
on to the River Vesle, the plan was to tie up reserves in
that region whilst leaving the way open for a German
fatal blow to the British on the Somme. The strength of
the attack needed to be convincing hence the 30 divi-
sions, but a far greater number of divisions were avail-
able for operations further north. The British and Amer-
icans had been forecasting this attack for some time but
the French ignored it, the French Commander failed to
anticipate the strength of the attack and subsequently
failed spectacularly to defend the French Positions. By
a stroke of fate the heaviest blows fell on the positions

held by the weary British soldiers on the right of the Chemin des Dames who were ostensibly resting. One could be forgiven for suggesting that there was something of a stink about the French tactics, they had ignored warnings of a pending German attack, the expendable worn out British divisions were used at the point of the heaviest thrust and Foch was accumulating divisions in the area of Montdidier and Noyon for a counterstroke, wherever that might be.

The order to open fire went out to the artillery units on the evening of May 26th and the British 18 pdrs opened up, in the distance could be heard the French 75's, the gunfire creating a fiery glow in the night sky. From the enemy lines there was no sign of movement but the attack was expected anytime. Around midnight the thunderous noise of heavy units moving up into position could be heard and at 0100hrs 27th May the German heavy batteries opened up with the roar of more than 5000 guns lasting more than three hours with a long end period of saturation with gas shell fire. The British were unable to return fire effectively as a result of the gas and the riflemen were sealed of below ground in sweltering conditions. The German observation balloons had picked out the British guns and the enemy fire was so accurate that most were smashed to pieces. When the enemy guns ceased fire the battle hardened British troops were out from below and firing toward the enemy that they knew were advancing, even though in the conditions they could see nothing. They came on with tanks and flamethrowers to brush aside all opposition. On the 29th the enemy were at Soissons and the 31st were again at the Marne only 50 miles from Paris.

The recent German offensive in the Ypres salient had been brought to a halt by the end of April and it had taken a huge toll on Plumers Second Army, up to this point there had been a stubborn resistance on the part of the British Govt. (Lloyd George) to send out replenishment troops. In the early months of the year to 21st of March there had been moderate numbers sent out, some 100,000, but now recognising the gravity of the situation they had unwittingly exacerbated, the War Cabinet tacitly acknowledged that it would have been better had they met Haig's demand for more men in order to have prevented the current rundown state of 4 of the 5 British Armies. Between the 21st of March and the end of August some 550,000 men were sent over of which about 50,000 were 'B' grade. Now with the Germans having broken through at the Chemin des Dames Foch was desperate for divisions. How different now the situation that the French were under heavy attack and being forced back, the Germans had made the longest advance attack of the whole war. Foch records in his memoirs[50]--- the Germans forced the British IXth Corps back up the heights of Chateau Thierry. These are the same weary British divisions taking their rest on the *Sectuers calmes du front Francais* after the week-long battles on the Somme. Foch makes no mention of this in his diary but he goes on to describe the reserves called on by Petain and himself from the British, French Eastern, the D.A.N. and the thinning out of Belgian Forces to cover for the divisions taken from the British Front.

In Foch's own words, '--- in fact, nearly every available French organisation was set in motion towards the battle'. Had Foch and Petain offered the same support to General Gough at the German March offensive, things may have been quite different. The Fifth Army prevented the Germans taking Amiens, an extremely important communications centre to both the French and the British. Had the Germans occupied Amiens the British and French armies would have been separated and in all probability Germany would have been victorious. The French had been given a bloody nose and it produced a change in attitude to the British following the German gains in March at St Quentin and later at the Lys. They were critical of the British Government in not providing more troops and the fact that conscription in Ireland had not been enforced, they had also openly said that that the Royal Navy contribution was not worth one gun to the French, when in fact it was critical to the Allied effort. Now there was a distinct change of attitude from the French.

On the 3rd of June Foch informed Douglas Haig that he had ordered the movement of four French reserve divisions from the Montdidier area and asked him to place 3 reserve divisions on the Somme, this Haig did at once. Having had first hand reports from Henry Wilson (who had visited Franchet D.Esperez's HQ) about the state of the IXth Corps (ostensibly resting in the quiet areas of the French Front) Haig asked that the corps be returned to British lines but this did not happen until the end of June. Foch followed these demands by asking that the four American divisions undergoing training on the British front should be released to take positions on the French Front, already Haigs French reserves had been taken along with 3 British divisions relocated to the Somme in of place them, above and beyond these he was asked to prepare to send all his reserves to wherever a crisis might occur.

When this was picked up by the C.I.G.'s, Sir Henry Wilson, from Haig's regular reports he mistakenly thought that it was intended to be an appeal to the Beauvais Authority against the authority of General Foch so brought the matter to the attention of the War Cabinet.The relationship between Haig and Foch had already deteriorated before all this and of course Foch's current demands did not help. Wilson disapproved of

378

Foch's plans and had been pressing for saltwater inundations along the coast with the object of shortening the line and releasing divisions, for that reason it may well have been that Wilson was only too ready to take up the cudgels on Haig's behalf and deliberately read the report wrongly. No appeal was made to the Beauvais Authority but Wilson and Milner crossed to France where they arranged to meet Clemenceau and Foch, present also were Douglas Haig, General Weygand and General DuCane the British Liaison Officer. At the meeting Haig said, [51] "--- the situation was quickly reaching a stage in which circumstances might compel me to appeal to them (the British Cabinet) under the Beauvais Agreement. In my opinion the order about to be issued by Foch imperilled the British Army in France".

By all accounts it was a hostile affair but matters were brought to reason by the politicians present, Foch said that he had not touched any of Haig's reserves, that he had only asked him to make preparations for any necessary move. He was playing at semantics since the object of asking for the reserves was to have them available for his use, in which case they were not available to Douglas Haig. Clemenceau obviously valued Haig's contribution to the war and banned the French GQH from ordering the movement of any units, French or otherwise from the British line without consultation with Haig. Perhaps what he meant was that Foch needed to issue a direct order to Haig before moving Divisions rather than act first and tell Douglas Haig later. Also at Clemenceau's suggeston it was agreed that Haig and Foch should meet more often. Foch suggested that Haig should not protest unless Foch committed *des imprudences*, if that arose then Foch would agree with Haig. It was suggested that the meeting had served to strengthen Foch's position and also the working relationship between the two Army leaders. In his memoirs

Foch stated that Haig had appealed to the Beauvais Authority but in actual fact that never occurred, however Douglas Haig did see more clearly the implications of the Beauvais Agreement, and it indicated that Foch had been empowered to do whatever he saw fit. Haig now felt that if he was charged with the responsibility for the safety of the British Army, then he needed that confirmed in writing, otherwise that responsibility devolved to Foch under the terms of The Beauvais agreement.

Since the end of the Lys offensive the British Front was relatively quiet, the French were now under pressure and the Germans were across the Marne, the outskirts of Paris was being bombed and on the 9th of July the Germans again attacked on the Noyon-Montdidier line. During the next two days the US troops saw there first action of the war in what was known as the Battle of Belleau wood and the German advance was brought to a halt on the 11th July. At this same time Haig was expecting an attack by the forces of Prince Rupprecht who were massed on Haig's front with some 35 divisions in reserve. Information had been gleaned from enemy prisoners and from German deserters telling when the offensive was to begin; the indications were that the attack on Ypres depended on finishing of the French at the Vesle before turning to the British Front. Foch on the other hand was expecting the Germans to make a further push again on the 14th July, and had developed a side operation that would release the railhead at Siosson, but as events unfolded he saw the possibility of a more far reaching offensive. With his assembled reserves to the south west of Amiens he planned a flanking attack on the expected German assault, but Foch was keeping his plans absolutely secret from everyone. Just as Ludendorff was ready to change his initial plan if the opportunity arose, so was Foch who,

380

having planned the small diversionary attack to relieve the railway to Soissons, saw an opportunity and changed his plan into a trap that turned the tide in favour of the Allies.

On the 12th July Haig's Chief of Staff, General Lawrence visited Foch's HQ at Bombom whilst Douglas Haig was away in England. Whilst he was there Foch informed him that he required the release of four British divisions, Lawrence, not wanting to fulfil the demand without Haig's authority, made an interim arrangement for one division to move. On his return Haig sanctioned the transfer of the divisions, two days later Foch asked that 4 more divisions be transferred to the reserve pool based to the south west of Amiens with which Haig again complied. The reserve force eventually amounted to 38 infantry and six cavalry divisions, General Mangin also had 18 infantry divisions, including two American divisions and 3 cavalry divisions. On the 17th July Lloyd George wrote a stiff letter to Clemenceau pointing out the dangerously exposed position of the British Army in Flanders and he instructed Sir Henry Wilson to liaise with Foch on the matter, Wilson wrote to Foch saying that Lloyd George would not allow our four divisions to go south unless Haig could give an assurance that Rupprecht would not attack. At this stage Foch had revealed his plans to no one, had Haig been aware that Foch intended to allow the enemy to overstretch it communications in reaching the Marne, no doubt he would have given his full support as he later did. In the end Milner managed to persuade Lloyd George to be less confronational and to write to Haig saying that if he thought that his force was being put in danger, he (Haig) should appeal to the Beauvais Authority. L.G. then sent Lord Smuts (the South African Prime Minister) and Gen. Radcliffe the D.M.O. to see Douglas Haig and get across L.G.'s views on the matter. Whether Haig was able to deduce what Foch was about and had decided to give his support is perhaps an interesting thought.

Haig complied with Foch's demands and moved the divisions south, and in doing so was fully aware of his actions, he knew exactly the position he found himself in and what he was doing, he said. "I will take the risk, I accept responsibility. I have acted in the Allied cause". He gave Smuts a note that he had prepared, which read,

"I take the risk, and I fully realise that if the dispositions of Foch prove to be wrong, the blame will rest with me. On the other hand if they prove to be right, the credit will lie with Foch". [52]

He then said to Smuts "that is in case the British Government cannot find a verbal undertaking sufficient to relieve their anxiety, with this the Government should be well satisfied".

It was a tails you win, heads I lose situation for Haig, but he was fully aware of that and let Lloyd George know that if Foch had fouled things up he (Haig) would be another scapegoat. Haig was keen to see the Germans knocked back in the Champagne region leaving him the opportunity to attack along the British Front and bring the war to a close, perhaps he saw through Foch's intentions and with that a strong possibility that an opportunity would occur for him to mount an offensive that would see the Germans pushed back over the Rhine. Meanwhile, Foch was contemplating a winter in the trenches and a renewal of operations in the Spring of 1919 with the support of an increased American army, that of course would have given the Germans time to regroup and raise morale in the divisions making the task that much harder.

Meanwhile the Germans had attacked on the 15th, and Marshal Petain, not being privy to Foch's secret plans, ordered the general reserves to be ready to go to Rheims, which is exactly what the Germans wanted and had planned for, to tie up the Entente reserves and leave the way clear for a huge offensive on the Somme. Foch heard of Petain's order that morning whilst visiting General Fayolle's HQ and immediately countermanded it. He held back the reserves and allowed the Germans to advance for another 3 days, stretching their lines of communication, and then on the 18[th,] Mangin's Army struck them a massive flanking blow. Haig had observed mass troop movements from Rupprechts reserves moving south and now it was obvious that Ludendorff had called off the expected attack on Ypres. This immediately opened the way for the BEF to attack even though they still faced strong German opposition, the British had been preparing heavily for what was expected to be a crushing attack that no longer existed, as a result Sir Henry Rawlinson presented plans for a Fourth Army attack in the Villiers Bretonneux area.

At a meeting of commonwealth Prime Ministers at Downing St. on July 31st Haig's proposals for an attack on the Somme were discussed. Also discussed was a memorandum presented by Henry Wilson, in this Sir Henry set forth his views on the likely course that the campaign would take in 1919? Milner said that it is clear we shall never beat the Boche; Smuts said that we will never beat the Boche in the west and there was some doubt in the minds of all that were present. It was some time later as the BEF drove the Germans back over the Hindenberg line that, with a sense of bewilderment, they looked back to that meeting and tried to understand what it was that created so pessimistic an outlook.

It seemed unbelievable that only weeks ago the Entente forces had been so fragmented, Haig was being set up by Lloyd George as a scapegoat when things looked dire and L.G. was keen to distance himself from Haig, it was Haig that offered to follow Foch's advice in the knowledge that, firstly there was a desperate need to coordinate the allied operations in order to maximise their effort against the enemy. Secondly he recognised the need to take risks and allowed Foch to stretch his own resources in order to bring the Germans to their knees at the 2nd Marne, thus opening the way for the British to attack. Douglas Haig demonstrated this when he gave to Smuts the message for Lloyd George. He also wanted an end to the war in 1918 and showed that he would cooperate in any plan that would achieve that. Without the resolve of Foch it would not have been possible anyway, allied manpower resources were badly depleted, the British could not have done it alone and France was prepared to defend and wait for a build up of American troops. But Foch did not waver, he stuck to his plan and took the criticisms that were thrown at him, the risks he took in allowing the German advance to the Marne were enormous, but as German enthusiam gave way to caution, Foch struck a heavy blow, something he could not have done without Haigs support, it cleared the way for British and Commonwealth troops to smash through the Hindenberg line, it broke the Germans back.

On the 24th July Haig, Petain and Pershing met with Foch at his HQ, He informed them that bringing the German offensive to a standstill had taken the initiative from them, their victories have now become defeats. True to Clauzwitz's theory that was exactly the case. The opportunity was now to turn from defence to attack, and at a meeting on the 26th plans by Haig and Rawlinson were presented for discussion, certain objectives were identified and it was decided that British supported by French divisions should attack on a common front, Rawlinson's Fourth Army with the XXXIst

French Corps on the British right. On 8th August the Allied offensive kicked of, [53] 'it was destined to end with the total defeat of the German armies in the great rolling battle of the 'Hundred Days.' In the first phase, the operations known in British despatches as the Battles of Amiens, Bapaume and Scarpe (lasting for nearly one month), with the First, Third and Fourth armies along with the XXXIst French Corps under Rawlinsons command, the Germans received a blow from which they never recovered. Ludendorff called that fateful August 8th 'the Black Day' or 'Day of mourning' of the German Army. The Canadians and the Australians fought brilliantly throughout this period and the credit is mainly theirs for the successes gained.

By the 21st of August Byng's Third Army operating north of Albert found the Germans giving ground, to the south the Fourth Army were driving the enemy back and by the 26th Horne's First Army was pushing east of Arras, as one area came under pressure the enemy were rushing in reserves only to find that the situation was deteriorating on another portion of the line, a few days later the line was extended when a mixed force of Belgians, British and French attacked out of the Ypres salient.

In England at the end of August the Police went on strike, Henry Wilson was highly indignant about it and offered a novel solution that probably brought the Police to the negotiating table and to accept the terms offered. On the 31st a small cabinet meeting was held at which Lloyd George, Bonar law, Milner and Sir Henry Wilson were present along with two or three others. Suggestions were put forward as to how the matter should be resolved to which Henry Wilson added "if they do not accept then they should be conscripted forthwith and put in the trenches, Bonar law and Lloyd George were in agreement. Needless to say the Police accepted the terms offered and the strike ended. It was an indication of the strength of feeling amongst the General Staff that civilian workers should take to strike action for something they were not satisfied with whilst men were laying down their lives at the front with no such privileges, for them to strike would be to mutiny, and that would incur the death penalty.

Douglas Haig was now on the way to winning the final Battles of the war, the relationship between Foch and Haig was working well, Foch was obviously very confident in Haig's ability to take the battle forward just as Haig was confident in his own ability to take back lost ground and maintain a momentum that would see the Germans back behind the Hindenberg line. By the first week in September the First, Third and Fourth Armies had swept everything before them taking some 80,000 prisoners and around 700 guns. On the 2nd of September the Group of Armies Northern, G.A.N were given the task of recapturing the Passchendaele – Clercken Ridge. Now that it could be seen that the Germans were being driven back all along from the Aisne to La Bassee, King Albert felt that the Belgians should take a greater part in any operations aimed at liberating their Homeland, to that end Foch had created G.A.N, this consisted of the 9 Belgian divisions, 6 French divisions and 6 divisions of the British Second Army operating under the Command of King Albert. It was not what Herbert Plumer wanted, he preferred to attack to the East through Messines on the assumption that the Germans were already leaving Passchendaele, but Haig wanted the Belgians moving back into their own territory.

28

The Final Roundup – Armistice

On the 2nd September Douglas Haig received a 'Personal' dispatch from Henry Wilson as he prepared for the assault on the Hindenberg line, --- [54]"just a word of warning, in regard to incurring heavy losses in attacks on the Hindenberg Line as opposed to losses when driving the enemy back to that line ---- the War Cabinet would become very anxious if we receive heavy punishment in attacking the H.L. without success. Haig wrote in his diary "It is impossible for a C.I.G.S. to send a telegram of his nature to a C.in C. in the field as 'Personal'. The Cabinet are ready to meddle and interfere in my plans in an underhand way but do not dare to say openly that they do not mean to take responsibility for any failure, though ready to take credit for any success! The object of this telegram is, no doubt, to save the prime Minister in case of any failure. So I read it to mean that I can attack the Hindenberg line if I think it right to do so. The C.I.G.S. and the Cabinet already know that my arrangements are being made to that end. If my attack is successful I will remain as C.in C. If we fail and our successes are excessive, I can hope for no mercy". " I wrote to Henry Wilson in reply. What a wretched lot of weaklings we have in high places at the present time".

Haig had found himself in the same unenviable position from the time he took Command. On the 8th of September Marshal Foch (He received his Marshal's Baton on 23rd August) asked Haig to undertake the most important operation, an attack on, "the most formidable line of resistance of all" He referred of course to the Hindenberg Line that the German's considered impregnable, the conversation was brief, Haig thought for a moment and then Foch said [55]"You will do it, there is nothing the British cannot do", Sir Douglas Haig agreed. Again Haig knew what he was doing, he was fully aware of what needed to be done to end the War and as events progressed the British and Commonwealth Forces under his command exceeded anything that Foch or the Allied Governments could have thought possible prior to the first week in August.

In accepting the challenge from Foch, Haig made his own decision; the War Cabinet had already given its tentative approval. An entry in Sir Henry Wilson's diary for 23rd September gives some inkling of just how much out on a limb Douglas Haig was. --- "Long talk with Milner today on his return from 10 days in France. He thinks Haig ridiculously optimistic and is afraid that he may embark on another Passchendaele. He warned Douglas Haig that if he knocked his present army about there was no other to replace it". The circumstances however that applied now were different in several significant aspects. Foch was now supremo and coordinating allied efforts, the war was now a mobile one where the Germans had been pushed back over a considerable distance and that, according to Ludendorff had a demoralising effect on the opposing German Forces. Breaching the Hindenberg line was, as pointed out by Foch, a huge task, but had it not been possible then neither he nor Haig would have consented to it.

On the 27th of September the British Forces (That is British, Australian, Canadian and two US army divisions) began an assault on the Cambrai and St Quentin fronts where they breached the Hindenberg line on a 6 mile front taking some 22,000 prisoners and by the 30th Haig's forces were seven miles across the Hindenberg line on a front of 25 miles taking a reported 36,000 prisoners and almost 400 guns. It was the final blow for the central Powers from which they would never recover. On the 29th Ludendorff called a conference at Spa and the decision was taken to approach the American President Wilson with a view to accepting the peace proposals he had put forward in January. Von Hindenberg demanded that an Armistice should be arranged the very next day, it was a week later when the German Government attempted talks with President Wilson but these failed. In January the US President had drawn up terms for a peace proposal and had asked the Allies to state on what terms they were prepared to make peace with Germany, the proposal was ignored by the Allies, there was no incentive for them to go down that route.

The G.A.N. attack was launched on the 28[th September] and was a complete success, the Belgians took the Passchendaele Ridge with ease, which vindicated Plumer who correctly forecast that the enemy was pulling out anyway. With that Plumer issued orders for an assault on Wytschaete and the Messines Ridge the next day, the weather changed and the rain turned to mud, but by evening the ring of hills around Ypres had been taken and were in Allied hands. With the capturing of the Hindenberg line there was distinct feeling that the war could be over soon. General Rawlinson records in his diary, "D.H. came to see me, he is in great form, delighted with the way things have gone in the North, and with the First and Third Armies. [56]*He thinks we shall finish the war this year,* and I hope he may be right, but it is no certainty. 'Rawly' was adamant about the need to send troops through to Berlin to ensure an end to hostilities.

On 5th October Rawlinson's records that the 2nd Australian and the 25th division had broken through the Hindenberg reserve line and that his leading troops were out in the open "my victory is won". The Hindenberg Line followed the line of the Canal du Nord that went through a 5000yds tunnel, the cutting was very deep and the enemy had use it as a forward defence, they had also made the tunnel, which was 160 feet underground, into an impregnabe barrack with carefully concealed exits and machine gun emplacements to cover all the approaches. Since the 8th August the Fourth Army had taken 62,000 prisoners. The allies had now some 100 divisions against the Germans 70 divisions and the initiative was with the Allies.

At this stage Germany had accepted all fourteen points of the US peace proposals and said that they would withdraw from all conquered territories. But Foch emphatically refused to talk terms with Germany while they were being driven back and told them "Get your armies behind the Rhine" The German peace proposals were a great worry to Rawlinson, it was directly linked to the lack of railway communications behind the British lines and the broken ground that lay ahead, he felt that the inability of the British to keep the Germans on the move because of these difficult communications would favour the Germans in any peace negotiations should the politicians accept the German offer. When he heard on the 12th of October that Germany had accepted the U.S. Wilson terms in full it prompted Henry Rawlinson to write to C.I.G.S. Sir Henry Wilson advocating that the Germans should not be allowed to 'wriggle out of a hole', ---- we cannot get the railways repaired in this broken part of the front before October, but we should be able to start marching in November. On the 6th of October Haig visited Foch at his HQ where he produced a newspaper article outlining the German proposals, he said, "Here you have the immediate result of the British piercing the Hindenberg Line" it was a big-hearted gesture that must have given great satisfaction to Sir Douglas, a sincere recognition of the recent huge achievements of the British Army.

On the 8th October the Third and Fourth Armies again mounted an intensive attack that drove the Germans out from their last defensive positions, the Australians had fought there last battle and moved back on the 5th October, there were two American Corps involved and Rawlinson was full of praise for the way they fought and told them so by telegram. The success of this operation prompted Lloyd George to write a grudging letter of congratulation to Douglas Haig, it was a letter of congratulation to Haig and all the officers under his command on their brilliant victory. It was however belittling and obviously intended to deny Haig of any gratification that he may have had at spiking L.G.'s guns.

Again on the 17th the a main assault was mounted against the enemy lodged on the Selles (where II Corps under General Horace Smith Dorian turned and stood against Von Kluck at Le Cateau in August 1914) and drove them out, on through the Great Forest of Mormal and over the Oise Canal taking prisoners and guns up to the 3rd November when the Fourth Army was now thirty miles in front of their railheads.

SPOILS OF WAR

I have a big French rifle, it's stock is riddled
clean,
And shrapnel smashed its barrel, likewise its
magazine.
I've lugged it from Bethune to Loos and back
from Loos again,
I found it on the battlefield, amidst the soldiers
slain.

It's a little battle souvenir for one across the
foam,
That's if the French Authorities will let me take
it home.
I've got a long, long sabre, as sharp as any
lance,
It was carried by a shepherd boy from some-
where South in France.

Where grasses wave and poppy flowers are red
as blood is red,
I took the shepherds sabre for the shepherd boy
lay dead.
I'll take it back, a souvenir for one across the
foam,
That's if the French authorities will let me take
it home.
That's if our own authorities will give me leave
for home.

***

Just as they had devastated everything as they withdrew
to the Hindenberg line in 1917 so the enemy were do-
ing the same as they pulled back out of France, destroy-
ing roads, railway and bridges etc, the more they could

392

delay the attacking forces the easier for them to retreat in good order, they were leaving no 'spoils of War' for the Allies and reports came in that they were taking their guns and everything else with them, they were not ever going to attack again but they were certainly not a destroyed army and given the chance to settle on lenient terms there was the potential for Germany to rearm and again create grounds for war. Lloyd George wrote to Douglas Haig in mid October ordering him to press on as hard and as fast as he could and on the 19th D.H. was in London. Haig records in his diaries that he went first to see Henry Wilson at the War Office ([57] Wilson diary 19th Oct --- Douglas Haig came to see me at 10.15am) after which they attended a meeting of the War Cabinet. [58]L.G. asked Haig his opinion regarding the German call for an armistice. Haig gave his report and said that the German army has been badly beaten but has not broken up. It is still capable of serious resistance. ---- "In my opinion the German Army is quite capable of making an orderly retreat to a predetermined line of defence and holding that line against equal, or possibly superior forces. ----- The British Army is the most formidable fighting force in the world, but there seems to be no prospect of its strength being maintained long term, it alone of the Allied armies could be capable of bringing the German army to its knees, but for what, why risk more lives in a cause aimed purely at enabling the French to exact revenge on German soil, there would be no incentive for the British army in that, in any event it would ultimately, be down to the British to achieve a victory since the Americans and the French were not capable of a serious offensive action."

According to another version of the presentation of Haig's report at that War Cabinet; his report was presented not by him but by his Chief of Staff and is described as follows. [59] When the Cabinet telegraphed fresh orders to Haig on the 15th of Oct. they therefore instructed him to to 'continue fighting night and day to the utmost limit of your capacity', but Haig was doubtful and sent a paper by return which his Chief of Staff read to the Cabinet. For some reason Denis Winter refers to Cabinet minute 23/16 he makes no reference to the fact that Haig was present at the meeting to give a verbal account, but refers only to his chief of staff presenting Haig's views in a report.

The conclusion that Haig draws is that the Allies would, at a later stage, be heavily dependent of the fresher American troops who would probably succeed in pushing the Germans over the Rhine, but having had the winter to resupply and build new defences, the task of finishing the German menace would probably not be achieved until 1920, and at great cost in human life at that. It was a change of attitude and a rather pessimistic one from Douglas Haig but nonetheless realistic, the British Army had carried the brunt of the fighting in the last three months and Haig had no time for exacting demands on the Germans that exceeded what would be considered adequate settlement terms for the British Government. Haig was right when he said that everyone wanted an end to the war, not a continuation on German terms beginning in the spring of 1919 having let the them off the hook. Henry Wilson was in agreement but was quite adamant that if the Armistice was to hold, real guarantees would have to be put in place and that meant the occupation of German territory British and French divisions over the German border.

From a tenuous start, Haig and Foch got along well together, barring a few minor differences Foch was obviously pleased to work with Sir Douglas Haig ready to accept his point of view as being sound and to support him in the objectives that he set. One occasion occurred when this partnership was sorely tested, Plumers Second Army was at this stage not under Sir Douglas's command, he was not happy about that and wanted it returned to his command in order to successfully keep the Germans on the run.

On the 24th C.I.G.S. was informed by General Du Cane (British liaison Officer to Marshal Foch) of a spat between Foch and Douglas Haig who had requested the return of the British Second Army, under Gen. Plumer, to his Command. The Second Army had for several weeks been under the Belgian King in the Lys area, Foch refused the request which prompted D.H to telephone C.I.G.S. to ask him to intervene. After consultation with Lloyd George, Henry Wilson set off for France on the 26th and set up a meeting with Clemenceau with Lord Milner present. This is his diary entry.

[60]---- "What a bother, it sounds to me as if Haig was right, Foch wants us to do all the work. The French are not fighting at all, and the Americans don't know how, so all falls on us. We took 8000 prisoners and 200 guns yesterday and no one else did anything. In the Aegean and France the French are being very tiresome".

Clemenceau agreed that Haigs request for the return of the Second Army was quite in order and went to see Foch at Senlis the next day, however Foch was adamant that he would not accede to the wishes of D.H. and under the circumstances Henry Wilson felt that he had no choice but to go and see Foch personally. In his diary he writes.

--- "If I can't persuade Foch to give up his position then I shall have to order him. But this of course is the last thing I want to do". Wilson said that he had a rather stormy meeting with Foch and managed to get his point across before they eventually parted excellent friends. That same day Haig had a pre arranged meeting with Foch for 4pm, over lunch at the Embassy Wilson suggested to D.H. that he met Foch half way by agreeing the Second Army return to British Command on reaching the Scheldt. That evening Gen. Du Cane (Liaison Officer to Foch) rang Wilson to say the meeting had gone splendidly. Foch[61] records the dialogue with Douglas Haig.

---- 'he sought to have restored to him the Second British Army which had been temporarily attached to the Flanders Group. I had no difficulty in showing Sir Douglas that if the Flanders Group was to do the work expected of it, the British Second Army must remain with it until it had conquered Belgium as far as the Scheldt'. When Foch had set up the Northern Army group (GAN) under the King of the Belgians on the 2nd of September, it consisted of the existing Belgian forces to which were added several French divisions and the run down divisions of (10) Plumers Second Army. Douglas Haig Had readily agreed to this assuming it was a short term measure, but when the initial objectives had been taken and new objectives set, taking the Second Army north east into Belgium in a secondary role covering the flank of the French and Belgians, Haig was not too pleased. Foch passes off the altercation as something and nothing. But Haig saw it differently as his diaries show.

----"Foch declines to return the Second Army to me because of the political value of having the King of the Belgians in command of an Allied army when he re enters his capital, Brussels! His real object is to use the British Second army to open the way for the 'dud' divisions (of which the rest of the Kings Army is composed) and ensure that they get to Brussels. France would then get the credit for clearing Belgium and putting the King back in his capital. De Goutte is nominally Chief of Staff to King Albert; really he is the Army Commander.

I explained my military reasons why my Second Army must now be under my orders. If there were political reasons requiring the Second Army to remain under King Albert, then the British Government must direct me on the subject. Until I was so informed I must contine to view the situation from a military standpoint and insist on the return of he Second Army without delay. F(och) asked me to submit my request in writing."
The Second Army under Plumer had raced ahead ignoring orders from Haig and the French Chief of Staff, although they were a flanking army they left the rest of the GAN behind in capturing Roubaix and Courtrai, so successful were they that they reached and crossed the Scheldt (Escaut) within a week of Douglas Haig asking Foch for their return to his command.

Without doubt Foch and Clemenceau were manipulating things to the advantage of the French, to be in the spotlight as it were, with Britain in the shade. The one thing they could not hide was that the British Army was doing all the work, having held on at the Somme and Arras from March 21st, the French then collapsed under enemy attacks in May to July from the Chemin des Dames to the Marne. It was the British who provided a significant number of divisions for Foch's reserve, this whilst holding on at the Lys against an all out German attempt to reach the coast, another exhausted British Corps was moved by Foch to the right of the Chemin Des Dames before the German attacks in May, again releasing 5 more French divisions for reserve.

In the meantime Erich Von Ludendorf, the German Chief of staff had met with the Kaiser and resigned his post, either voluntatily or otherwise, he was replaced on the 27th of October and retired to Sweden to write his memoirs. The Kaiser himself would very soon follow, but in his case the country was Holland.

Foch's terms for an Armistice were that the Germans should evacuate the occupied territories including Alsace and Lorraine within 14 days; within a further eleven days they should evacuate all territory on the east bank of the Rhine and Allied occupation of bridge-heads each forty kilometres radius east of the Rhine at Mayence, Koblenz, Cologne and Strasbourg. Further to this they were to hand over to the Allies 5000 guns, 8000 trench mortars, 30,000 machine guns, 2000 air-craft, 5000 trains and 100,000 railway carriages in per-fect condition, 10 battleships, 6 battle cruisers, 8 light cruisers, 50 destroyers and 150 submarines, plus repa-ration would be paid in full by Germany for all damage done. Although the British Govt. considered these terms to be too harsh, it was felt by comparison, that Douglas Haig's proposals were too lenient, but in arriv-ing at his conclusions, Haig was mindful of the position of the War Cabinet with regard to casualties when he was required to attack the Hindenberg line, the losses had been high during the September/October offen-sives. There was generally an understanding of Haig's position; that he wanted to see a peace settlement signed to ensure there was no further fighting. Howev-er, on the 1st Nov at a meeting of the Supreme War Council at Versailles, the terms as laid down by Mar-shal Foch were approved provisionally leaving Germa-ny the only belligerent after Italy and Austria had al-ready signed peace terms. Douglas Haig wrote to his wife on November 1st,[62] --- "I am afraid the Allied Statesmen mean to exact humiliating terms from Ger-many. I think it is a mistake, because it is merely laying up trouble for the future, and may encourage the wish for revenge in the future". Haig really was concerned to create lasting peace and this coupled with his own pre-ferred peace proposals are clear evidence of that, he did not live to see his views justified in 1939.

The Comment that Henry Wilson had made in his

diary regarding the Americans not fighting; was to do with the fact that General Pershing was not cooperating with Foch in his efforts to coordinate the battles that raged along the front in a concentrated push to bring Germany to negotiations. Pershing's intransigence had prompted an infuriated Clemenceau to write to Marshal Foch in a very long letter with the sole objective of having Pershing removed. The General opinion amongst the leaders of the Allies was that the American divisions would be better spread amongst the British and French armies where they would operated well under experienced command. They were great and keen soldiers just straining at the leash. In the letter Clemenceau says,

---- In spite of heavy losses they have failed to conquer the ground assigned to them as their objective. nobody can maintain that these fine troops are unusable; they are merely unused.

The American troops were making the mistake of not clearing ground as they advanced, with the consequence that the enemy were reappearing from the trenches and machine-gunning them from behind; this had been a hard lesson that had to be learned by the British New Army in a new type of warfare fought from the trenches in 1916. The U.S. divisions that were fighting with the British Fourth Army attracted unending praise from Gen. Rawlinson, the Army Commander; they sought to learn by seeking advice from the more experienced French, and British that they fought alongside. Whilst Foch struggled to bring Pershing into line, Haig was complying with the Marshal's request that the British First, Third and Fourth Armies should attack in the Mons – Avesnes area supported on the right by General Debeney's 1st Army. This was another fatal blow for the German Army when on the 5th November the British took Le Quesnoy and the Mormal

Forest.

In the memorandum sent to President Wilson in late October accepting the terms of the Wilson peace settlement that they had received in January, the German Govt. indicated that they would assume that Allied military advisors would complete the detail within the broad terms of the US settlement. On that assumption the Germans made certain suggestions that were immediately rejected by Foch who records.

[63]---- 'the conditions of the Armistice, were to be left to the military advisors, and that the proportion now existing between the troops at the front would serve as a basis for the arrangements which would assure and guarantee these conditions. The German Govt. leaves it to the President to draw up the conditions necessary for regulating details. It is confident that the president of the United States will countenance any demand that would be irreconcilable with the honour of the German Nation and the making of a just peace'.

This of course was a direct attempt to have the US President recognized as arbiter in the terms of the Armistice, but the allies could smell a rat and made it clear that the communication between The Germans and Washington should be terminated and future negotiations directed to the Supreme War Council at Versailles. The terms of the Armistice needed be agreed in the main by the Allied heads of Government to ensure that they were not the losers. At a meeting on the 4th of November the Supreme Council finalised the definitive text of the Armistice that was agreed by the Allied heads of Government and a copy cabled to President Wilson. Listed in the U.S. fourteen points was the principle of 'Freedom of the seas' in view of that it was agreed that a British Admiral should be Aide to Marshal Foch as he was charged with the duty of communicating the Armistice terms to representatives of the German Govt.

At 0.30hrs on the morning of the 7th of November Foch received a communication from the German High Command naming its delegates and asking that he arrange a meeting place. A reply stated where the delegates should present themselves, an outpost on the Belgian French Border near La Capelle, from where they would be transported to a meeting place. Information was received that they would arrive at the agreed place in the late afternoon of the 7th but they were badly held up by road conditions behind the German lines. They eventually arrived a tired, ragged group at General Debeney's 1st Army HQ at around 9pm; they then travelled by train and arrived at Compiegne at 7.00am the next morning. Two hours later at 9.00am Marshal Foch and his staff, accompanied by Admiral Wemyss (First Sea Lord) heading the British Naval delegation, met with the German Delegation of six in a carriage of Marshal Foch's train. It is interesting to read an account of that meeting in an extract, the Marshal asked for the delegates credentials which were presented and after withdrawing with Admiral Wemyss to examine the documents the two sides sat down at the conference table.

[64] ---- *'The Marshal asked the purpose of their visit.*

Herr Erzberger replied that the German delegation had come to receive the proposals of the Allied Powers looking to an Armistice on land, sea and in the air, on all the fronts and in the Colonies.

Marshal Foch replied that he had no proposals to make.

Count Oberndorff asked the Marshal in what form he desired that they express themselves. He did not stand on form; he was ready to say that the German delegation asks the conditions of the Armistice.

The Marshal replied that he had no conditions to offer.

401

Herr Erzberger read the text of President Wilson's last note, stating that Marshal Foch is authorized to make known the armistice conditions.

Marshal Foch replied that he is authorized to make these known if the Germans ask for an Armistice. "Do you ask for an Armistice? If you do, I can inform you of the conditions subject to which it can be obtained."

Herr Erzberger and Count Oberndorff declared that they asked for an Armistice.

Marshal Foch then announced that the Armistice would be read; as the text was rather long only the principle paragraphs would read for the present, later on the complete text would be communicated to the plenipotentiaries.'

Herr Erzberger went on to describe the disorganisation and lack of discipline in the German Army, also that the country was in a state of famine and that revolution was on the rise, in view of this he asked for a cessation of hostilities whilst the terms were considered. General Von Winterfeldt also asked that he also be heard, that he had a special mission to fulfil on behalf of the German Government. His request was also for a cessation of hostilities reiterating the request made in the initial German communication, the grounds for this request being that in this final stage many lives would be lost unnecessarily at such a late hour of the conflict.

To both Marshal Foch went on to say that hostilities couldn't be ceased until the armistice is signed. Not only did he refuse to order a temporary halt to hostilities, he also, on the basis of the knowledge that he had received with regard to the state of discipline in the German army, immediately wrote to the chiefs of the Allied Armies with the message; "redouble your energy in order to consolidate the results attained by your victories." After the full draft had been sent by courier to the German HQ at Spa, the German delegates asked to speak personally to the members of the Allied delegation, the first question that they asked was whether or not the terms of the Armistice had been dawn up so severe in order to ensure refusal by the German Government. The reply was that the Allies were making known the conditions under which they would grant an Armistice; there were no hidden intentions.

The decline for acceptance of the terms was the eleventh hour of the 11th day of November, at about 8pm on the tenth of November a the German Government sent a wireless message to the German delegation at Compeigne saying that the German Govt. accepts the conditions of the armistice and, by using an agreed code word in the message, authorized the German Secretary of State to sign the agreement. The Armistice was not a peace treaty or even the start of peace, it was an agreed break in hostilities that would prevent bloodshed whilst giving the belligerents time, in peaceful circumstances to draw up plans for a permanent peace treaty. A meeting was convened in the same railway carriage at 2.15am on the 11th and final agreement reached and the armistice signed at 5am. A few days later the Allied armies started to move toward the three bridgeheads over the Rhine where they remained until 1929, 10 years before the whole thing started again.

Henry Rawlinson commented, ----[65] "looking back on the events of March, it seems incredible that all this should have come to pass. We owe it to three things; to the spirit of the troops – their recovery after the events of the 1918 spring is a glorious testimony to British grit; to the way old Foch pulled the operations of the Allies together; and to Douglas Haig's faith in victory this year – he believed in it long before I did, and when all the people at home were talking about plans for

1919, He not only believed in it, but also went all out for it, and he must be a proud and thankful man today. I have written him a letter of congratulation. I have been looking at the figures of the Fourth Army [66]*alone* since August 8th. We have captured 79,000 prisoners and 1,100 guns, and our casualties have numbered 110,000. It has been very truly representative of the English speaking peoples. I have commanded British, Australians, Canadians, South Africans and Americans, and, if we make a proper peace it is with these peoples that the future of the world should rest. From Amiens to Avesnes has been a wonderful story, may I live to write it some day."

Sir Douglas Haig replied to Rawlinson in a very warm and sincere letter, he also wrote in his diary on the 27th November 1918 a very enlightened comment.

---- *"We must not forget that it is in our interest that we return to peace methods at once, to have Germany a prosperous, not an impoverished country. Furthermore we ought not to make Germany our enemy for years to come."*

The Military Historian; Maj.Gen. J.F.C. Fuller commented about Haig saying that 'unlike his contemporaries he realised, that peace is the true aim of War.'General Pershing the American Military Commander credited Haig with having won the war. After the signing of the Armistice Haig ordered the Second and Fourth British Armies to move up to the Rhine from where they would cross and occupy bridgeheads for the next ten years. For the British Forces this was the original BAOR, the British Army of the Rhine, in 1945 BAOR was back again along with America, Russia and France to occupy not only bridgeheads, but the whole of Germany again for a period of ten years until May 1955, by coincidence the date that the author joined the colours and went to Germany.

The soldiers of the British army returned to England to pick up life were they had left off, there was of course the generation that would not come back and just as Germany's suffering did not end with the war, neither did the British. Millions had died and millions more were permanently disabled, Germany and Russia suffered something in the region of two million deaths each, France and Austro-Hungarians some 1.5 million each, Britain some one million deaths and America 100,000 mainly as a result of the influenza epidemic of 1918. Marshal Foch returned to Paris to take centre stage, to a triumphant welcome, he was feted throughout France and Britain; a never-ending train of parades and celebrations in the larger cities, immersing himself in the glory of Victory. Sir Douglas Haig on the other hand paraded through London with Foch and the King and then retired to a more sedate life, for him there was great joy only in that the war was over and the Allies victorious. Unlike Foch he could find no glory in the loss of a generation of young men, there was nothing to celebrate about the death and destruction the last four years had brought, a war that would take years to get over, his only consolation was in the fact that it was over. He was showered with honours and medals but was offered no part in military or public life, his nemesis, Lloyd George saw to that. He lived at the historic Bemersyde mansion house in the Scottish lowlands on the banks of the River Tweed, from there he threw himself into providing support for the men who had so gallantly fought under him, his concern was for them, and he worked tirelessly for the rest of his life building up the British Legion.

Lord Rawlinson was sent out to Murmansk in Arctic Russia to see what help could be given to the White Russians in their struggle against the Bolsheviks. On his return he took over as G.O.C Aldershot Command.

In 1920 he was offered the post of Commander in Chief of the Indian Army where he lived until he died aged 61 in 1925.

Field Marshal Sir Herbert Plumer took Command of the British Occupation forces in the Rhineland for a short time before becoming Commander in Chief of the Forces in Malta. At the end of his tour the Australian Government asked that he be made the next Governor General of Australia, something that appealed to him, however, he felt that since there would be a heavy financial cost to him, it was something he could not afford and therefore accepted the post of High Commisioner to Palestine.

Field Marshal Sir William Robertson replaced Field Marshal Plumer as GOC British Army of the Rhine.

Field Marshal Sir Henry Wilson who was contemplating entering political life, was shot dead by two IRA assassins as he entered the doorway of his home at Eaton Place in London in June 1921. He had been to deliver a speech in Liverpool and was walking from a taxi to his front door when one of the two assailants fired on him, he drew his sword to defend himself but was struck by several bullets, two in the chest from which he died within minutes. The two men were caught, tried and hanged.

After the signing of the Armistice Lloyd George made a speech about the Fifth Army, it was full of inaccuracies and falsehoods that in the fullness of time were wholly disproved, he went on to further reveal his churlish nature when in the years that followed he never ever took the time to correct his destructive mistakes, something that hurt Sir Hubert Gough intensely.

29

Conclusion

At this point the story pauses whilst the people of Europe try to return to some sort of normality, to recover from the trauma of war and build that 'better world'. Alas! They went on to suffer the onset of the great depression, followed by a repeat attempt by Germany to dominate Europe in 1939. By 1945 our enemies were beaten and our Russian ally became the west's new enemy in the Cold War. France and Germany agreed that there should never be another European war and united to form the Common Market, a misnomer if ever there was one, the other fear of course was Communism and the need for EU countries to unite against that evil threat, and so NATO came into being. Britain was not invited to join the EU club and as time went on had to almost beg to be admitted, Nato was the only club open to us. Eventually, the perfidious Edward Heath conned the British people into thinking that we were joining a Common Market, he gave away our fishing industry, and anything else to appease the arrogant, anti British General De Gaulle so as to clear the way for British membership, what a laugh that has turned out to be, along with the distorted Human Rights Act.

It cannot be argued, by a long shot, that what we have now is what those generations fought for, we have blundered along the way so badly that almost every person one meets is disillusioned with the life we lead, hide bound by Human rights laws, racial discrimination laws, uncontrolled immigration, political correctness balanced in favour of any religion other than Christianity, overbearing policing, a welfare state that provides for the rest of the world, and the marginalisation of Parliament and the Law of the land by diktats from Europe. We are all but an occupied country, nobody wants that, but not enough of those with the power to do anything about it can see the way to changing it. Germany, not having fired a shot, is master of Europe, Kurt Waldheim was right, we are not masters in our own house, and those that went would never understand that. All that Churchill stood for, that this country should never be dominated by any other power has been stood on its head, even if we get out of Europe we are not masters in our own house because that is only half of it, what about the high level of political correctness that has permeated every aspect of our lives. Our forebears faced machine guns, knee deep in mud to bring back the wounded, they didn't have a multitude of weapons to hand in a designer flak jacket. Now the public services will not enter a children's paddling pool to save a seriously ill person from drowning!

We need to hold sacred the memory of those who strived in vain for a better world to live in. For some forty years leading up to the Millenium the armed Forces were by and large, ignored, as if they did not exist, but following the Iraq and Afghanistan campaigns there has been a greater recognition by the younger generations, of the courage and selflessness of our armed Forces when weighed against the everyday life of the average person. How heartening it would be to think that perhaps our politicians could show the same spirit. The signs are that 'Remembrance' will, thankfully, be an important part of our lives for years to come, would it be too much to hope that in another 100 years time that all those British servicemen who have given their lives or suffered serious injury will be remembered in the same way?

Lawrence Binyon says it all in the first lines of his poem, 'For the Fallen.'

With proud thanksgiving, a mother for her children,
England mourns for her dead across the sea.
Flesh of her flesh they were, spirit of her spirit,
Fallen in the cause of the free.

End

Material Sources

Douglas Haig. The Educated Soldier. By John Terraine. Hutchinson 1963

The Fifth Army. By General Sir Hubert Gough. Hodder & Stoughton 1931

The Fifth Army, March 1918. By W. Shaw Sparrow. Bodley Head 1921

1914. By Field Marshal Viscount French of Ypres. Constable. 1919

The Life of General Lord Rawlinson of Trent. By Major General Sir Frederick Maurice. Cassell & Co 1928.

Haigs Command. By Denis Winter. Viking. 1991

Field Marshal Sir Henry Wilson. By Major General Sir C.E. Callwell.
Cassell & Co. 1927

Plumer. By Geoffrey Powell. Pen and Sword. 1990

Spectamur Agendo. By Lt. Hopkinson. Privately published. Printed by Heffer and
Sons Cambridge. 1926

The Lancashire Fusiliers. By Cyril Ray. Published by Leo Cooper 1971

The Western Front. By Richard Holmes. BBC Publication. 1999

Biography of the Late Marshal Foch. By Maj. Gen.

George Aston.
Hutchinson. 1929

The Memoirs of Marshal Foch. Col. T. Bentley Mott.
Doubleday Doran 1931

Napoleon The Final Phase. By Lord Rosebery. Constable. 1900

Europe Since Napoleon. By Prof. David Thompson.
Longmans Green. 1957

In Flanders Fields. By Leon Wolff. Longmans, Green
& Co. 1959

History of the First World War. By B.H. Liddell Hart.
Faber and Faber. 1930

For the Sake of Example. By Anthony Bebington. Leo
Cooper. 1983

Story of a Royal Regiment. By Col. J.M. Cowper. Published by the Regiment.

History of the East Lancashire Regiment in the Great
War. By Maj. Gen.
Sir C.L. Nicholson. Littlebury, Liverpool. 1936.

See How They Run. By William Moore. 1970 (The
Fifth Army)

Regiments and Corps of the British Army. By Ian. S.
Hallows. Arms and Armour press. 1991

Schoolboy Into War. H.E.L Mellersh. Pub. 1978 by
William Kimber & Co. Ltd.

1 This is supported by the German author Fritz Fischer in his book 'Germany's aims in the First World War' 1961.
2 Esther St. Blackburn, Lancashire. Demolished in the 1970's
3 George Haslam, photo of him in the book cover and on the cover.
4 Napoleon. The Last Phase. Lord Rosebery 1900
5 The Fifth Army. By Gen. Sir Hubert Gough
6 '1914'. Sir John French. Published 1919
7 Spectamur Agendo. Lt. E.C. Hopkinson.
8 A long term German Plan to deal with Russia and France.
9 Sir Henry Wilson Diaries
10 Spectamur Agendo. Capt. Frank Hopkinson
11 Spectamur Agendo. Capt. Frank Hopkinson
12 '1914'. Sir John French
13 Forty years of service, General Horace Smith Dorrien.
14 Two of the battalions covering the withdrawal of II Corps had difficulty in disengaging and were involved in severe rearguard actions until they were eventually over run and taken prisoners, these were the Cheshires and the Norfolks.
15 Decisive battles of the western world. Maj. Gen. J.F.C Fuller
16 Sir John French's private secretary
17 It had left England on the 4th over 4000 strong.
18 BEF allocated La Bassee – Menin. The French allocated Menin – Dixmude. The Belgians allocated Dixmude –The coast
19 The Memoirs of Marshal Foch. Translated by T.Bentley Mott.
20 Taken from 'The First Hundred Thousand' - 'K (1)' - by Ian Hay published 1915
21 1914. Field Marshal Sir John French
22 Life of General Lord Rawlinson of Trent. Maj. Gen. Sir Frederick Maurice.
23 Field Marshal Sir Henry Wilson. Maj.. Gen. C.E. Callwell
24 Schoolboy at War. By H.E.L. Mellish.

25 War Diaries of the Kings Own Royal Regiment (Lancaster)
26 Lloyd George War Memoirs. Vol I

27 The life of General Lord Rawlinson of Trent. Maj.Gen. Frederick Maurice.
28 The life of General Lord Rawlinson of Trent. By Maj. Gen. Frederick Maurice
29 The Fifth Army. General Sir Hubert Gough.
30 Field Marshal Sir Henry Wilson. Maj. Gen. C.E.Callwell
31 Flanders Fields. Leon Wolf. 1959.
32 Field Marshal Sir Henry Wilson. Maj. Gen. Sir C.E. Callwell
33 Decisive Battles of the Western world. J.F.C.Fuller.
34 Fifth Army. General Hubert Gough.
35 The Fifth Army in March 1918. Walter Shaw Sparrow.
36 Memoirs of Field Marshal Foch. Translated by Col. T. Bentley Mott.
37 Biography of the late Marshal Foch. Maj. Gen. George Aston
36 Field Marshal Sir Henry Wilson vol ii. Cassell. Mj. Gen. C.E. Callwell
38 Fifth Army in March 1918. Shaw Sparrow. P266.
39 ibid

39 Douglas Haig. The Educated Soldier by John Terraine. P427.
40 Plumer the Soldiers General. By Geoffrey Powell. P259
43 The Fifth Army in1918. W. Shaw Sparrow
      42 C. In C. German 18th Army facing Gough's Fifth Army.
43 Sir Henry Wilson Diaries
44 Ibid
47 Memoirs of Marshal Foch. Translated by T. Bentley Mott.
48 Field Marshal Sir Henry Wilson Memoirs. By Maj. Gen. C.E. Callwell.
49 The Educated Soldier. John Terraine.

[50] Memoirs of Marshal Foch. Translated By Col. T Bentley Mott.

[51] Haig the Educated Soldier. John Terraine

[52] Authors italics.

[53] Memoirs of Marshal Foch, Lt. Gen. Aston.

[54] Extract from, Haig the Educated Soldier. John Terraine P.463

[55] Biography of Marshal Foch. Maj. Gen. Aston. Footnote.

[56] Authors italics.

[57] F.M. Sir Henry Wilson. Maj. Gen. C. E. Callwell.

[58] Version taken from The Educated Soldier. John Terraine.

[59] Haig's Command a Reassessment. Denis Winter.

[60] Field Marshal Henry Wilson. Maj.Gen. Sir C. E. Callwell

[61] Memoirs of Marshal Foch. Translated by T. Bentley Mott.

[62] The Educated Soldier. John Terraine.

[63] The Memoirs of Marshal Foch. Translated by Col. T. Bentley Mott.

[64] Ibid

[65] Life of Gen. Lord Rawlinson of Trent. By Maj. Gen. Sir Frederick Maurice.

[66] Authors italics